'It's a cliche to describe books as "timely". In this case, however, it could not be more true. Sam King's theoretically informed and meticulously researched analysis of whether and how probation supervision can support the early stages of desistance from crime will be a vitally important resource, not just for researchers and policymakers, but also for those charged with commissioning and providing probation services – not just in the strange new landscape of criminal justice in England and Wales, but also much further afield.'

Fergus McNeill, Professor of Criminology and Social Work,
University of Glasgow

'Sam King makes an invaluable contribution to our understanding of the attitudes and opportunities that lead offenders to stop offending. His reliable and scholarly summary of current research is enlivened with many vivid quotations from his own interviews with people struggling to get out – and stay out – of crime. This engaging and readable book offers many perceptive insights into the contribution that probation officers could make to support the process of change.'

Professor Rob Canton, De Montfort University

Desistance Transitions and the Impact of Probation

Moving away from criminal behaviour can be fraught with difficulties. Often it can involve leaving behind old habits, customs and even friends, while at the same time adopting a new way of life. How do individuals go about making a decision to give up crime? How do they plan to sustain this decision? And in what ways does probation help? This book explores these questions.

Based on in-depth interviews with a group of men under probation supervision, Sam King investigates the factors associated with making a decision to desist from crime. The book examines strategies for desistance and explores the factors that individuals consider when they are thinking about how they will desist. In doing so, the book sheds new light on existing understandings of desistance from crime and helps to develop our understandings of the role that individuals play in constructing their own desistance journeys. This book also highlights the role of probation in this process, offering a timely and critical review of the nature of probation under the New Labour government in the UK between 1997–2010.

The findings indicate that we should allow Probation Officers greater autonomy and discretion within their roles and that we should free them from the bureaucracy of risk assessment and targets. Moreover, the book warns against the potential fragmentation of community supervision. As such, the book will be of interest to criminology students, researchers, academics, policymakers and practitioners, particularly those who work with ex-offenders in the community.

Sam King is a Lecturer in Criminology at the University of Leicester. Previous to this appointment, he taught at the University of Birmingham and the University of Derby. His main research interests are desistance from crime, community supervision of offenders and experiences of community supervision. He has published in several journals, including: *Punishment and Society*, *Criminology and Criminal Justice*, and *Probation Journal*.

International series on desistance and rehabilitation

General Editor
Stephen Farrall, *University of Sheffield*

Editorial Board
Ros Burnett, *University of Oxford*
Thomas LeBel, *University of Wisconsin-Milwaukee, USA*
Mark Halsey, *Flinders University, Australia*
Fergus McNeill, *Glasgow University*
Shadd Maruna, *Queens University Belfast*
Gwen Robinson, *Sheffield University*
Barry Godfrey, *University of Liverpool*

Desistance Transitions and the Impact of Probation

Sam King

Routledge
Taylor & Francis Group

LONDON AND NEW YORK

First published 2014
by Routledge
2 Park Square, Milton Park, Abingdon, Oxfordshire OX14 4RN

and by Routledge
711 Third Avenue, New York, NY 10017

First issued in paperback 2015

Routledge is an imprint of the Taylor & Francis Group, an informa business

British Library Cataloguing in Publication Data
A catalogue record for this book is available from the British Library

Library of Congress Cataloging-in-Publication Data
King, Sam (Lecturer in criminology)
Desistance transitions and the impact of probation / Sam King.
    pages cm. – (International series on desistance and rehabilitation)
    1. Criminals–Rehabilitation–Great Britain. 2. Recidivism–Great
    Britain–Prevention. 3. Probation–Great Britain. 4. Criminals–
    Rehabilitation–United States. 5. Recidivism–United States–Prevention.
    6. Probation–United States. 7. Change (Psychology) I. Title.
    HV9345.A5.K56 2014
    364.3–dc23   2013013722

ISBN 13: 978-1-138-92237-2 (pbk)
ISBN 13: 978-0-415-64228-6 (hbk)

Typeset in Times New Roman
by Wearset Ltd, Boldon, Tyne and Wear

Contents

Illustrations

Figures

Tables

Preface

Desistance Transitions is about the early stages of the desistance process, how individuals plan to move away from crime, and the coming together of social obstacles and individual will. More specifically, it is about the experiences of a group of men under probation supervision during late-2009 and early-2010, and it represents the findings of my doctoral research undertaken in this subject area. I would like to thank Bob Matthews and David Prior for their support during this aspect of my research. I also owe a great deal to the Probation Officers who agreed to participate and helped me to recruit other participants, and to the men who were under probation supervision and who agreed to share their stories with me I am also very grateful. I would like to thank the many individuals, especially Steve Farrall, Fergus McNeill and Nathan Hughes, who also provided me with support, advice and guidance with this book and with other publications on the same topic. I would like to thank Nicola Hartley for her friendly encouragement and support during the writing of this book. I am thankful most of all to Teresa, frankly without her this research would never have begun and this book would not have been possible.

I began the research upon which this book is based at a time when the National Offender Management Service (NOMS) was in its fledgling stages, there was critical talk of the development and implementation of C-NOMIS, and concerns were being raised about the introduction of end-to-end offender management, contestability/privatisation and an increase in the level of bureaucracy within the work of the Probation Officer. The Probation Officers who I began talking with at the very early stages of the research were astoundingly optimistic in the face of such change, and demonstrated great determination to have a positive impact upon the lives of those individuals who they worked with. During the course of the research I spent many hours in probation offices, and I witnessed many staff working under immense pressure and confronted by a whole range of obstacles, but still with a positive frame of mind and willingness to initiate change. That would prove to be an enduring theme throughout this research – strength in the face of adversity and a willingness to help others. When I began interviewing the men under probation supervision I often encountered similar characteristics – a motivation and willingness to change, often to help not only the individual but also for the benefit of others as well.

Unfortunately, the men under probation supervision were also under real pressure in a variety of areas of their lives: financially, emotionally and, in some cases, physically. They also spoke about a whole range of obstacles that they faced, either in terms of rejection or exclusion from other people, or social problems in relation to employment, housing, finance, or addiction to drink or drugs. The circumstances that the men described made it clear that making any kind of change, let alone meaningful and long-lasting change, would be extremely difficult. That said, many of them were extremely positive and showed a real desire to overcome these barriers. I hope that I have encapsulated these themes within this book.

General editor's introduction

The *International Series on Desistance and Rehabilitation* aims to provide a forum for critical debate and discussion surrounding the topics of why people stop offending and how they can be more effectively reintegrated into the communities and societies from which they came. The books published in the series will be international in outlook, but tightly focused on the unique, specific contexts and processes associated with desistance, rehabilitation and reform. Each book in the series will stand as an attempt to advance knowledge or theorising about the topics at hand, rather than being merely an extended report of specific a research project. As such, it is anticipated that some of the books included in the series will be primarily theoretical, whilst others will be more tightly focused on the sorts of initiatives which could be employed to encourage desistance. It is not our intention that books published in the series be limited to the contemporary period, as good studies of desistance, rehabilitation and reform undertaken by historians of crime are also welcome. In terms of authorship, we would welcome excellent PhD work, as well as contributions from more established academics and research teams. Most books are expected to be monographs, but edited collections are also encouraged.

Sam King's book is another very welcome addition to the (now quite sizable) series. At first glance Sam's book may appear to be simply a further attempt to explore the initial phases of desistance, yet that would be a grossly unfair reading of his contribution. What Sam accomplishes is a deeper reading of how and in what ways probation services are able to assist individuals to stop offending. He locates the recent developments in probation supervision in England & Wales in terms of the wider political context of New Labour's managerialism, highlighting how these changes altered what happened in probation offices up and down these countries. Against this much wider background, Sam goes on to develop his thinking on individual agency and how certain configurations of agency may be more likely to result in the sorts of changes which people are commonly required to attempt in order to 'produce' desistance. In so doing, Sam's book develops the knowledge-base surrounding desistance via his focus on the specifics of the *initial* changes which the men in his sample undertook as they started to stop offending. Sam's aim was to uncover and illuminate to a greater degree than had hitherto been the case the role of his sample's attitudes and their experiences as they started to desist from crime, and to show these related to their strategies for maintaining their desistance. Sam wanted to explore the social context of men whose lives he had studied in the initial stages of their efforts to desist, and in particular to relate these to those structural factors which have been shown to influence desistance, and how individuals mediated these factors, building them into their future strategies. He has certainly managed to achieve that goal. But moreover, Sam's contribution has developed our understandings of how probation interventions (or whatever replaces these) can influence individuals' personal and social contexts, and the ways in which those being supervised perceive these to enable or constrain their attempts to desist.

Stephen Farrall,
Sheffield,
July 2013

1 Introduction

Introducing desistance transitions

Desistance from crime emerged as an area of interest following the somewhat unexpected findings from a number of longitudinal studies in the UK and North America which began in the late-1950s. Prominent studies included the Philadelphia Birth Cohort Study in the USA (Kempf, 1990; Wolfgang *et al.*, 1987), and the Cambridge Study in Delinquent Development in the UK (Farrington, 1989, 1995; Farrington *et al.*, 2006a, 2006b). The researchers undertaking these projects had expected to study crime over the life-course but found that by the 1970s many within the cohorts that they were observing ceased their involvement in crime as they began to enter early adulthood. Thus, the pattern that was observed followed the now well-established 'age-crime curve', and researchers were left to explain how and why so many members of the cohorts had ceased offending at this time in their lives, and why a smaller group of persistent offenders remained after the majority of offenders had desisted (Farrall and Calverley, 2006: 3). In other words, the pattern of offending identified at the macro level by the age-crime curve concealed disparities in patterns of offending at the micro level between individual offenders. The task for researchers would be to explore how individual offenders were able to desist from crime at different stages of the life-course (Farrall and Calverley, 2006: 3–4).

Different views of desistance

Indeed, following these findings, desistance became a field of research in its own right, and a number of authors began to publish their findings on how offenders ceased their involvement in crime (for example: Burnett, 1992; Cusson and Pinsonneault, 1986; Shover, 1983). This has led to the identification of a number of factors associated with successful desistance, including: marriage/family formation (Osgood and Lee, 1993; Shover, 1983); employment (Fletcher, 2001; Uggen, 1999); detachment from delinquent peer groups (Maruna and Roy, 2007; Osborn, 1980); the impact of criminal justice interventions (Burnett, 1992; Hughes, 1998; Rex, 1999); motivation and confidence in the ability to desist

(Burnett, 1992; Farrall, 2002); the development of a pro-social sense of morality (Weaver, 2009: 18); and the adoption of an alternative, non-criminal identity (Giordano *et al.*, 2002).

Drawing upon the empirical observations outlined above in relation to the factors that support desistance, a number of theoretical explanations have been proposed to explain how and why individuals move away from offending and offending-related behaviours. Generally, there are three broad theoretical categories: structural (which relate to the social context within which desistance takes place), agency (which relate to the individual's attitudes, values and other personal characteristics), and integrated (which seek to combine structure and agency elements) (Barry, 2010a). 'Structural theories' are those which explain desistance as resulting from particular life-course events, which usually accompany processes of ageing and maturation. These may prompt desistance, for example through experiencing some form of 'external shock', such as sustaining injury whilst committing a crime (Cusson and Pinsonneault, 1986). However, structural theories most often explain desistance in relation to particular life-course transitions which alter the socio-structural context of an individual's life, such as employment, marriage, or detachment from delinquent peer groups (Laub and Sampson, 2003). 'Agency theories' generally explain desistance in relation to some conception of free will or rational choice (Clarke and Cornish, 1985; Cornish and Clarke, 1986). Often these theories explain that would-be desisters have some form of plan or vision for an alternative future that does not involve offending (Maruna, 2001), and some perception of past behaviour as being morally wrong and incongruent with their future vision (Weaver, 2009: 18). Generally, therefore, agency theories explain desistance as resulting from enhanced decision-making skills in relation to the risks and rewards associated with crime.

Structural and agency theories have been criticised for reducing the role of the desister to either that of a 'super-dupe', whose actions are wholly constrained and determined by structural factors, or that of a 'super-agent', who is entirely free to take whatever course of action they desire (Farrall and Bowling, 1999). 'Integrated theories' aim to overcome these shortcomings, not only by combining structure and agency dimensions in their explanations but, moreover, by exploring their interaction (Bottoms *et al.*, 2004; Byrne and Trew, 2007). Generally, these theories explain that desistance occurs when changes to an individual's attitudes, values and decision-making lead to the individual seeking to alter their socio-structural context by searching for, or engineering, particular pro-social life-course transitions. Once these transitions take place, new behaviours are learned and new pro-social roles become cemented (Barry, 2010a).

Although researchers have studied desistance more extensively in recent years, more research is still required on how desistance is perceived and experienced prospectively from the perspective of the individual offender. The rationale for this is that an understanding of this nature will offer a greater insight into understanding 'how' and 'why' successful desistance occurs for some but not for others (Maruna, 2000: 12). An integrated theory, of the type discussed above, is clearly relevant to this endeavour, as it allows for an incorporation of structural factors in relation to particular obstacles or life-course turning points in the individual's social context, and agency factors in respect of the individual's attitudes, values and decision-making that influence behavioural intentions. However, despite the growing body of research that employs an integrated theory, structure-agency interaction remains a relatively under-explored aspect of desistance research. In particular, theoretical and conceptual accounts of agency remain vague, and there is a dearth of research which explores notions of 'active agency' in desistance, which, it is argued, refers to the notion that individuals may be able to engineer their own desistance pathways, although not necessarily under conditions of their own choosing (Bottoms *et al.*, 2004; Vaughan, 2007). Indeed, there is considerable research which has paid little attention to the role of agency in the desistance process (for example: Gottfredson and Hirschi, 1990; Laub *et al.*, 1998; Sampson and Laub, 1993), and where the concept has been applied it has generally been considered from a rational choice perspective (for example: Paternoster, 1989; Piliavin *et al.*, 1986; Uggen and Shelton, 1998).

Exploring prospective strategies for sustaining desistance may reveal a great deal about the desistance process, not least because existing evidence suggests that successful desisters tend to have a plan that they adhere to (Maruna, 2001). It is likely that one aspect of such a plan will entail overcoming certain obstacles. Previous research has identified a number of obstacles that offenders are likely to face as they attempt to move away from crime, in relation to employment, alcohol, drugs and so forth (National Audit Office, 2002; SEU, 2002), and it has been shown that individuals are more likely to desist if they are able to successfully overcome such obstacles (Farrall, 2002). An examination of the individual's prospective viewpoint can offer a greater insight into the types of obstacles offenders face when attempting to desist, and how these obstacles are perceived by the individual. Further, such an approach is likely to reveal how such perceptions inform intended action (Forste *et al.*, 2010: 2), and how this influences actual behaviour, as behavioural intention is central to actual behaviour (Ajzen, 1991).

The probation context

The development of the desistance literature has broadly coincided with the resurgent interest in exploring 'What Works' in community interventions in the UK (for example: Burnett and Roberts, 2004; Mair, 2004; McGuire, 1995; Newman and Nutley, 2003). This, in turn, led to the New Labour government establishing 'reducing reoffending' as an explicit aim of criminal justice policy (Halliday, 2001; Carter, 2003; Home Office, 2004a). A rising prison population and public anxieties about the extent of reoffending – particularly among those under probation supervision – are contemporary concerns in the UK (Leapman, 2006; Doyle, 2008; Ford, 2009), so it is pertinent to explore the topic of desistance in relation to probation interventions at this time. It is also worthwhile reflecting on the impact of New Labour's policies in relation to probation and desistance from crime given the changes which are being proposed, if not already administered, within probation under the current Coalition government (see for example: Ledger, 2010; Neilson, 2010; Warburton, 2010; Burke, 2011; Hough, 2011; Ryan, 2011; Fox and Albertson, 2012; Teague, 2012). Numerous changes took place within probation, and within criminal justice policy more generally, under the New Labour government – not the least the introduction of the National Probation Service (NPS), the Carter Review of correctional services and the subsequent development of the National Offender Management Service (NOMS), the enhancement of National Standards, the creation of the Ministry of Justice and the passing of the Offender Management Bill.

However, much of the policy-focus on reducing reoffending under New Labour had been concerned with young offenders (Soothill *et al.*, 2003: 408), to the neglect of the needs of adult offenders (Soothill *et al.*, 2009: 84). Further, contemporary probation can be characterised in terms of its focus upon the management of offenders, targets and objectives, reflecting the rise and significance of risk within the criminal justice system (Denney, 2005; Hope and Sparks, 2000; Kemshall, 2003; O'Malley, 1998; Stenson and Sullivan, 2001). Thus, throughout the New Labour administration, despite many changes within probation, the predominant theme was public protection through the surveillance and management of offenders. The effect of this has been a shift towards an ethos of 'responsibilisation' and 'individualism', whereby the individual offender is held accountable for reducing their own risk of reoffending. In other words, recent changes within the Probation Service mean that the important relationship between officer and offender has been altered to the extent that individuals attempting to desist are likely to receive less help from their supervising officers. The significant changes that probation has undergone in recent years reinforce the importance of a desistance-focused research agenda, as it has become more uncertain how probation can support individuals in their efforts to move away from crime. This, combined with the arguments presented earlier in this chapter in relation to the lack of focus on 'active agency' within desistance research, supports the justification for further research in this area. If probation interventions assume that individuals are capable of exercising agency in order to reduce reoffending, then research needs to explore the nature of this agency and how individuals exercise it within the context of the probation interventions to which they are subjected.

This book is based upon a study of the impact of probation interventions on the construction of individuals' prospective strategies for desistance. A total of 20 men and their supervising officers were interviewed in-depth in order to gain an understanding of: the processes which led towards a decision to attempt to desist; the intended strategies that individuals would employ in order to try to sustain desistance; the expected or anticipated obstacles that individuals believed they would encounter; and how they intended to overcome these. The aim of this study was to contribute to the existing knowledge of desistance by exploring the early transitional stage of desistance through an examination of a sample of men's narratives about the prospect of attempting desistance. It was also intended that the study would contribute to existing knowledge about 'assisted desistance' (see for example: Rex, 1999; Farrall, 2002; Farrall and Calverley, 2006; King, 2013a). That is, the role of probation interventions in facilitating the transition towards desistance. This book aims to shed new light on these two factors relating to the wider process of desistance, but it also aims to offer something by way of an appraisal of the New Labour approach to probation and the implications that this may have for understanding desistance. At the time of writing, it is approaching three years since the formation of the Coalition government in May 2010. There has been much speculation and conjecture during that time about changes to the way that probation works with individuals, and about the future of the Probation Service more generally (see for example: Ledger, 2010; Burke, 2011; Hough, 2011; Dominey, 2012; Maguire, 2012). Therefore, it is timely to reflect on what could be learned about probation and desistance from the New Labour approach.

Overview of the book

Chapter 1 begins by providing an overview of the socio-political context within which the study took place. The nature and extent of persistent reoffending is outlined, before discussing the response from the Probation Service. This chapter provides an account of some of the key changes to probation implemented under New Labour. It is commonly accepted that criminal justice in general, and probation more specifically, experienced significant change during the period 1997–2010, and much of this change was part of the modernisation of public services (Whitehead, 2010). Chapter 1 outlines how these changes altered the nature of probation interventions, and the impact upon the relationship between the Probation Officer and the Probationer, which has been highlighted in the existing literature as a central aspect of assisted desistance.

Chapter 2 then turns attention to the topic of desistance. The concepts of persistence and desistance are explored in order to provide an understanding of how and why these phenomena may occur, and to account for the processes by which formerly persistent offenders may come to cease offending. Clearly most people will not abruptly stop offending, particularly if they have been involved in persistent offending over a period of time, so Chapter 2 introduces the concept of the transitional phase of desistance, in order to account for the dynamics of moving from criminality to conformity. Various life-course factors are examined which have been shown to facilitate desistance, and the role that the individual can play in their own desistance journey is explored. Chapter 2 also provides an overview of assisted desistance in order to develop a greater understanding of the ways in which criminal justice interventions can facilitate the process.

As a key aim of this book is to provide a greater understanding of the role of human agency in the desistance process, Chapter 3 provides a detailed account of the key aspects of agency found in the desistance literature to date. This chapter provides an understanding of the role of agency in desistance, and a particular focus is given to the impact of agency on the early transitions towards desistance. In this chapter it is argued that particular configurations of agency are more likely to lead to the transformations necessary to sustain desistance over a longer period of time, and that these configurations of agency may be present during the early transitional stages. Chapter 4 provides an overview of the methods employed to explore and understand desistance transitions.

Chapter 5 examines the men's accounts of the first tentative steps towards desistance. The role of agency is examined in relation to the process of making a decision to desist. In this chapter particular attention is paid to the way in which the men reflected on their past in order to consider alternatives for the future. Chapter 6 builds upon this by examining in greater detail the specific strategies that the men constructed in order to help them to achieve the goals that they had set for the future. Again, particular attention is given to the role of agency in this process. Most of the men highlighted employment as a crucial factor in their strategies, so this is explored in some detail, and the barriers to fulfilling the strategies are also identified. Chapter 7 examines the role, or the perceived role, of probation in enabling or constraining the transition towards desistance. Particular aspects of probation interventions are identified as enhancing individual agency, such that desistance becomes more feasible, while other dimensions of probation are identified as constraining the transition towards desistance.

Chapter 8 analyses the accounts of desistance transitions explored in the previous three chapters through the lens of Emirbayer and Mische's (1998) conceptualisation of the chordal triad of agency. Their work provides a framework within which an understanding is developed of how agency can either reproduce or transform social contexts and individuals' trajectories. This approach is relevant to research which examines the nature of agency in the desistance process as it can enable a greater understanding of how individuals approach the process of attempting to initiate change in their lives. The final chapter offers some concluding thoughts on the nature of agency in the desistance process, and the impact of probation under New Labour.

This book seeks to develop knowledge of desistance by specifically focusing on the initial transition towards desistance. The aim is to gain a greater understanding of individuals' attitudes and experiences in the immediate aftermath of making a decision to desist, and how these relate to their prospective strategies for sustaining desistance. More specifically, it aims to explore the social context of individuals in the early stages of desistance, particularly in relation to those structural factors which have been shown to be associated with desistance, and how individuals mediate these in relation to their future strategies. Finally, it also seeks to develop understandings of the probation interventions that these individuals are subjected to, how these influence individuals' personal and social contexts, and whether individuals perceive these to enable or constrain their attempts to desist.

2 Reoffending and the response from probation

The concern with reoffending

Criminal justice policy over the past three decades has emerged as a central theme in political rhetoric and governance in England and Wales, and within this two elements have constituted the dominant concerns surrounding crime: public protection and reoffending. The concern with public protection has, in part at least, been the result of the rise of the 'risk society' and the hegemonic discourse of risk within debates about crime and punishment (see for example: Hudson, 2003; Kemshall, 2003; Kemshall and Maguire, 2001). Risk in criminal justice has been most pervasive in the increased use of risk assessment tools and risk management strategies in policing and penal practice (O'Malley, 1998; Kemshall and Maguire, 2001). Risk in relation to crime more generally can, perhaps, be most readily characterised in terms of individuals' fear of crime victimisation. While fear of crime may not necessarily reflect actual experiences of crime and victimisation (Farrall *et al.*, 2009), successive governments – encouraged, or perhaps facilitated, by a populist press – have responded with a degree of punitive populism which has seen an inexorable rise in the prison population. Indeed, under New Labour the prison population increased by 33 per cent, from 61,000 in 1997 to almost 85,000 in 2009 (Vanstone, 2010). It could be argued that much of this punitive populism has been directed towards recidivist offenders, as 61 per cent of further offences resulted in a conviction (as opposed to a reprimand, warning or caution) in 2011, compared to only 11 per cent of first offences.[1] The concern with punitive populism has not been restricted to an increase in the prison population, community sentences have become more punitive as well, as successive governments have sought to demonstrate a tough approach to the use of probation (Worrall and Hoy, 2005).

These concerns resulted, in part at least, from the finding that a small number of offenders were responsible for a large amount of overall crime. Indeed, it has been alleged that 'in England and Wales, half of all crimes are committed by 10% of offenders' (Ministry of Justice, 2008a). Criminal justice policy since the early 2000s has been particularly focused upon persistent reoffending (Home Office Communications Directorate, 2004), and a concern with identifying specifically which interventions help to reduce reoffending among persistent offenders (Perry *et al.*, 2009). Thus, the growing concerns around public protection and reoffending in recent decades have led to the development of a 'recidivist sentencing premium' in various Western jurisdictions, whereby individuals are punished more severely for persistent reoffending (Roberts, 2008), and the introduction of various schemes designed to tackle 'the problem' of reoffending.[2] However, responding to reoffending is hampered, to a certain degree, by uncertainty about the term itself and how best to measure its occurrence. The term may be conflated with reconviction or recidivism, yet this may not be helpful, particularly from a methodological point of view in terms of measuring offending events.

Reconviction data as a measure of reoffending

Friendship *et al.* (2003a) distinguished between reoffending, reconviction and recidivism. Recidivism is, they argued, the broadest definition as it encompasses reoffending and reconviction, but it also refers to lapses into patterns of offending behaviour. Reoffending incorporates reconvictions, but also refers to offences which remain undetected. Consequently, Shapland *et al.* (2008) have argued that 'reoffending cannot, in itself, be measured' (2008: 3). They stated that reoffending can, in fact, only be measured if it is officially judged by the state as a conviction or other official disposal. Therefore, although the nature and causes of reoffending are highly complex, it is usually measured using relatively simple, binary reconviction data. Indeed, reconviction is frequently used as a proxy measure of reoffending (Friendship *et al.*, 2003b). A reconviction is generally considered to be a subsequent conviction of an offence within a fixed follow-up period. It is common to use reconviction data to measure reoffending as it is relatively easy to observe and is accessible through official sources (Friendship *et al.*, 2003a). However, numerous problems arise here, not least because of the difficulties associated with official crime statistics (Macdonald, 2002). For example, whether an individual is arrested but not convicted, or whether reconviction reflects patterns of policing or social attitudes towards particular offences. Furthermore, Friendship *et al.* (2002) stated that 'reconviction has traditionally been expressed as a dichotomous event (all or nothing)' (2002: 442), and consequently there is no reference to changes to the attitudes and behaviour of individual offenders. Rather, because the effectiveness of the criminal justice system is often measured by a binary 'yes/no' reconviction tool, this means that frequency and severity of offence are not often incorporated into the measure of reoffending which, in turn, means that a more nuanced consideration of changes in offending behaviour is not possible.[3]

McNeill (2009) wrote, with reference to a range of problems of using reconviction data to measure the effectiveness of criminal justice interventions, that:

> These are not minor methodological inconveniences; they call into question not just studies that seek to compare the efficacy of sanctions by comparing reconviction rates, but also much of the literature on 'what works' in which reconviction, despite its flaws, has tended to be the preferred measure of treatment effectiveness.

(2009: 13)

One corollary of this is that comparisons of the effectiveness of different interventions are often contested (McNeill, 2009: 13), and it becomes difficult to assess the marginal gains of particular interventions. Marginal gains, in this context, refers to gradual reductions in frequency or severity of offending. However, while it may be true to say that 'every known measure of reoffending has its drawbacks' (Shepherd and Whiting, 2006:1), reconviction data does provide an indicative picture of the extent of reoffending events in England and Wales.

The extent of reoffending

The criminological literature suggests that some form of low-level offending behaviour during childhood or adolescence is 'ordinary', and that many individuals cease offending during the transition between adolescence and adulthood (Piquero *et al.*, 2012). Moreover, while it may be true to state that most adult offenders had been antisocial or delinquent during childhood or adolescence, most adolescent offenders do not become adult offenders (Loeber and LeBlanc, 1990; LeBlanc and Loeber, 1998). This is evidenced in the Offending, Crime and Justice Survey (OCJS) 2003–2006. This provides self-reported data on offending among 10–25 year olds in England and Wales. The survey shows that over a four year period, almost half (49 per cent) of respondents stated that they had offended on at least one occasion over the past four years, and almost a quarter (23 per cent) reported offending in the previous 12 months, with the peak of offending occurring during the mid- to late-teens (see Figure 2.1) (Hales *et al.*, 2009). Similar findings have been reported in previous studies (Anderson *et*

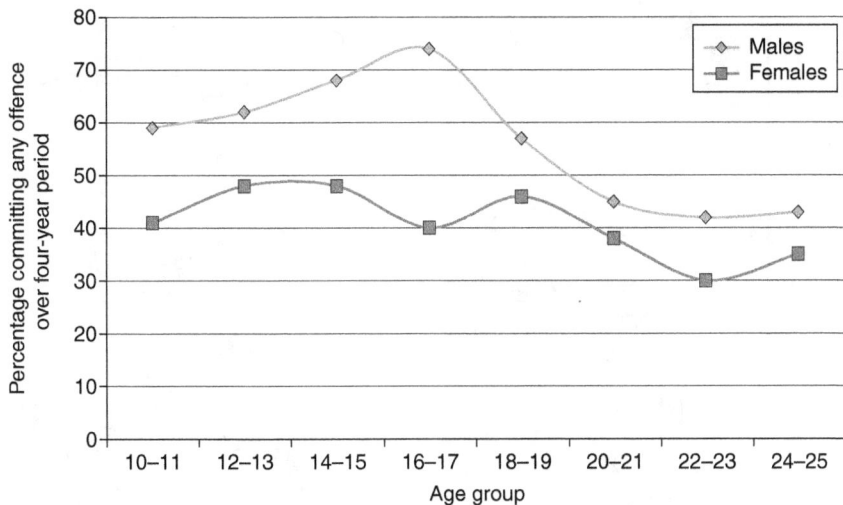

Figure 2.1 Percentage of OCJS sample offending over a four-year period, by age and gender (source: Hales *et al.*, 2009: 9).

al., 1994; Budd *et al.*, 2005a, 2005b; Flood-Page *et al.*, 2000; Graham and Bowling, 1995; Riley and Shaw, 1985; Roe and Ashe, 2008).

However, the literature on criminal careers shows that persistence in offending is an unusual event, insofar as many individuals cease offending after one conviction. Prime *et al.* (2001) reviewed the criminal careers of offenders born between 1953 and 1978, and found that more than half of the population of male offenders born in 1953 had only one court appearance before the age of 46. This was found to be consistent within subsequent cohorts, as shown in Figure 2.2.

In addition to the majority of offenders having only one conviction, most offenders also have criminal careers of less than one year. A criminal career is measured as the number of years between first and last conviction, so for those with only one conviction the career length is recorded as 'less than one year' (Prime *et al.*, 2001). Within the 1958 cohort, only 3 per cent of male offenders had a criminal career of two years or more, and a further 3 per cent had a criminal career of more than three years. Over half had criminal careers of less than one year, and two-thirds had careers of less than five years. For some, offending becomes a more entrenched aspect of their lives and their criminal careers endure for considerably longer. The data from the 1953 cohort of the Prime *et al.* study (2001) show that of the 114,740 males in the sample, 62,010 had criminal careers of less than one year. However, 29,280 had criminal careers of ten years or longer and 3,090 had careers of 30 years or more. This indicates that a smaller group of the offender population are convicted of disproportionately more crime than the rest of the offender population (Soothill *et al.*, 2003: 390). Indeed, the Farrington *et al.* (2006a, 2006b) Cambridge Study in Delinquent Development suggested that 7 per cent of males accounted for approximately half of all convictions up to age 50.

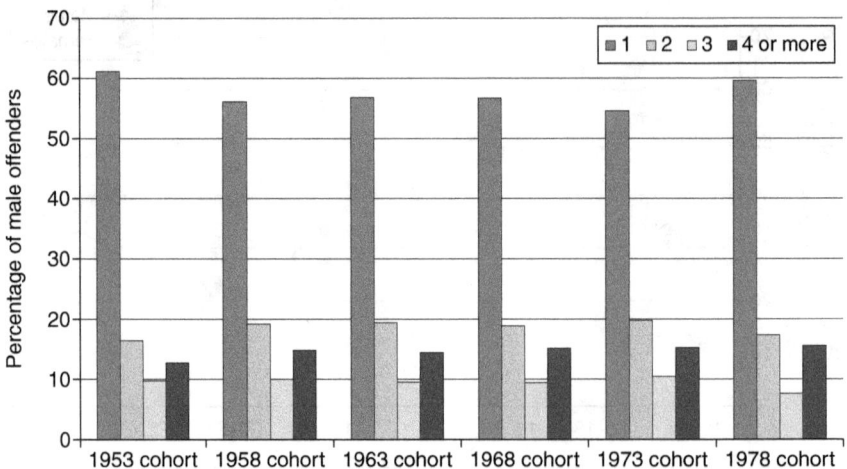

Figure 2.2 Percentage of male offenders, under 17, by number of court appearances (source: Prime *et al.*, 2001).

However, analyses of reoffending are not just concerned with persistent offending over a period of time, they may also be concerned with the extent of reoffending among the offender population in a given year. Reconviction rates in a given year may indicate how prevalent reoffending is among the offender population. Ministry of Justice (2013) data has shown that there were approximately 550,000 offenders between April 2010 and March 2011, and around 140,000 of these had committed a further offence within a year, giving a proven reoffence rate of 25.4 per cent. This figure has been broadly consistent since 2000, as illustrated in Figure 2.3.

Ministry of Justice (2013) data has also shown that those individuals who reoffend within a given year are likely to have committed more than one reoffence in that year. Figure 2.4 shows the average number of proven reoffences committed per adult reoffender in a given year from 2000–2011. Reoffenders committed an average of 2.88 reoffences in the 12 months to March 2011. Some figures show that reoffending rates in England and Wales have been between 51–55 per cent for those serving community orders, and 65–67 per cent for those released from prison (LGiU, 2009; Thomson, 2009). More recent data suggests that reoffending rates are considerably lower. However, some of the differences between these figures can be accounted for by changes to the recording and reporting of reconviction rates. In 2006, the government reduced the follow-up period from two years to one year, to make 'reoffending data timelier' (Ministry of Justice, 2008b: 3). However, reconviction rates over a two year period remain approximately the same as for previous years (Thomson, 2009).

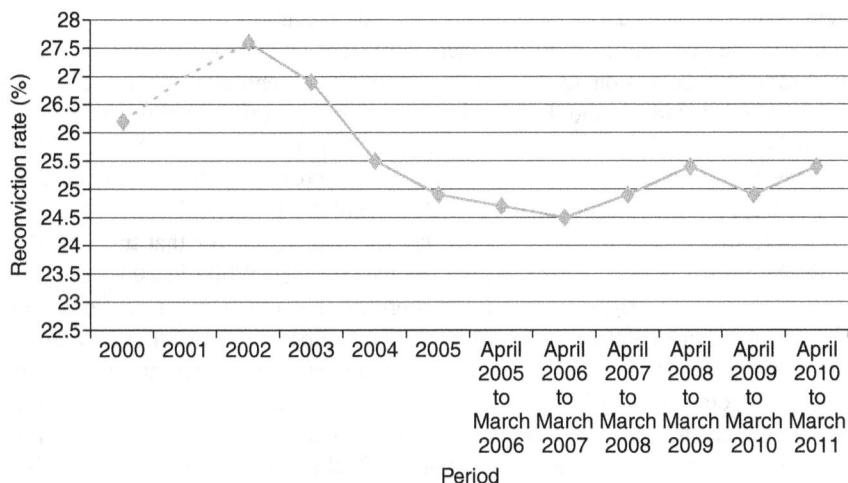

Figure 2.3 Reconviction rate, 2000, 2002–March 2011 (source: Ministry of Justice, 2013).

Note
Data unavailable for 2001 due to a problem with archived data on Court Orders.

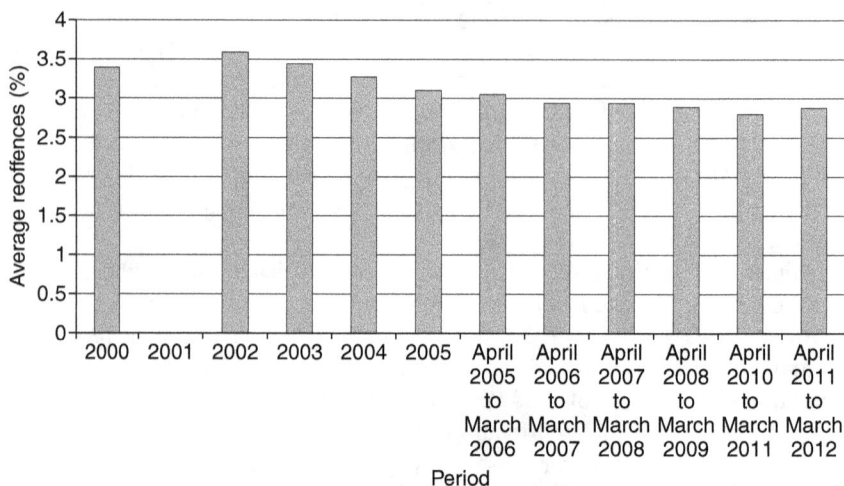

Figure 2.4 Average proven reoffences per adult reoffender, 2000, 2002–March 2011 (source: Ministry of Justice, 2013).

Note
Data unavailable for 2001 due to a problem with archived data on Court Orders.

Recent data (Ministry of Justice, 2012a) for England and Wales suggests an increase over the past decade in the proportion of those dealt with by the criminal justice system with offending histories. The data show that almost 90 per cent of offenders in 2011 had been convicted or cautioned previously. As this figure is the proportion of all offenders convicted or cautioned it could be that this reflects a reduction in the number of first-time entrants into the criminal justice system. Indeed, the data for the number of first offences show a decrease from 269,777 in 2001 to 208,292 in 2011, after a peak of 329,813 in 2006. However, the number of further offences has increased over the past decade. There were 544,372 further offences in 2001, and this figure had risen to 632,673 by 2011, after a peak of 678,251 in 2008. The data also show that the extent of offending histories has increased over the past decade. While in 2001 less than 18 per cent of all offenders had 15 or more prior convictions or cautions, this figure had risen to almost one third by 2011. The proportion of those receiving custodial sentences with 15 or more convictions is even higher, at 44 per cent. Within all other categories for the number of previous convictions or cautions there has been a decrease in the proportion of offenders with offending histories between 2001 and 2011. These figures may reflect a bifurcated approach to criminal justice, through the targeting of individuals defined as prolific or persistent offenders (see, for example: Home Office, 2002a, 2004b). Some have argued that the case against persistent offenders has been overstated (Garside, 2004), and others have raised doubts about the effectiveness of recent responses to so-called prolific and persistent offenders (Hopkins and Wickson, 2012), but it may still be surmised that reoffending in general is an issue of significance for policymakers and practitioners alike.

Responding to reoffending

While the task of reducing reoffending has been central to the work of the Probation Service since its inception, the concern here is with more recent developments in criminal justice in England and Wales.[4] While some may argue that the approach to probation under New Labour might be described in terms of 'missed opportunities' (Vanstone, 2010), the period between 1997–2011 is perhaps best characterised in terms of change and contradiction. The dominant form of change would be a modernisation of the service, a process which had begun under the previous Conservative administration (Lawrie, 2011). Change through modernisation would entail the introduction of managerialist techniques, which would become pervasive throughout criminal justice agencies (Ashworth, 2009), in an attempt to establish a more efficient and effective service. The contradictory nature of the changes initiated under New Labour occurred as a consequence of the juxtaposition between the rhetoric of tackling social exclusion, and the maintenance of a punitive stance (Whitehead, 2010). New Labour maintained the punitive toughness initiated under the previous Conservative regime under the slogan 'prison works', but also indicated a concern for the development of rehabilitative approaches through evidence-based practice. In a little over a decade, New Labour would seek to change the nature and use of community sentences, the organisational structure and working practices within the Probation Service, and the role of commissioning and contestability in probation. Further change would be introduced by the Coalition government formed in May 2010.

The nature and use of community sentences

The New Labour era (1997–2010) marked a shift away from the old social democratic underpinnings traditionally associated with the Labour Party (Whitehead, 2010), and the new era would be characterised by modernisation and 'national renewal' (White, 1994). The impact on probation would be seen as early as 1998, with the publication of the Home Office (1998) consultation document which outlined the intention to bring together the Prison and Probation Services. This suggested an ideological shift within probation, and a requirement for probation to modernise in an increasingly punitive fashion. It was also suggested that the Probation Service should be renamed (although this never materialised), in order to convey the message that advising, assisting and befriending offenders, the ideological approach traditionally associated with probation, would no longer be tolerated (Whitehead, 2010).

Early in New Labour's second term, the Halliday Report (2001) had stated that community sentences were too complex, and that sentencers should be given a set of options from which to construct a sentence. A number of recommendations from the Halliday Report informed the future sentencing reforms proposed in the White Paper, *Justice for All* (Home Office, 2002b), and the Criminal Justice Act 2003. The Act introduced a menu of possible sentence options (CJA 2003, s. 177), and indicated that community sentences should be tailored to suit individual needs:

> [A] requirement or requirements forming part of the community order must be … the most suitable for the offender [and that] the restrictions on liberty imposed by the order must be … commensurate with the seriousness of the offence.
>
> (CJA 2003, s. 148)

These requirements were also intended to be available for individuals who would have previously been given a short custodial sentence (that is, less than 12 months), which would be replaced by 'Custody Plus', involving a short custodial sentence and a period on licence in the community (Criminal Justice Act 2003, s. 181, 182). However, the 'shelving' of this sentence has meant that a significant group of offenders are denied access to resettlement interventions that could otherwise facilitate a reduction in reoffending (Lewis *et al.*, 2007: 49). Herein lay a contradiction within New Labour's criminal justice policy. On the one hand, the language of the Community Order suggested a focus upon the needs and requirements of the individual offender. On the other hand, the decision to shelve Custody Plus may be seen as a reluctance to support such needs.

However, as New Labour's tenure progressed, public protection and reducing reoffending clearly became the twin priority goals of the government's Offender Management strategy (Ministry of Justice, 2009d). In its 'Five Year Strategy for Protecting the Public and Reducing Re-offending' (Home Office, 2006b) the government outlined its commitment to these shared aims:

> As well as needing offenders to be punished, a healthy and safe society needs them to be given every opportunity to reform – to get back onto the straight and narrow and become constructive contributors to the good of society as a whole. This is not just because it is morally right to enable people to change their lives for the better and overcome their failures and mistakes. It is also a practical recognition that more than half of all crime is currently committed by people who have been through the system and have not yet changed their behaviour. Reducing re-offending will cut crime and make Britain safer. This strategy … explains how we will protect the public and punish offenders, but at the same time tackle the linked factors that make them more likely to commit crime again.
>
> (Home Office, 2006b: 5)

This strategy incorporated a mixed economy of providers, partnerships, and end-to-end offender management. Furthermore, the strategy built upon the provisions for sentencing established in Part 12 of the Criminal Justice Act 2003, in advocating the use of fines, unpaid work, custodial and community sentences (Home Office, 2006b). The New Labour government also transformed the community sentence, presenting it as a tough sentence designed to punish and deter offenders, while incorporating aspects designed to reduce reoffending through breaking the cycle of criminal activity. Prior to this, the community sentence had shifted from being an 'alternative to custody to punishment in the community', as the Conservative government of the early 1990s sought to portray probation as being a tougher option (Worrall and Hoy, 2005: 23).

However, following the 'What Works' movement, a rehabilitative ethos was restored to the community sentence, largely through the introduction, in the mid-1990s, of various programmes designed to help individual offenders to alter their attitudes and behaviour in order to reduce their own likelihood of reoffending (Raynor, 1996). The New Labour government began by committing to an evidence-based approach to criminal justice policy, under the guise of the 'What Works' movement. This underpinned the implementation of the Effective Practice Initiative (Robinson and Crow, 2009: 80), the publication of the 'Effective Practice Guide' (Chapman and Hough, 1998), the development of the Crime Reduction Programme (Maguire, 2004) and the evaluation of various 'Path-finder' projects (Lewis *et al.*, 2007; Rex and Gelsthorpe, 2002). The government established a commitment to evaluate the effects of various programmes, which could be delivered in the community, on reducing reoffending (Raynor, 2002a). Indeed, the National Probation Service was set the target of 60,000 accredited programme completions by 2004, with an expectation that this would result in a 5 per cent reduction in reconvictions among those under supervision (Raynor and Vanstone, 2002: 104).

The New Labour government also advocated community sentences as a means of rehabilitating offenders, and this was justified on the basis that 'It's great news if an offender becomes an ex-offender thanks to a community sentence. But the people who benefit most are the general public who want to see less crime' (Ministry of Justice, 2008a). The benefits of reducing reoffending are often stated with reference to the reduced cost to the taxpayer, as well as the benefits of 'fewer victims' and 'safer communities' (Ministry of Justice, 2008a). Similarly, the Social Exclusion Unit (2002) stated that 'crime can have a devastating impact on the lives of victims. It scars entire communities, and the costs to society as a whole are huge' (2002: 3), and efforts to reduce reoffending have also been justified by linking it with public protection: 'Public safety is not safeguarded when prisoners are released into homelessness, with no prospect of employment' (2002: 4). Community sentences are now designed to tackle criminogenic rather than non-criminogenic (welfare) needs, because the latter are not directly linked to risk and, consequently, attention towards them will not reduce the calculated likelihood of reoffending (Robinson, 2008: 432). Thus, the commitment towards community sentences and efforts to reduce reoffending have been established less with reference to the wider social structural factors that influence crime causation, or the difficulties that confront individual offenders in their attempts to move away from crime (Robinson, 2008: 432–3). Rather, the emphasis has been upon the positive effects upon wider society in terms of public protection, safer communities and reduced economic cost.

The use of community sentences increased during the period in which New Labour was in power. Indeed, community sentences were given in 196,424 cases in 2007, an increase of 56,434 since 1997. The most common disposal in 2007 was fines, accounting for 66.6 per cent of all sentences, although this has decreased from 72.1 per cent since 1997. Custody accounted for 6.7 per cent of all sentences in 2007, a slight increase since 1997, although the proportion of sentences resulting in custody has remained broadly consistent over this time period. The largest increase (from 0.3 per cent in 1997 to 2.9 per cent in 2007) was in the use of suspended sentences, largely as a result of the introduction of the Suspended Sentence Order (SSO) in the Criminal Justice Act 2003. The SSO was introduced for offences committed after April 2005 and replaced the Fully Suspended Sentence (FSS) (Ministry of Justice, 2009a: 16).

Thus, while the prison population increased rapidly during the New Labour era, the use of custody as a proportion of total sentences remained broadly the same between 1997 and 2007, largely as a result of increases in the use of the Community Order and the SSO. The introduction of the Community Order and the SSO marked a significant change in sentencing policy in England and Wales. These changes were intended to replace the 'mishmash' of community sentences that existed beforehand (Mair and Mills, 2009: 5); to provide probation with a single order; facilitate offender resettlement through narrowing the divide between custody and community; and to address the issue of 'uptariffing' (Mair *et al.*, 2007: 7). However, the new orders also raised the issue of 'sentence over-load', as has been evidenced when sentencers are given greater options (Hedderman *et al.*, 1999), as combinations of multiple requirements could be included in the original sentence, or additional requirements imposed if the order was breached (Mair *et al.*, 2007: 13–14).

Trends in the use of the new sentences between 2005–2008 revealed a steady decline in one-to-one supervision, an increase in the use of punitive requirements, and a decrease in the use of accredited programme requirements. Over this time period the use of one-to-one supervision and group work activities declined, while the use of more punitive requirements, such as unpaid work, remained high. This would indicate that New Labour's approach had been to administer a punitive community sentence, with rehabilitation as the individual's responsibility. Over the same time period, five requirements (supervision, unpaid work, accredited programmes, drug treatment, curfew) accounted for over 90 per cent of all those used. Increased workloads and limited resources are likely explanations for the narrow administration of possible sentence options (Mair and Mills, 2009: 11; National Audit Office, 2008a; Oldfield and Grimshaw, 2007).

Indeed, caseloads in the Probation Service have increased at a significant rate during the last decade,[5] and this may have discouraged sentencers from impos- ing supervision or accredited programme requirements. Alongside this, budget allocations have been reduced (Oldfield and Grimshaw, 2007: 12), and this is also likely to have affected the use of requirements in individual areas. In addition to this, the number of 'frontline' staff diminished, while the number of senior managers increased considerably, and the ratio of offenders to supervising officers also rose.[6] The evidence presented in the tables below reflects the view that New Labour's approach to probation had been to enhance the punitive dimensions of community sentences, in order to ensure that they did not appear as 'soft options'. Further, the approach may be seen as encouraging individual offenders to become more 'self-realising' in their efforts to move away from crime, offering less direct support, while also demonstrating the 'surveillant managerial' discourse that underpins criminal justice policy (Nellis, 2005).

Organisational structure and working practices

While pragmatism and a commitment to evidence-based practice might be offered as the underpinning rationale for these developments, changes to the Probation Service indicated a desire to portray probation as less of a 'soft option' and more as a punitive sentence, and there was also a desire to establish a more managerialist structure and organisation. A new vocabulary emerged to define the sentences that probation would deliver, in part in an attempt to ensure that probation would not be seen as a 'soft option'. Table 2.1 indicates the transition in vocabulary within probation sentences. This new vocabulary placed 'community', 'rehabilitation' and 'punishment' at the heart of probation work and the remit of the new National Service was 'enforcement, rehabilitation and public protection' (Robinson and Crow, 2009: 45).

Indeed, in practice these changes entailed a greater emphasis upon enforcement, such that offenders had to fulfil the requirements of their sentence or face prosecution for failure to cooperate (Raynor and Vanstone, 2002: 103–4). Moreover, in practice these changes reflected an attitude that rehabilitative work was a 'consequence of crime', as opposed to something that offenders received as a result of their difficult circumstances. Indeed, rehabilitative work was regarded as something which would benefit the wider community, rather than just helping the individual offender (Raynor and Vanstone, 2002: 113–14). Hence, the identity and philosophy of probation altered at the turn of the century, as did its organisation and delivery.

In 2001, following the Criminal Justice and Court Services Act 2000, the 54 Probation Services were replaced by a National Probation Service, establishing 42 Probation areas and a National Directorate (Worrall and Hoy, 2005: 92). This

Table 2.1 Changes to community sentences for adults

Former sentence	*Became*
Probation orders	Community Rehabilitation Order
Community service order	Community Punishment Order
Combination order	Community Punishment and Rehabilitation Order

Source: adapted from Raynor and Vanstone, 2002: 101.

made crime reduction and public protection explicit aims of the Service, and would remove powers considerably from the local level. Under the previous arrangement, each of the 54 Probation Services were responsible to a local Probation Committee, and initiatives and delivery could be driven by local priorities, which was responsible for some area variation in the implementation of services (Underdown, 1998). With the introduction of the National Probation Service, policy became centralised and a national organisational structure was introduced. The 42 Probation areas corresponded with the police, courts, and Crown Prosecution Service to enhance the possibility of partnership and multi-agency working. Shortly after the introduction of the National Probation Service, the government introduced the National Offender Management Service (NOMS) (Home Office, 2004c), in response to the recommendations made in the Carter Report, a review of the correctional services in England and Wales (Carter, 2003). This 'would ensure the end-to-end management of offenders, regardless of whether they were given a custodial or community sentence' (2003: 33). Raynor (2002) argued that the rationale behind the introduction of the National Probation Service was to introduce a centralised service capable of greater efficiency and effectiveness, driven by national policies and targets, and the same may be true of the introduction of NOMS.

The explicit setting of objectives, and later targets, began in the 1980s, inscribed within the framework of New Public Management. Under New Labour, targets were central to the approach to improving public sector services as a whole, and probation more specifically (Whitehead, 2007: 39–40). Targets pervaded considerable areas of probation work including: OASys assessment completions within set time frames; breach proceedings initiated within set time frames; attendance at arranged appointments by offenders; unpaid work requirement completions; and pre-sentence reports completed within set time frames (Ministry of Justice, 2007b). In 2007–2008, for example, the target for accredited programme completions was 17,319 (NPS, 2008: 10), and specific targets were introduced for individual areas, for example the target for completed unpaid work requirements in South Wales in 2007–2008 was 1,318 (National Audit Office, 2008a). The emphasis on targets of this nature was a concern for the timeliness and number of completions of certain aspects of probation work, rather than the engagement with the offender or the quality of the work completed. Thus, the concern was with inputs, process and outputs, rather than content, quality or meaningful outcomes.

Indeed, of the targets contained in the Integrated Probation Performance Framework, 20 per cent focused on timeliness and 18 per cent on the number of requirement completions, whereas only 11 per cent related to quality and those were almost all in relation to risk assessments and pre-sentence reports (National Audit Office, 2008a: 60). No targets measured the quality of engagement with offenders, despite evidence to suggest that this can be a key factor in facilitating a reduction in reoffending (Mason and Prior, 2008), and there was a lack of focus on measuring the quality of offender management (National Audit Office, 2008a: 35). Whitehead (2007) wrote that targets are arbitrary devices that give the impression of precision, whereas they are actually subjective and are formed on the basis of human judgement. He continued to argue that a target culture, as opposed to a person-centred service, is 'much more bureaucratic, mechanised and subject to routine, and reflects a one-size-fits-all approach' (2007: 41). There are also issues to be considered in relation to the influence of target achievement in other areas of the criminal justice system, and of competing targets within probation (Whitehead, 2007: 43), which could lead to undesirable consequences. For example, it is possible that an offender could escape breach for not attending a supervision session as reporting this would affect the service's attendance target. Further, budgets, and performance-related pay for senior managers, were linked to target achievement, which could have led to questionable information in relation to sentencing advice (Whitehead, 2007: 44). Despite these potential consequences, targets were a dominant feature of probation in England and Wales under New Labour. The qualities and tasks involved in working with people within various organisations – such as, listening, understanding, empathising, and problem-solving – are distinct from those which are measured within the target culture, but the latter eclipsed the former through the pursuit of 'more bureaucratic forms of accountability' (Whitehead, 2007: 45).

Commissioning and contestability

Further efforts to increase efficiency and effectiveness were driven in the latter part of the New Labour tenure through processes of contestability. Arguably, contestability also began under the auspices of New Public Management, with its emphasis upon explicit standards, valuing outputs over processes, and encouraging constraint in the use of public resources. Contestability, therefore, has roots in the Conservative government of the 1980s, with its aim of 'opening up the market' through the disaggregation of public sector units, competition in the public sector, and the introduction of private sector management styles and techniques within the public sector (Canton, 2011: 187). Contestability was a prominent theme in the Carter Report (Carter, 2003). Carter argued that more effective service delivery could be achieved through greater use of contestability, 'using providers of prison and probation from across the public, private and voluntary sectors' (2003: 34), although this claim was not evidenced in the report. The government's vision for contestability derived from the experience of contracting-out prison services to private firms (Home Office, 2004c: 14). Some have argued that the use of the private sector increased efficiency and effectiveness (Hutto, 1990; Logan, 1990, 1996; Logan and Rausch, 1985; MacDonald, 1990, 1992; Young, 1987), while others have argued that such successes have been overstated (Dilulio, 1988; Mobley and Geis, 2001; Robbins, 1988; Ryan and Ward, 1989), and that private sector companies can manipulate policy to achieve their own ends (Shichor, 1995). Despite the apparent lack of supporting empirical evidence, Carter clearly identified contestability as playing a central role in the future delivery of services, claiming that 'within five years ... contestability would have been introduced across the whole of prisons and community interventions' (Carter, 2003: 41).

The Probation Service offered strong opposition to the introduction of contestability, and a number of authors highlighted the potential consequences of pursuing this objective (see for example: Nellis, 2006). Similar questions have been raised in regard to the government's introduction of a purchaser-provider split within the Probation Service (Bhui, 2004: 99; Lewis, 2008: 74), particularly in relation to the supervision of individual offenders and the potentially deleterious effects upon the officer-offender relationship (see Robinson and Dignan, 2004). However, the Management of Offenders and Sentencing Bill 2005 provided the Home Secretary with powers to direct probation boards to commission services from specific providers (s. 2). Although the 2005 Bill was not passed during the 2004–2005 Parliamentary session, the government demonstrated a continued commitment to introducing contestability, publishing a consultation document (NOMS, 2005) and, shortly afterwards, in a summary of responses to the consultation the government stated the intention to 'introduce legislation to restructure the Probation Service as soon as Parliamentary time allows' (NOMS, 2006a: 8). Later that year the government outlined further plans to increase the use of contestability:

> This year and next year we are requiring local probation areas, on a voluntary basis, to double and then double again the proportion of services they contract out. From April 2008, legislation permitting, we will go further and compete a much larger proportion of the interventions they provide – up to £250m worth of services a year.
>
> (NOMS, 2006b: 2)

The Offender Management Act 2007 received Royal Assent in July of the same year, and gave the Secretary of State powers for full commissioning and contestability to be introduced to probation services (s. 3).

Responsibilisation in probation

Some readings of probation's history may give the impression that what was once a rehabilitative/welfarist model of probation has been replaced by a punitive/risk-focused service. However, it is rather the case that 'at times correction and reform have held centre stage, though punishment was *never fully displaced* – and ... the reverse is also true' (Hutchinson, 2006: 444, emphasis added). Indeed, some commentators suggest that certain accounts of penal history have overstated the extent of the rehabilitative ideal during the penal welfare era (O'Malley, 2004; Zedner, 2002), and Vaughan (2000) has argued that punitiveness and reform are always entwined in forms of modern punishment (2000: 26–7). It is argued here that this is also the case for contemporary probation practice.

In theory, the approach adopted by New Labour involved a more balanced approach to working with offenders, suggesting a concern for punishment, public protection, resettlement and rehabilitation, as outlined in the Management of Offenders and Sentencing Bill 2005 (s. 1). Furthermore, New Labour's approach appeared to show a concern for 'social rehabilitation' (Robinson and Crow, 2009), through the targeting of various factors which may contribute towards experiences of social exclusion (SEU, 2002). However, programmes of prison expansion (Home Office, 2006a), contestability, the expansion of risk assessment, and the continuation of populist approaches to sentencing (Lewis, 2008: 78) appeared to contradict the more humanitarian proposals. Indeed, initially the election of New Labour offered hope of an 'upturn' in probation's fortunes, but the pervasive managerialism, target-setting and bureaucratic culture would detract from the one-to-one work of practitioners, and would focus too heavily upon measurable outcomes rather than quality or processes (Burke and Collett, 2010: 242). Furthermore, the shift towards 'bureaucratic positivism' in the use of targets, quantification and measurement (Whitehead, 2007) indicates that probation work had become more detached from face-to-face work with offenders, with concerns moving away from exploring 'why' particular behaviours occurred towards the more immediate questions of 'what' had taken place (2007: 39).

Within contemporary approaches to responding to reoffending, the needs of the offender have become narrowly redefined as 'criminogenic needs', or individual risk factors (Hannah-Moffat, 2005). Structural constraints upon the decisions and motivation of offenders to desist, including access to social, cultural and economic resources, are of little concern (Gray, 2005: 939), and interventions which target the causes of crime are directed, largely, at moral deficiencies and personal shortcomings (Hannah-Moffat, 1999). Put simply, individuals are responsible for the consequences of social structures which shape their lives, yet which they may be unaware of (Squires, 2006: 155). The emphasis which is placed on the offender to take responsibility for reducing their own risk of reoffending mirrored the wider approach to social inclusion adopted by New Labour. Rather than attempting to remove the structural constraints which socially exclude sub-groups of the population, the focus has instead been on equality of opportunity (Jordan, 1998: 18). This responsibilisation, then, created an environment within which failure to take advantage of the opportunities created would be seen as an individual deficiency. The implication of this is that processes of moral engineering were regarded as the most appropriate intervention to reintegrate offenders, rather than approaches which would tackle structural inequalities (Gray, 2005: 940).

One of the key distinctions between rehabilitation in penal modernity and the approach adopted by New Labour is that the offender was no longer regarded as a disadvantaged and marginalised individual, but rather was recast as a rational decision-maker whose criminality was a response to situational circumstances. As such, offending could be controlled through the actuarial identification of an individual's risk of offending (Garland, 1996), and interventions were designed to encourage offenders to reduce this risk themselves. This was exemplified by the focus upon risk assessment and programmes designed to challenge individuals' cognitions and behaviour. Programmes were also offence-focused, which provided the explicit message that the offender's actions were wrong (Robinson and Crow, 2009: 121). This suggests an ideology within probation policy and practice under New Labour that 'irrational' choices were blamed upon the individual, rather than upon structural constraints:

> Citizens who do not make the desired choice are recast as imprudent and reckless, blameworthy and responsible for their own misfortune. Disadvantage and exclusion are reframed as matters of choice and not of structural processes, crime itself becomes a matter of irrational and imprudent choices. Citizens who fall into the imprudent category are seen as ripe for remoralization....Offenders are of course a key group for such a remoralization and responsibilization agenda.
>
> (Kemshall, 2003: 19)

Such approaches suggest that as the offender recognises the immorality of their actions, they will draw the conclusion that they need to alter their behaviour, and the attitudes that underpinned it, in order to prevent future offending (Duff, 2001: 101). Thus, offending behaviour programmes were underpinned by a philosophy of responsibilisation, with respect to the fact that they emphasised the personal responsibility and moral wrongdoing of the individual at whom they were targeted.

Of course, an argument can be made that New Labour introduced proposals which recognised the influence of structural factors on offending, and it was acknowledged, particularly through the Social Exclusion Unit, that offenders are likely to experience multiple disadvantage. Evidence suggests that a more holistic approach to interventions is the most effective method of reducing reoffending (McGuire, 2002), and research has suggested that delivery of such an approach requires multi-agency partnerships and communication to provide services both in custody and the community (Partridge, 2004). Such findings, for example, informed the development of Offender Management (Home Office, 2004d). However, it is argued here that within such developments there was an underlying discourse of agency, as there was an implicit emphasis upon notions of individualism, responsibility, reflexivity and risk (see Giddens, 1990, 1998 for further discussion of these concepts). A consequence of this is that individuals were, ultimately, defined as being responsible for seizing the opportunities available to overcome the structural barriers to reducing their own risk of reoffending.

This ideology reflected a shift in welfare paradigms, towards greater individualism, as 'state institutions must now develop concurrently with the idea of the "self-monitoring individual", and the "reflexive agent"' (Fudge and Williams, 2006: 588). As such, under New Labour the state became responsible for enabling individuals to confront challenges independently. This is because the individual agent was regarded as being responsible for their own destiny, and it was assumed that they have the power to change the conditions in which they live if they choose to do so (Greener, 2002: 692–3). As Giddens (1998) suggested: 'We have to make our lives in a more active way than was true of previous generations, and we need more actively to accept responsibilities for the consequences of what we do and the lifestyle habits we adopt.' New Labour's approach, therefore, can be regarded as one which emphasises equality of opportunity, rather than one which sought to tackle structural barriers to reducing reoffending (Gray, 2005). Within this it can be argued that individuals who were perceived to have failed to take advantage of such opportunities to rehabilitate themselves would be punished further still (Bennett, 2008). An example of this responsibilising approach can be found by exploring employment, which was at the heart of New Labour's strategy for reducing reoffending and in-keeping with the wider programme of social inclusion (HM Government, 2005; Young and Matthews, 2003: 20). Yet New Labour's policies, designed to facilitate (re-)entry into employment, were premised upon a hybrid of 'work-first' and 'human capital' approaches. The former 'prioritise labour market attachment on the premise that any job is better than none', while the latter emphasise the development of personal attitudes and skills 'that will equip people to find and retain suitable jobs' (Dean, 2003: 442). Thus, the emphasis of New Labour policy was upon 'manipulating agency', rather than tackling structural barriers to employment (Young and Matthews, 2003: 20).

A consequence of this approach is the perception that any work is better than no work (Young, 2002: 473), and there is little consideration of variability in demand for labour. For the majority of offenders, who are more likely to live in communities characterised by deprivation, poverty and unemployment, there is a greater probability that demand for labour will be scarce. Further, the desistance literature has suggested that it is not merely having a job that decreases the likelihood of recidivism, but that it is the quality of employment and the subjective attachment the individual has to it (Weaver and McNeill, 2007a: 90), a finding which is also supported by Harper and Chitty's (2005) review of 'What Works'. However, policy and practice related to the employment of offenders has predominantly been focused upon efforts to increase employability (see also Haslewood-Pocsik *et al.*, 2008), thus reflecting an underlying discourse of agency. Further, while there is some evidence of attempts to try to engineer structural barriers to employment (see, HM Government, 2006), the overriding emphasis is upon getting offenders into any kind of work, regardless of quality or sustainability – in 2006–2007, for example, a target was set to place 15,000 offenders into employment, with a target of 12,000 sustaining employment for a period of just four weeks (NPS, 2006).

It can be seen, therefore, that in recent years probation policy and practice have become increasingly managerialist, retributive and punitive. This is, at least, partly the result of an emerging discourse around community penalties and community justice which has seen probation move away from its traditional rehabilitative roots (see also Feeley and Simon, 1992, 1994). Such changes have also been reported, to a greater or lesser extent, in the USA (Taxman *et al.*, 2010) and elsewhere in Europe (Durnescu, 2008). Rehabilitation, in this context, has become something which is done to offenders, in the interests of the wider community and society in general (McNeill *et al.*, 2012). The importance of this is the potential effect upon efforts to reduce reoffending through interactions between Probation Officers and individual Probationers. As will be explored in greater detail later in this book, the interactions between Probation Officers and offenders are central to efforts to reduce patterns of reoffending. These interactions may be influenced by the organisational culture of probation, and the wider criminal justice system (Mawby and Worrall, 2011a, 2011b; Phillips, 2011). In order to ensure that successful reductions in reoffending occur, an understanding is required of the processes by which people cease offending and the interfaces between this and community-based interventions.

3 Persistence, desistance and the transitional phase

In the 1980s research which found that a small proportion of offenders were responsible for a significant amount of overall crime led to the emergence of academic concerns with criminal careers (Blumstein *et al.*, 1988; Elliott, 1994; Farrington, 1995; Kempf, 1988; Petersilia, 1980; Piper, 1985; Shannon, 1991). The term 'criminal careers' in this context refers to the sequence of events or behaviours related to offending over the period of a lifetime, rather than referring to the manner in which an individual may sustain themselves financially (Blumstein *et al.*, 1986). Researchers examining criminal careers have since been able to shed considerable light on the factors associated with the onset, continuation and termination of offending within an individual's lifetime. The development of this research agenda has made it possible to elucidate the factors which are associated with the beginning of a criminal career, and also the patterns which might explain why some people persistently offend. Various factors during childhood, for example, may lead to the early development of antisocial behaviours, which may increase the likelihood of criminal behaviour and persistent offending in adolescence and adulthood (Farrington, 1986, 2007; McAra and McVie, 2012).

Understanding persistence

Various risk factors have been identified which can increase the likelihood that an individual may become involved in crime. These may include: poor parental supervision; poverty and deprivation; poor educational experiences; having delinquent family members; child maltreatment; parental conflict; peer associations; and neighbourhood environment (McCord *et al.*, 2001; West and Farrington, 1973; Farrington, 1997b, 2000; Denno, 1990). Various studies have shown that these factors have a cumulative effect, whereby the more risk factors that are present in a particular case the greater the likelihood of that individual becoming involved in crime. Indeed, some studies, such as the *Cambridge Study in Delinquent Development*, show that the effect of childhood risk factors is likely to endure during adulthood (Piquero *et al.*, 2007). The identification of these risk factors may be perceived to be a deterministic explanation of offending, wherein individuals who present such risk factors are destined to engage in a lengthy criminal career. In reality, however, pathways through crime are more likely to be characterised by change and variability (Healy, 2010), and several authors have examined different patterns of offending and reoffending at different points of the life-course (Blokland and Nieuwbeerta, 2005; Farrington, 2003; Horney *et al.*, 1995; Moffitt, 1993, 2008; Nagin, 2004; Paternoster and Brame, 1997; Patterson and Yoerger, 1993; Piquero *et al.*, 2003).

Studies such as these have shown that while adolescent delinquency is indicative of adult offending, not all individuals who offend during adolescence will continue to offend during their adulthood. It is more likely that a smaller number of individuals who offend during adolescence will be responsible for a disproportionate number of offences during adulthood. However, even those who persistently reoffend during adulthood are likely to cease offending at some point as they become older. Indeed, the relationship between age, crime and desistance is 'one of the surest things in all of criminology' (Griffin, 2006: 1). As individuals age they are more likely to decrease the frequency of their offending, until they cease offending altogether. This is illustrated by the age-crime curve, which suggests that most criminal careers follow a similar pattern. Offending begins during pre- or early adolescence, and peaks at around late adolescence. There is a sharp decrease in offending between late adolescence and early adulthood, and criminal activity levels off by middle age (Nagin *et al.*, 1995). Indeed, there is evidence to suggest that once they have ceased offending, 'many ex-offenders manage to create conventional lifestyles that are often indistinguishable from those of non-offenders' (Healy, 2010: 4).

Explaining persistence

Various explanations have been offered to account for why some people persistently reoffend over the life-course. There is an argument to be made that persistent reoffending may be a product of 'suspended maturity', which in this context refers to the presence of certain attitudes or behaviours in adulthood which are more characteristic of adolescence. Indeed, early explanations of offending identified a decline in offending with maturation and the transition to adulthood (Goring, 1913), and Glueck and Glueck (1945, 1968, 1974) suggested that persistent reoffending is the result of suspended maturation – that is, that persistent offenders, regardless of their age, are yet to develop the maturity necessary to cease committing crime. Glueck and Glueck (1945) wrote of the individuals featured in their 13-year study of discharged prisoners, that it is 'the achievement of adequate maturation regardless of chronological age at which it occurred that was the significant influence in the behaviour change of our criminals' (1945: 81). More recently, however, Hayford and Furstenberg (2008) found no evidence to support the contention that an offender's behaviour might be incongruent with their stage of the life-course.

Glueck and Glueck's work prompted subsequent longitudinal research in the UK and elsewhere. Such research was underpinned by an assumption that criminality and offending behaviour are changeable. Gottfredson and Hirschi (1987,

1990; Hirschi and Gottfredson, 2001), on the other hand, suggested that longitudinal studies are futile because the cause of crime remains stable over time, and
once it is identified early in the life-course it will then remain constant. They
made reference to individuals' capacities for self-control, arguing that the propensity to commit crime remains stable over time between individuals. They
argued that self-control is formed in early childhood and, therefore, some individuals will have relatively lower self-control than others. However, as socialisation processes continue throughout the life-course, absolute self-control can
increase. Therefore, persistent offenders are likely to have relatively low levels
of self-control, but as absolute self-control increases they are more likely to be
able to desist later in their lives. The authors gave no consideration to the influence of life-course events or environmental context upon persistent offending,
however, and instead wrote that:

> maturational reform is just that, change in behaviour that comes with matu-
> ration; [Gottfredson and Hirschi's theory] suggests that spontaneous desist-
> ance is just that, change in behaviour that cannot be explained and change
> that occurs regardless of what else happens.
>
> (Gottfredson and Hirschi, 1990: 136)

Ezell and Cohen (2004) found little evidence to support the key tenets of Gottfredson and Hirschi's (1990) theory and, while Gottfredson and Hirschi's theory
underestimates the degree of self-control that many offenders have when planning criminal activities, they do not provide any detail about the variable of
criminal opportunity (Soothill *et al.*, 2009). Laub and Sampson (2003) were also
somewhat critical of these approaches, arguing that theories based on self-
control imply that persistent offending results from individual deficiencies with
respect to coping with the demands of society.

Moffitt (1993) also argued that a group of offenders existed whose offending
behaviour would remain stable over the life-course. Her often-cited offender taxonomy of offender development sought to explain the apparent difference
between those who only offend during their teenage years, and those who continue to offend into adulthood. Moffitt distinguished between adolescent-limited
(AL) offenders and life-course persistent (LCP) offenders. AL offenders aspire
to certain goals of adulthood (such as employment, money, or status), but are
unable to achieve them – what Moffitt referred to as the 'maturity gap'. As a
result, they imitate the behaviour of LCP offenders and offend as a means of
mimicking the status of young adults (see also Greenberg, 1977). As they
approach adulthood the maturity gap narrows as they are able to achieve goals
more easily through legitimate means.

LCP offenders, by contrast, are individuals who begin offending at an earlier
age (often early childhood), and continue to offend throughout adolescence and
well into adulthood. LCP offenders are more likely to have neuropsychological
deficits, which could include low levels of self-control which lead to an inability
to control impulses. During childhood, LCP offenders are likely to present

difficult and challenging behaviour which is likely to elicit parental responses. But, as Moffitt (1993) suggested, these parental responses are often inadequate or inconsistent as the family finds it difficult to cope with the challenges presented. As a result, the antisocial child develops into an antisocial adolescent, and the LCP offender does not experience the socialisation necessary to cease offending in late adolescence. It is, as Moffitt (1994) has pointed out, the interaction between the LCP offender's personality traits and the environmental reactions to them that diminish the likelihood of change (1994: 28), rather than simply the early experiences of offending. Crucially, for Moffitt, continuity of offending behaviour is more likely for LCP offenders than the possibility of change and the adoption of a more 'conventional' state.

Numerous studies have examined this typology since its inception, and it has received mixed support. Some have found evidence to support the view that neuropsychological and family environment deficits are more likely to lead to persistent offending in adulthood (Moffitt and Caspi, 2001; Raine *et al.*, 1994), and Ezell and Cohen (2004) found evidence of the presence of AL offenders. However, they also found six groups of LCP offenders, as opposed to the one group identified by Moffitt (1993), although Moffitt (2003; Moffitt and Walsh, 2003) later acknowledged the possibility of other offending typologies. Other studies have found some support for Moffitt's typology, but have questioned the extent of the distinction between AL and LCP offenders. For example, Nagin *et al.* (1995) found that while LCP offenders were responsible for a significant amount of overall crime, there was evidence that AL offenders continued to participate in offending and offending-related behaviour well into adulthood.

Massoglia and Uggen (2010) have also argued that growing out of offending behaviour is a crucial aspect of the transition from adolescence to adulthood. Drawing upon the work of various researchers examining transitions over the life-course (Arnett, 2000, 2003, 2007; Elder *et al.*, 2003; Furstenberg *et al.*, 2004), Massoglia and Uggen (2010) argued that age-appropriateness of various behaviours is embedded within a society's culture. Various formal and informal social controls and sanctions emerge from this culture and this conditions the onset, persistence and cessation of particular behaviours. Writing from an interactionist perspective, they suggested that certain behaviours or transitions are associated with particular ages or points in the life-course. Those whose behaviour or transitions do not match social expectations are unlikely to see themselves as adults, because they have not made the transitions that would be expected of someone their age, and because they have not progressed from an earlier point in their lives. Crucially, they posited that offending is not regarded consensually by society as age-appropriate and, therefore, that those who persistently reoffend in adulthood will not be perceived by key reference groups as being adults. The authors developed this line of argument by suggesting that because of the perceptions of these reference groups, persistent offenders were more likely to believe that others see them as not being adults, and therefore were more likely to see themselves as not having adult status. This, they argued, explains why many individuals who offend in adolescence but grow out of offending behaviour during the transition to adulthood seem to acquire adult status, roles and responsibilities, and see themselves as adults.

This is similar to Maruna's (2001) argument that persistent offenders live according to a 'condemnation script'. Those who reoffend during adulthood regard the onset of their delinquent behaviour as being conditioned by poor upbringing, social inequalities or a lack of opportunities. Although they may want to lead a legitimate lifestyle, they feel powerless to make changes in their lives. They regard themselves as being victims of circumstance, constrained by poverty, drug dependency, or social stigma, and that they sought refuge in alcohol, drugs and crime. Maruna (2001) suggested that, for some, crime was a means of 'escaping the burden of choice', in that individuals would intentionally offend in order to receive a prison sentence and avoid the burden of responsibility for making decisions about their own lives. For Massoglia and Uggen (2010) the experience of punishments such as incarceration would prolong or disrupt socially expected life-course transitions, such that individuals do not acquire the roles and responsibilities associated with adult status. Consequently, reoffending becomes more likely, as a continuation of delinquent behaviour would be associated with how the individual is perceived by others, how they believe others perceive them, and how they in turn perceive themselves.

This may suggest a somewhat pessimistic view for persistent offenders, and Maruna (2001) also argued that for persistent offenders the future outlook is 'dire' (2001: Chapter 3). However, this is not because of personal deficiencies or particular personality traits, but may instead be because of their common social circumstances and poor life chances (McNeill and Whyte, 2007: 46). Similarly, Laub and Sampson (2003) argued that persistent offending results from a lack of positive turning points in an individual's life. Drawing upon the case study of 'Boston Billy' in their research, they wrote that he had:

> little opportunity or ability to engage successfully in the traditional pathways away from crime. He did not serve in the military, he did not have a steady job that he was willing to invest in (or an employer willing to invest in him), and he did not have any strong ties to a wife.
>
> (2003: 160)

Laub and Sampson (2003) also wrote that the excitement of crime can be an attractive alternative to conformity for persistent offenders (2003: 165), and that many persistent offenders have to contend with serious alcohol problems. As such, many offenders face considerable challenges to moving away from crime and, therefore, are condemned to persistent offending behaviour, at least until they are able to overcome such obstacles. Indeed, individuals who persistently reoffend are likely to retain several obstacles in their personal and social contexts. Persistent offenders are unlikely to be able to cease offending by addressing one or two obstacles. Massoglia and Uggen (2010) similarly argued that the transition from adolescence to adulthood will not occur as a consequence of one event, but rather as a result of a constellation of life-course events. Consequently, many persistent offenders will continue to reoffend over a prolonged period of time as they seek to address the various factors which may contribute to their reoffending.

This is illustrated in Leibrich's (1993) work, where she described offending careers as curved; the offenders in her sample could not be divided into 'neat' categories. It is unlikely that many offenders will be able to overcome all obstacles, and desist from offending behaviour that they may have engaged in from a young age, in an instant. This is also illustrative of the argument which suggests that desistance does not occur merely as a function of chronological age (Loeber and LeBlanc, 1990: 452), but rather particular life-course events are likely to correspond with certain periods of transition such that desistance is more likely. The theories developed by Giordano *et al.* (2002) and Rumgay (2004) suggested that individuals must be both open to change and regard particular life-course events as opportunities, or 'hooks', for change. As such, life-course events which are associated with desistance exist only as potential opportunities to change until they are acted upon by the individual concerned.

These opportunities (employment, housing, and so forth) are more likely to be available at different times during the life-course, such that factors associated with offending are likely to have a differential impact depending upon the individual's age. According to Jamieson *et al.* (1999), desistance among younger adolescents (14–15) is more likely to be associated with a negative evaluation of crime. For older adolescents (18–19), increased maturity, often linked to life-course events such as employment or relationships, and the transition to adulthood, are more likely to prompt desistance. For young adults (22–25), desistance is associated with the assumption of new roles, such as 'parent' or 'breadwinner' (McNeill and Whyte, 2007: 51). Therefore, while variation may result from differences in age, motivation, and personal and social circumstances, most individuals, including persistent offenders, are able to overcome various obstacles and cease offending (McNeill and Whyte, 2007: 46).

The blurred boundaries between persistence and desistance

The observation that even the most persistent offenders are likely to eventually cease offending has prompted considerable interest in the field of desistance from crime (for example: Bushway, *et al.*, 2001; Giordano *et al.*, 2002; Laub *et al.*, 1998; Laub and Sampson, 2001, 2003; Loeber *et al.*, 1991; Maruna, 2001; Sampson and Laub, 2005a). Yet, despite a burgeoning interest in the subject in recent years, there remains a certain degree of ambiguity with regard to the definition and conceptualisation of the term. In some respects the lack of agreement results from the tendency of some researchers to conflate the definition of desistance with the measurement of the concept. Indeed, there is considerable variability in the operationalisation of desistance within the existing research (Kazemian, 2007: 8). Farrington and Hawkins (1991), for example, defined desistance as occurring where there has been a conviction at age 21 but no convictions between ages 21 and 32. Shover and Thompson (1992), on the other hand, defined desistance as being the absence of arrest in the 36 months after release from prison. Alternatively, Warr (1998) has defined desistance as being the lack of self-reported offending during the previous year. Within these three definitions of desistance there are differences with regard to age, duration of non-offending, and measure of offending (conviction, arrest, self-report). Setting aside any discussions about the methodological implications of measuring offending using official or self-report data, these three definitions illustrate the complexity of desistance and the variation in understanding about when desistance has (or has not) occurred. Laub and Sampson (2001) noted in their research review that there was no consensual definition of desistance. This has led to disparate research findings and some commentators have suggested that 'because conceptual and operational definitions of desistance vary across existing studies, it is difficult to draw empirical generalisations from the growing literature on desistance from crime' (Uggen and Massoglia, 2003: 316–17). Many commentators would agree upon the meaning of desistance in its simplest form as termination of offending. Maruna (2001) suggested that 'the criminal career literature traditionally imagines desistance as an event – an abrupt cessation of criminal behaviour' (2001: 22). Farrall and Bowling (1999) defined desistance as the 'moment that a criminal career ends' (1999: 253), but it is also a process which culminates in the ending of a criminal career. As Maruna (2001) has argued, criminal activity is sporadic, and many offenders have a tendency to drift or zig-zag in and out of crime (Glaser, 1964; Matza, 1964). Evidence from the desistance research also shows that many initial attempts to desist are unsuccessful (Maruna, 1997). As such, it is highly likely that instances of reversals and relapses are common (Burnett, 2004). Studies which regard desistance as purely a termination, and not therefore as a process which leads to termination, are more likely to observe a lull in offending and to conceal progress made towards desistance. Healy (2010) described the ambiguity surrounding when desistance has actually occurred as 'different shades of grey' (2010: 5). She cited various studies which have shown that many offenders gradually reduce the frequency and severity of their offending, and may sometimes participate in antisocial or illegal acts which present a lower risk of conviction so as to avoid jeopardising the aspects of their lives which might be considered to be more 'conventional' or 'mainstream' (such as employment, marriage, parenthood, and so on).

That some people may be considered to be 'desisters' while continuing to engage in offending or offending behaviour may be reflected in Uggen and Kruttchnitt's (1998) distinction between behavioural and official desistance. Behavioural desistance is defined as the absence of self-reported illegal earnings during a three year follow-up period. Official desistance refers to the absence of arrest over the same time period. In this regard, individuals may be able to avoid arrest by reducing the frequency or severity of their offending. As such, the boundaries between persistence and desistance may often appear to be blurred, as most offenders are likely to continually shift between offending and non-offending, and 'complete criminality' or 'complete conformity' are unlikely to be states of being which are achieved by many individuals (Bottoms *et al.*, 2004: 383).

Consequently, it is preferable to regard desistance as a dynamic process, as opposed to a static condition, primarily because 'the dynamic model is much more articulate than the static [termination] model about the nature of the desistance process' (Bushway *et al.*, 2003: 146). In doing so, researchers attempt to overcome the caveat inherent to static definitions – that a focus on the termination of offending ignores the progress made by the individual towards desistance. Such progress may be examined by exploring the transitions between crime and conformity in greater detail.

The transitional phase

The criminal careers research discussed earlier in this chapter has highlighted the considerable heterogeneity that exists in patterns of offending both between different individuals and within the same individual over time. While for many individuals offending is clearly of an ephemeral nature (often during early adolescence), for others the duration of offending behaviour is more protracted. Also, some individuals will engage in a wide variety of criminal acts, while others may specialise in a very narrow type of offending behaviour. This heterogeneity is also evident in the transitions that individuals make between offending and non-offending. While there is a possibility that some individuals may cease offending with almost immediate effect following a particularly critical event (Cusson and Pinssoneault, 1986), many offenders are more likely to gradually move from criminality to conformity over a period of time.

There are identifiable attempts within the desistance literature to provide a theoretical or empirical examination of this phenomenon. Maruna and Farrall's (2004) work is, perhaps, the most well-known and often-cited conceptualisation of the desistance process (see also Maruna, Immarigeon and LeBel, 2004). They identified two categorical phases of desistance: primary and secondary. Primary desistance refers to a lull or break in criminal behaviour, while secondary desistance refers to 'the movement from the behaviour of non-offending to the assumption of the role or identity of a "changed person"' (Maruna *et al.*, 2004: 19). Support for this proposition may be found in the evidence which suggests that desistance is accompanied by a change in identity, from that of 'offender' to 'non-offender' (Giordano *et al.*, 2002; Maruna, 2001). As individuals experience such a change, they are likely to come to regard criminal activity as incompatible with their new identity, while simultaneously distancing themselves from their past identity (Vaughan, 2007: 394). Essentially, primary desistance is identified as a condition, or a state of being, which does not require any significant commitment from the individual concerned. Secondary desistance, on the other hand, marks a fundamental shift within the individual themselves, such that they will be perceived, and will perceive themselves, as being a 'changed person' who now lives a conventional non-offending lifestyle. Maruna *et al.* (2004) argued that because gaps in offending are so common, primary desistance is of little theoretical interest and that empirical research should instead focus upon secondary desistance.

However, the conceptualisation of primary and secondary desistance as dis-creet categorical phases, may not offer as much clarity as has previously been assumed. It is argued here that desistance should be viewed as a process, rather than an event, which is likely to involve periods of vacillation. Also, it is argued here that the usage of the term desistance requires greater clarification than that which it receives in much of the existing literature, and that the delineation between primary and secondary desistance provides a useful means of doing so. Furthermore, secondary desistance can, indeed, provide fruitful insights into the process of moving away from crime. Maruna (2001) argued that exploring *how* people manage to refrain from offending is of greater importance to the study of desistance than developing an understanding of *why* people choose to desist (2001: 24), and secondary desistance is clearly related to the former question. There are also a number of reasons to support the argument that primary desist-ance is worthy of empirical investigation, not least because only a proportion of primary desisters will make the transition to secondary desistance, and therefore research which explores individual experiences during the early stages of desist-ance can provide useful insights into how this transition might be achieved (Healy and O'Donnell, 2008; Healy, 2010). Investigations which focus on sec-ondary desistance are able to uncover the factors which might allow for the long-term maintenance of non-offending and the adoption of 'conventional' identities, while those which focus on primary desistance are able to explore in detail the factors which might cause a shift between criminality and conformity. There-fore, there would appear to be merits in researching both phases of desistance.

However, it could also be argued that it is the conceptualisation of the trans-ition between primary and secondary desistance which is problematic here. In the literature to date, secondary desistance is presented as an 'end state'. It is considered to be the final stage of the desistance process, where the individual acquires the identity of, and is perceived to be, a 'non-offender'. Yet there is little acknowledgement here regarding the possibility that individuals might be able to achieve secondary desistance and then subsequently return to offending again, nor that individuals might be able to achieve secondary desistance while still retaining some of the characteristics that they portrayed during primary desistance (King, 2013b). The evidence which supports the conceptualisation of primary and secondary desistance is largely based upon the retrospective accounts of individuals who have desisted over a certain period of the life-course.

There is limited empirical evidence to support the view that these are distinct categorical phases, and it is possible that individuals may portray characteristics usually associated with secondary desistance much earlier in the desistance process and, likewise, aspects of primary desistance may endure much later in the process (King, 2013b). This would call not only for a reconsideration of the characteristics usually associated with primary and secondary desistance, but also of the sequential nature ascribed to these phases. Carlsson's (2012) concept of intermittency in the desistance process, developed from findings from the Stockholm Life Course Project, is relevant here. The Stockholm Life Course

Project was a longitudinal study examining the life histories of 287 men born in Stockholm between 1943 and 1951. The original sample included 192 boys who were known to have committed a non-trivial offence, and a control group of 95 boys who had not. A follow-up study was conducted in the 1980s, where the 192 known offenders were divided into two groups, the first comprising those boys who had been involved in relatively low levels of offending, and the second comprising boys who might more likely be considered as persistent offenders. A subsequent follow-up study was conducted with the second group in 2010–2011.

From this second follow-up study, Carlsson identified two forms of intermittency in criminal careers. The first type of intermittency is where an offender 'holds up' their offending. There is no will to desist at this time, and the individual may intentionally 'restart' their offending behaviour. In the second type of intermittency a will to desist is present, but it is not fully realised. Here, though, the individual does not intentionally restart their offending behaviour, but rather occurrences of reoffending are the result of a relapse or a failure to refrain from situations or circumstances which are likely to lead to criminal activity. Essentially, Carlsson (2012) argued that the second form of intermittency is dependent upon a willingness to desist, and that this will may be conditioned by a combination of routine activities, life-course events, and social context. However, it has been shown previously in the desistance literature that there is no direct correlation between motivation to desist and success in avoiding recidivism (Burnett, 2000; Farrall, 2002), and it is argued here that the dynamics of desistance transitions are conditioned by greater complexity than the will of the individual alone. This is not to suggest that Carlsson focused solely on individual will, but rather that greater consideration could be given to the dynamics in which personal and social contexts can condition how an individual thinks and behaves in relation to desistance from crime. Carlsson's findings offer a useful starting point from which to consider the nature of desistance transitions. Indeed, his work may suggest that desistance can be constituted of transitional phases which contain elements of both primary and secondary desistance. Within these phases the individual may be more or less conforming, and this may have a concomitant effect upon the likelihood of sustained desistance. His work also shows that there may be qualitative differences between patterns of transitions between crime and conformity often found in quantitative studies. While the nature of these transitions may vary considerably from one person to another, there are particular life-course events or social contexts which can have an influential effect upon the initiation of desistance transitions.

Life-course events and desistance

The existing literature has shown that there are particular life-course events which can influence the process of desistance. These may include relocation to an alternative geographical area (Osborn, 1980; Sampson and Laub, 1993), changes to peer group association (Warr, 1998; Maruna and Roy, 2007), obtaining work (Sampson and Laub, 1993; Benda *et al.*, 2005), getting married

(Farrington and West, 1995; Blokland and Niuewbeerta, 2005; Blokland *et al.*, 2005; Sampson and Laub, 2005; Bersani *et al.*, 2009), and becoming a parent (Graham and Bowling, 1996; Moore and Hagedorn, 1999; Edin *et al.*, 2001; Uggen *et al.*, 2004; Farrall and Calverley, 2006). The desistance literature, generally, contends that particular life-course events can prompt a move away from crime, as well as helping the individual to sustain a crime-free lifestyle.

Marriage

There is a large body of literature on the correlation between marriage and desistance. Petras *et al.* (2010) found that marriage helped individuals to decrease their participation in criminal behaviour, and the frequency with which they committed crime. Blokland and Nieuwbeerta (2005) argued that 'during marriage offenders seem maximally inhibited; no other life circumstances equal the effect of marriage' (2005: 1228), while Shover (1983) found that for desistance to occur it was important for the offender to establish a 'mutually satisfying relationship with a woman' (1983: 213). The association between marriage and desistance has also been shown to be significant among research with female offenders, although the findings are less robust than studies concerned with male offenders (King *et al.*, 2007).

Sampson and Laub (2005: 17–18) found four mechanisms through which marriage can affect desistance. First, marriage can enable individuals to 'knife off' the past, drawing a distinction between their past, present and future. While the individual's past may be characterised by deviant behaviour, their life after marriage will not entail any criminal activity. Second, marriage can allow for the emergence of a new sense of self, where the individual adopts a new identity which is incongruent with offending behaviour. Third, marriage allows for the development of new pro-social relationships which, in turn, can offer new opportunities and sources of support, as well as new sources of supervision and control (see also, Nagin and Paternoster, 1994; Maume *et al.*, 2005). Fourth, marriage can alter routine activities, reducing bonds with deviant peers.

Some have argued that marriage may have a positive effect on recidivism, such that the marital relationship may actually encourage further offending. Simons *et al.* (2002) and Sampson *et al.* (2006) found that when men entered into relationships with deviant women they were more likely to reoffend. Other studies have suggested that marriage has a more positive effect for men than it does for women, which may be because men find it easier to marry into pro-social relationships (Giordano *et al.*, 2003; King *et al.*, 2007).

Taking an alternative view of the marriage effect, some other researchers have attempted to examine the relationship between cohabitation and desistance. This is a relatively new area of desistance research, and existing findings are limited and somewhat contradictory. For example, Savolainen (2008) found that cohabitation could have a greater effect on reducing recidivism than marriage, while Forrest's (2007) study found that recidivism rates increased with cohabitation. The evidence base may be too small to draw any firm conclusions, but it is possible that this dissonance may reflect the nature of the bonds that individuals develop. Laub *et al.* (1998) found that marriage could help to facilitate desistance, but only where a spousal bond had developed over time. Simons and Barr (2012) studied the impact of non-marital romantic relationships on desistance among 600 African-American young adults. While they found no evidence to support a connection between desistance and romantic relationships per se, they did find that quality of relationship and desistance were correlated. They argued that desistance became more likely because romantic relationships would help to reduce the commitment to a criminogenic knowledge structure, such as hostility towards others and an aversion to conventional norms. Such findings support the argument that it is the strength and quality of the relationship which is more important (Mischkowitz, 1994).

Employment

Several authors have also found that obtaining employment can play a crucial role in successful attempts to desist from crime (Laub and Sampson, 2001; Metcalf *et al.*, 2001; Webster *et al.*, 2001; Visher and Travis, 2003; Haslewood-Pocsik *et al.*, 2004; Crow, 2006; Rhodes, 2008). The importance of employment to the desistance process can be illustrated by the centrality of approaches aimed at enhancing employment opportunities to wider reducing reoffending strategies (HM Government, 2005, 2006). It has been suggested that stable employment can reduce the risk of reoffending by between one third and a half (LGA, 2005). In a similar vein to those accounts of the relationship between marriage and desistance, the influence of employment on desistance has been explained as a consequence of an alteration of social bonds, peer associations, and routine activities.

Wright and Cullen (2004), using data from the National Youth Study, found that employment influenced desistance as a result of the relationships formed with pro-social co-workers. The young adults in their study who perceived their co-workers as rejecting of delinquent behaviour were more likely to desist from crime. This, they argued, was because the development of pro-social relationships with co-workers fractured previous relationships with delinquent peers, and led to an increase in pro-social peer networks. Wright and Cullen's (2004) findings can be seen to complement Sampson and Laub's (1993) prior assertion that employment increased the likelihood of desistance because it demands a certain set of behaviours and obligations. Employment increases levels of supervision and monitoring, while also enhancing pro-social networks, such that conformity becomes more likely.

Other studies have found that the relationship between employment and desistance is not as strong as much of the existing literature suggests. Tripodi *et al.* (2010) examined the relationship between employment and recidivism among parolees in Texas, USA. They found that employment did not have a significant effect upon reducing the likelihood of reincarceration. However, they did find that the parolees in their study who were able to find employment were likely to spend longer in the community before being reincarcerated. In other words, employment kept those individuals out of prison for longer than those who did not find employment. Disparities in research findings surrounding the effect of employment on desistance may be due to variations in the quality of employment experienced by individuals being studied. Sampson and Laub (1993) argued that employment alone is insufficient to maintain desistance, but rather it is 'employment coupled with job stability, commitment to work, and mutual ties binding workers and employers' that reduces criminality' (1993: 146). Uggen (1999) also found that high quality jobs were more likely to reduce criminal behaviour. For Uggen, jobs need to be perceived to be satisfying by the would-be desister in order to initiate a reassessment of lifestyle and attitudes, and for the social controls provided by the job to have a meaningful effect on the individual's determination of the 'relative attractiveness' of criminal or pro-social behaviour (1999: 145).

Fatherhood

The existing literature has tended to focus upon the relationship between motherhood and desistance (Graham and Bowling, 1996; Fleisher and Krienert, 2004; Byrne and Trew, 2008; Brown and Bloom, 2009; Kreager *et al.*, 2010; Michalsen, 2011), and it has been argued that parenthood may have a more efficacious impact on desistance for mothers than is the case for fathers (Bersani *et al.*, 2009). That said, there is some evidence to suggest that fatherhood can have a positive effect upon the likelihood of an individual moving away from crime (Shannon and Abrams, 2007; Mills and Codd, 2008; Savolainen, 2009). Niven and Stewart (2005) found that men who were better able to adapt to family roles were less likely to reoffend, and LeBel *et al.* (2008) found that men who identified themselves as being a 'family man' were more likely to avoid further offending. In a recent contribution to the dearth of research, Lösel *et al.* (2012) conducted a longitudinal study which collected data on standardised measures examining the interaction between prisoners' families and resettlement expectations and outcomes, as well as data from semi-structured interviews. Prisoners from 13 prisons and their families were interviewed on two occasions, comprising 40 family sets in total. These authors found that reoffending was more significantly associated with communication during imprisonment, quality of parents' relationship before imprisonment, and the quality of the parental relationship after imprisonment. They measured the effect of these variables against reincarceration and difficulties in avoiding criminal activity. The father's involvement with children before imprisonment and frequency of family contact during imprisonment did have a negative effect upon recidivism, but these were not found to be significant.

Lösel *et al.* (2012) also found that fathers were likely to have less involvement with their children after imprisonment than before. This may be because of a breakdown in relationships between father and child during imprisonment, or it could be the result of a poor quality relationship between father and mother.

Helyar-Cardwell (2012) has argued that there are a number of barriers which young fathers face when attempting to move away from crime, and that where a positive parental relationship exists, the mother is more likely to consent to contact between father and child. She also suggested that parenthood may not facilitate desistance for some individuals because support to cope with the demands of parenthood is limited to short courses, so the positive effects may be short-lived.

Becoming a father has also been identified as a possible correlate for desistance. It is argued that fatherhood enhances motivation and offers a 'hook for change' (Helyar-Caldwell, 2012). Although the rebuilding of father-child relationships can positively influence desistance, becoming a father can have an even more dramatic effect on the process of moving away from crime. Helyar-Caldwell's (2012) interviews with five young fathers under probation supervision revealed that all of the men regarded fatherhood as a positive aspect of their lives, and that having a child had altered their attitudes towards criminality. Although three of the young men admitted to reoffending, this was of a less serious and infrequent nature, suggesting that the desistance process for these young men was, at least partly, successful. Some accounts have suggested that ex-offenders' stories of becoming fathers are akin to religious testimonies, where individuals clearly distinguish between 'before and after fatherhood' scenarios, and herald fatherhood as fundamentally changing behaviours and attitudes (Eden *et al.*, 2004).

Explaining life-course events

While it is commonly accepted in the literature that certain life-course events can positively influence desistance (Sampson *et al.*, 2006), there is less agreement over the answers to the questions of *how* and *why* life-course events might matter in the desistance process. Life-course events may act as a trigger, prompting within-individual change perhaps as a consequence of being shocked by a wounding, by the last crime taking place in circumstances of panic or intense fear, or the receipt of a very severe sentence and the collateral consequences that would ensue from it[1] (Cusson and Pinsonneault, 1986: 73). Another explanation for the impact of life-course events on desistance may be found in the suggestion that such events alter the routine activities of individuals, such that opportunities to commit crime become curtailed. Marriage, for example, may lead to the individual spending more of their time with their partner, leaving less time to associate with delinquent peers (Osgood and Lee, 1993; Warr, 1998). Farrall (2002) argued that employment can offer 'a reduction in "unstructured" time and an increase in "structured" time' (2002: 146), and Laub and Sampson (2003) offered a similar explanation for the effect of marriage. Indeed, Shover (1983) suggested that employment provided the desister with 'a pattern of routine activities' and that these then 'left little time for the daily activities associated with crime' (1983: 214).[2] In other words, life-course events may create conditions which constrain opportunities for criminal activities, while also generating and reinforcing opportunities to engage in pro-social behaviours.

Life-course events may provide a source of direct social control upon the individual desister. If an individual gets married or finds work it is unlikely that their spouse or employer will be accepting of criminal behaviour. The perceived or real threat of disappointment or rejection as a consequence of offending behaviour may be enough to help the individual to desist. It has also been argued that life-course events such as marriage may allow individuals to develop and exercise greater levels of self-control, which may enhance efforts to desist (Forrest and Hay, 2011). Life-course events may also provide a form of social support, through the enhancement of an individual's social networks. Following marriage, or through gaining employment, an individual may be more likely to develop links with pro-social individuals and networks, which can provide social support and enhance social capital (Laub and Sampson, 2003). Enhancing social capital can be a crucial aspect of the desistance process, as it entails creating opportunities for change and it makes it harder to renege on certain responsibilities (McNeill, 2009). While the explanations for the impact of life-course events discussed so far suggest that they somehow alter the behaviour of the individual, an alternative explanation may be that life-course events mediate within-individual changes to cognitions, identity, biography and narrative (Giordano *et al.*, 2002; Maruna, 2001; Rumgay, 2004). When individuals introspectively reformulate aspects of their lives and identities this may prompt changes to their social circumstances, such that life-course events become more likely. In other words, individual change may already be occurring by the time marriage, for example, takes place (Giordano *et al.*, 2003). From this perspective it could be that within-individual changes lead to life-course events, or that life-course events concretise and confirm the changes to identity that individuals have already sought to make.

One of the key theoretical constructs within the existing desistance literature is Sampson and Laub's (1993; Laub and Sampson, 2003) age-graded theory of social control. They suggested that life-course events may alter the social bonds that an individual has with society. Particular events may help to establish bonds between the would-be desister and wider society. Involvement in criminal activity is more likely when social bonds become undermined or do not exist altogether, and less likely when the bonds are intact and strengthened (ibid.). Individuals invest more time and more of their own resources in these attachments and their commitment to conventional values and goals is strengthened. This may result from the socialising effect of various life-course events (ibid.). Their work was based upon a longitudinal study involving the life histories of 500 men who were remanded to reform schools in Massachusetts during adolescence. The men were originally the subjects of studies by Glueck and Glueck (1950, 1968). The Gluecks followed the men until age 32, and Laub and Sampson reanalysed the original data and tracked a subset of the men as they approached age 70 (Laub and Sampson, 1988, 1993, 2001; Sampson and Laub, 1990, 1992, 2003, 2004). By contrast to the self-control theory of Gottfredson and Hirschi (1988, 1990), which posited that crime and criminality are stable over the life-course, Laub and Sampson argued that patterns of crime were variable and that individuals would persist and desist at different rates and at different ages across the life-course. They developed an age-graded theory of social control, which stated that as individuals mature they are likely to encounter particular life-course turning points, such as marriage or employment, which would have a positive effect upon desistance. They explain persistence in offending as the result of the 'cumulative disadvantage' of weakened social bonds over the life-course, from incomplete education to low-level job stability and delinquent peer associations.

Sampson and Laub's (1993; Laub and Sampson, 2003) theory stated that this continuity in offending behaviour could be altered following the establishment of a stronger social bond. Social bonds, they argued, are connected to life-course events, and these produce greater forms of social capital in the form of knowledge about role expectations and increased informal social controls. Essentially, Sampson and Laub argued that social bonds, such as marriage and employment, enhance obligations and sanctions and make further offending too costly. Over time, the individual invests more in these social bonds and the levels of informal social control increase, which makes longer term desistance more likely. More recently, Skarohamar and Hovde Lyngstad (2009) have suggested that attachments to social bonds may be more complex within increasingly pluralistic societies. They have argued that new configurations of family formation within modern society present a range of alternatives for the would-be desister, and that the 'traditional' attachment to social bonds such as marriage may no longer be relevant for some individuals. For example, their research found that becoming a father can have a negative effect on crime when it is independent of any firm commitment to the mother. Skarohamar and Hovde Lyngstad (2009) also found that cohabitation may have a negative effect on further offending, a finding which is not supported by earlier quantitative studies (Horney *et al.*, 1995; Forrest, 2007). This may suggest that new forms of family formation can alter the social bonds or attachments that individuals may forge en route to desistance. In a similar vein, Fletcher (2007, 2008) has suggested that changes to the nature of labour markets have altered the nature of the bond between the would-be desister and employment.

The individual and desistance

While external life-course events undoubtedly can have a profound effect on desistance, individual-level changes can also impact on the process of moving away from crime. Often these may involve changes to an individual's identity, either as perceived by themselves or by others (Giordano *et al.*, 2002), or changes to an individual's motivation (Shover, 1983). Both Burnett (1992, 2000) and Farrall (2002) identified a connection between motivation and desistance. Farrall's (2002) work involved interviews with 199 men, and their supervising officers, who had been subject to a probation or combination order.[3] His findings suggested that those who wanted to stop offending and felt that they were able to were the most likely to desist. However, this is not to suggest that being motivated to desist necessarily entails that it will happen. Burnett (1992) interviewed 130 men for the Oxford Dynamics of Recidivism Study, once shortly before release from prison and again four to six months after release.[4] She found that while 80 per cent of the sample stated that they wanted to desist, 60 per cent of the original same sample reported reoffending after release. Only one in four stated that they felt definitely able to desist. Interestingly, in both studies an external factor was identified which forged a stronger resolution among those who were more successful at desisting from crime. In Farrall's sample the most confident and resolute Probationers were those whose supervising officer also perceived that they were able to desist. For the men in Burnett's study those who were most steadfast in their approach to desistance were those who had been able to reinterpret their value systems following a particular life-course event (such as starting a relationship, becoming a parent, gaining employment and so on).

A number of authors have found that changes to an individual's sense of morality can influence cessation from criminal activity (Paternoster, 1989), as Shover (1996) writes that desistance can follow the 'acquisition of an altered perspective on their youthful self and activities' (1996: 131). Leibrich (1993) was among the first to explore the relationship between desistance and probation. Her book provided an account of the desistance experiences of 48 men and women who had been sentenced to probation, but who had subsequently remained crime-free for approximately three years. For her, remorse was found to be the primary reason behind making a decision to desist (Leibrich, 1993, 1996). By contrast, Giordano *et al.* (2002) suggest that remorse is associated with a repudiation of past actions, and occurs at a later stage of the desistance process. Sampson and Laub (1995) argue that desistance can result from a realisation that offending behaviour can incrementally 'mortgage' future life chances, and that individuals come to regret offending in terms of its impact upon limiting opportunities (1995: 147). These individual-level subjective changes can be 'triggered by an individual offending against their personal morality – [as they come] to think that their offending was wrong' (Weaver, 2009: 18).

Bringing the threads together

The discussion so far has identified a range of factors that have been shown, in the existing literature, to support the process of desistance. The work of Burnett (2000) and Maruna (2001) has suggested that a dynamic relationship between structure and agency underpins this process, and that a particular interaction occurs between these two dimensions which will affect the likelihood of successful desistance. For Maruna (2001) there are three broad theoretical positions in the desistance literature, each attempting to explain how desistance occurs. 'Ontogenic', or maturation, theories are based upon the long-established relationship between age and crime. 'Sociogenic' theories explain that there exists a bond between the individual and certain social ties, including family and employment. As these bonds develop, individuals have a stake, or an investment, in society that future criminal activity could jeopardise, so there is an incentive to conform. 'Narrative' theories, which are the primary concern of Maruna's (2001) study, explain how desistance can result from changes to identity and an alternative future outlook.

McNeill (2003; McNeill and Whyte, 2007) has argued that desistance occurs somewhere within the interaction between the three dimensions outlined by Maruna (2001), and that the success or otherwise of desistance is dependent upon the interrelationship between each area. These areas are age/maturation, life-course events and social bonds, and narratives and identity. On the one hand, if there is correspondence between each area, moving away from offending, then desistance will be more likely. However, it is likely that most individuals will experience some correspondence and some dissonance between each of the areas throughout the desistance process (McNeill and Whyte, 2007: 148). Indeed, it is the interrelationship between aspects of structure and agency, rather than discrete factors, which underpins desistance: 'the process of desistance is one that is produced through an *interplay* between individual choices, and a range of wider social forces, institutional and societal practices which are beyond the control of the individual' (Farrall and Bowling, 1999: 261, emphasis in original). However, desistance does not occur simply through the choices made by individuals from a range of available options. Rather, desistance occurs as a result of the objective and subjective circumstances of individuals' lives at a given time.

Indeed, it is not just the incidence of particular life-course events that matters to desistance, but the relationship between these and an individual's subjective attachment to the event. This offers an explanation as to how individuals with similar backgrounds living in similar environments can experience desistance in alternative ways. Individuals' reactions to particular situations can be explained in terms of a manifestation of individual characteristics, as people acquire different ways of reacting to similar situations (Zamble and Quinsey, 1997: 146–7). As Farrall (2002) argues:

> the desistance literature has pointed to a range of factors associated with the ending of active involvement in offending. Most of these factors are related to acquiring 'something' (most commonly employment, a life partner or a family) which the desister values in some way and which initiates a re-evaluation of his or her life, and for some a sense of who they 'are'.
>
> (2002: 11)

The nature of the subjective attachment to a particular life-course event may be affected by various individual characteristics, including: age, other personal and social circumstances (distinct from the event in question), and existing social ties, in addition to personal attributes such as motivation. As a result of the nature of interaction between subjective and social factors, the desistance process is likely to be complex, lengthy and non-linear (Maguire and Raynor, 2006b: 24). However, despite the complexity, various contingencies and the highly individualised nature of the desistance process, there are approaches which can help to facilitate the transition away from crime.

Assisted desistance

Desistance research can have significant implications for policy and practice. Findings can suggest which factors are likely to encourage someone to desist, those which are likely to sustain it, and how obstacles might be overcome during the process. Despite this, there have been relatively few studies which have explicitly examined the impact of criminal justice interventions on desistance from crime, although there are also several notable exceptions. Some researchers have focused upon the process of resettlement, or re-entry, into the community following a custodial sentence (Petersilia, 2003; Maruna *et al.*, 2004; Samuels and Mukamal, 2004; Travis, 2005; Maruna, 2006; Burnett, 2010; Serin *et al.*, 2010; Moore, 2012). Others have examined more explicitly the nature of supervision in the community and the impact that it can have upon the process of desistance. This small, but growing, body of literature provides an alternative to much of the 'What Works', or evidence-based practice, literature, which has entailed a predominantly quantitative analysis of reconviction data and the outcomes of particular interventions (Farrall, 2002). Such analyses are, largely, evaluation studies which assess the outcome effect of interventions, and these suffer from severe limitations. Research which seeks to examine the interface between criminal justice interventions and desistance tend to be more exploratory or explanatory in style, and are better equipped to identify the contextual factors that can lead to change (McNeill *et al.*, 2012).

Farrall (2002) reviewed the existing research related to the outcomes of criminal justice interventions (2002: 11–16), and suggested that the literature can be divided between two research paradigms: the smaller, criminal career research which focuses upon cessation from crime and reveals little about probation supervision; and the much wider literature exploring the outcomes of criminal justice interventions. This latter body of work is predominantly positivist and focuses upon criminal history variables and official recorded data. The limitation, therefore, of this literature, is that little can be said about how or why particular interventions work. The recent emphasis underpinning research on outcomes of interventions has been upon assessing the outcomes of cognitive behavioural approaches, coupled with a focus upon specialist interventions as opposed to the generic process of probation (Farrall, 2002: 13). This reflects the rise of the 'What Works' literature in the 1990s, which, in turn, reflects a concern for evidence-based practice, the forerunner of which has been 'cognitive behaviouralism', and the increase of specialist programmes which focus on specific activities.

Rex (1999), in her study of 60 Probationers and their experiences of probation, found that a number of individuals attributed behavioural change to work undertaken by their supervising officer. Most Probationers believed that probation supervision served a rehabilitative purpose (a finding also supported by McCulloch, 2005: 17), and that 41 (68 per cent) of the Probationers she interviewed felt that they would be less likely to offend as a result of probation supervision. Her participants suggested that feeling engaged with probation and being given the opportunity to take an active role in their own change processes were important. Probationers were also willing to accept direct guidance from their supervising officers about their problems and behaviour, and this was related to the perception that supervising officers were concerned for them and interested in their wellbeing. The dedication and loyalty of supervising officers was interpreted as a crucial aspect of facilitating behavioural change, as Rex wrote (1999: 380): 'The commitment shown by probation officers in a whole variety of ways was crucial in preparing probationers to take quite directive guidance from supervisors whom they saw as concerned about their wellbeing.' Rex's (1999) research, therefore, resonates with the pro-social model that has emerged from practice in Australia (Trotter, 1993, 1996, 1999). Within this model the supervisor encourages the offender to be actively pro-social, and supports this through praise as a reward for their actions. For this model to be successful, the supervisor needs to provide a framework within which the offender is guided towards a 'pro-social lifestyle', involving the encouragement of reliability, honesty and respect.

The importance of the 'relational' aspect of the desistance process is also highlighted by Barry (2000, 2007, 2010a, 2010b, 2012) and McCulloch (2005), among others (see, for example: Burnett, 2004; McNeill, 2006b; Healy, 2012; Weaver, 2012). There are various ways in which these relationships can influence the desistance process, not least in terms of providing practical support and nurturing pro-social narratives (Burnett and McNeill, 2005: 236). As part of the Scottish Desistance Study, Barry (2007) asked people for their perceptions about what helped them to reduce offending and their opinions on good practice as 'expert witnesses'. The Scottish Desistance Study involved interviews with 40 current or previous persistent offenders, 20 males and 20 females, aged 18–33. With respect to the factors that helped individuals to reduce offending, most stated that resolving personal and social problems were key, but that the process of achieving this was often initiated and maintained by developing significant relationships with friends or family (although this was more often the case for women than men) (Barry, 2007: 413). With respect to respondents' opinions on good practice, the majority of respondents in the sample suggested (2007: 416) 'that the best approach was for supervising officers to talk and listen to their clients, about the problems, fears and consequences of offending … so as to encourage personal development, learning and meaningful interaction'. Most respondents suggested that intensive probation, where individuals were able to build a rapport with their supervising officer, and community service, as it gave people a sense of purpose, were good examples of effective practice in facilitating desistance (Barry, 2007: 416–17). McCulloch's (2005) research also supports the finding that talking and listening are crucial aspects of probation work, and that this can help to develop relationships between the supervising officer and the offender wherein the Probationer is likely to be more receptive to direct guidance (2005: 18).

However, not all studies of desistance and criminal justice interventions have shown the relationship between supervising officer and offender to have a positive effect on the desistance process. The Sheffield Desistance Study[5] followed 113 young (born between 1982–1984) male persistent offenders over four interviews between 2003 and 2008. The individuals who participated in this study suggested at the second interview that they received little assistance from probation (14 per cent stated it was 'fairly useful' or 'very useful', while 30 per cent stated it was 'a little useful' or 'not at all useful'). In part this could be because contact with probation was regarded as only involving a fairly minimal level of reporting to the supervising officer in a very general manner. In later waves, reflecting on their experience over the past three years, 35 per cent stated that they found probation 'fairly useful' or 'very useful', but 65 per cent stated that it was 'a little useful' or 'not at all useful'. As such, individuals did not report that probation had been of much assistance in helping them to move away from crime (Bottoms and Shapland, 2011; Shapland and Bottoms, 2011). The Sheffield Study also found that desistance was 'a process of learning new ways of living in the community' (Bottoms and Shapland, 2011: 70), and it could be argued that one of the purposes of probation could be to facilitate this learning process.

Farrall's longitudinal study with 199 men subject to probation supervision explored the impact of probation on individuals' efforts to desist. Initially, Farrall found that while more than half of the original sample evidenced the emergence of desistance, very few cases attributed this success to probation. Both officers and offenders suggested that overcoming personal and social difficulties was contingent upon a range of factors, many of which were out of the direct control of either party (Farrall, 2002: 207). This has been supported by McCulloch (2005), who found that it was more common for 'improvements' to be made to probationers' social problems, rather than 'resolutions' (2005: 20). In the final wave of interviews, the participants suggested that for 57 per cent of the problems they had identified, their supervising officers had done nothing to help overcome or resolve them. Farrall (2002) found that Probation Officers were reluctant to become involved in working on desistance-related needs, such as employment and family formation, but where this did occur greater rates of success were seen (2002: 227).

This led Farrall to question 'conversational' approaches to probation work, where these might focus on the individual while neglecting the wider social context.

Farrall's (2002) argument is that these interventions can develop agency – for example, through enhancing decision-making and reasoning skills, or through increasing an individual's employability – but that interventions are also required which are 'aimed at altering some aspects of an individual's social and personal circumstances' (Farrall, 2002: 214). The argument was not that probation is irrelevant to the desistance process, but rather that probation has an indirect effect upon factors which contribute to desistance and, as such, probation interventions should incorporate a greater degree of direct assistance in relation to personal and social contexts. In their follow-up study, Farrall and Calverley (2006) interviewed 51 of the original sample, and found that some individuals attributed some positive developments to the work of probation. Individuals suggested that probation had 'planted a seed', and that from this they might develop the motivation to desist from crime. In other words, the effects of probation appeared to become more obvious over a longer period of time. This was also found during the fifth, and most recent, wave of interviews with this sample. The research found that probation could have an impact on individuals a long time after their sentence had ended, and that where individuals experienced greater levels of impact from probation (in terms of learning, receiving help and being given advice) the likelihood of reconviction decreased (Farrall, 2013).

Differences in experiences of the impact of probation may, in part, be due to differing perspectives about the prioritisation of tasks within probation supervision. In a review of the literature on quality in probation practice, Shapland *et al.* (2012) found that practitioners tended to regard attitudinal and behavioural change as a higher priority than addressing practical issues, whereas Probationers were more likely to regard the resolution of social problems as being more important. The literature review found that both Probationers and practitioners regarded quality and effectiveness in probation as involving trusting relationships, talking and listening, and providing motivation and encouragement to change and reduce reoffending. However, while Probationers were more likely to suggest that practical support directly from the supervising officer, alongside referrals to external agencies, supervisors' opinions were much less likely to mention practical assistance, whether directly or through referrals to other agencies.

It is also likely that the cultural context of probation will have an impact upon how supervising officers facilitate desistance. Healy's (2010, 2012) research was based in Ireland, which has largely retained an inclusive and social work oriented underpinning (Fernee and Burke, 2010; Kilcommins, 2011). Healy's (2010) findings suggested that both the offender and their supervising officer perceived probation to be a relationship which aimed to provide practical assistance to overcome problems and a supervisory relationship characterised by talking, listening and motivation. Within this context, Healy found that Probation Officers in Ireland were more attuned to providing desistance-related support, and Probationers generally found probation to be helpful.

McNeill (2006a) identified findings from the desistance literature to suggest which factors would be more likely to facilitate moves away from crime. He argued that the evolving culture of probation in England and Wales over the last century could move towards desistance-focused practice, and he suggested a desistance paradigm for offender interventions. Such a paradigm, he argued, would refocus the work that is carried out with offenders in the context of contemporary penal policies and public discourses around crime, punishment, public protection and reoffending. Further, he argued that desistance should be supported by work with offenders and, therefore, that interventions need to be based upon an understanding of the processes of desistance, particularly as a means of reducing harm and making good to both offenders and victims (2006a: 56). He also emphasised the need to develop interventions which could enhance both social and human capital, while also recognising strengths as well as needs and risks (2006a: 55). Finally, he also highlighted some of the 'practice virtues', which are often identified as valued aspects of the officer-offender relationship (see above), as being relevant to desistance-focused work (McNeill, 2006a: 52).

This desistance paradigm for work with offenders can be incorporated with the conceptualisation of desistance, suggesting that supervising officers and those delivering interventions can play an integral part in the desistance process. The desistance literature highlights that attitudes and motivation are significant to the desistance process (Burnett, 1992, 2000; Farrall, 2002), and that being open to and ready for the possibility of change are likely to be prerequisites for change to occur (Giordano *et al.*, 2002; Rumgay, 2004). Assessing the extent to which an individual is ready to change will necessarily impact upon the practical strategies that are employed during formal work with the offender. This suggests a collaborative working relationship between officer and offender to explore each discrete area, as well as the interrelationships between them, to discover which factors in the individual's life are likely to enable or constrain desistance, as McNeill and Whyte (2007: 48) wrote:

> If there were consonance between the three areas such that all are 'pulling together' in the direction of desistance, then a reinforcing support plan might be relatively straightforward to construct. If all aspects were conso-nant in the direction of continued offending, by contrast, this would suggest both implications for risk assessment and, if community supervision were appropriate, the need for an intensive and multifaceted intervention. If, as is perhaps likely in most cases, there were some dissonance within and between the three areas, then the task becomes one of reinforcing the 'posi-tives' and challenging the 'negatives'.

Both Farrall (2002) and McNeill (2006; McNeill and Whyte, 2007) have argued that the role of probation work should incorporate methods of supporting change by developing human and social capital. While human capital – in the form of individuals' skills and knowledge – is already targeted by probation work, devel-oping social capital remains largely neglected (Farrall, 2002: 217). This is, at least partly, the result of the current emphasis upon the individual offender and their criminogenic needs, as highlighted in the previous chapter. Essentially, the argument for supporting desistance in probation practice relates to the contention that the body of work that has developed from recent desistance studies chal-lenges the correctionalist paradigm that has emerged as the hegemonic discourse in penal policy, public discourse and discussions of effective practice (McNeill, 2004: 241).

Indeed, recent probation policy and practice has been primarily geared towards challenging individual deficits and responsibilisation (Whitehead, 2007: 90). Largely this is due to current thinking being dominated by a concern with criminogenic need rather than desistance facilitators, while practice is often led by heavily managerialised and homogenous accredited programmes that challenge individuals' thinking skills. Therefore, the knowledge and understanding about desistance that has emerged in recent decades has, to date, been relatively unable to effectively influence work that is undertaken with offenders. From the discussion of probation practice presented in the earlier chapters, and the discussion of desistance presented here, it can be observed that there is incongruence between the two. The early transitional stages of desistance remain relatively under-explored, and there is a dearth of knowledge surrounding the consonance or dissonance between probation interventions and this transitional phase.

4 Agency, narratives and social contexts

A key aim of this book is to examine the nature of agency in the desistance process in more detail. Despite frequent references to the concept of agency within the desistance literature, usage of the term remains vague (Bottoms *et al.*, 2004). In order to consider the role of agency in the desistance process it is important to examine the meaning of agency in a wider sociological sense, before deconstructing the key aspects of agency in relation to the desistance process as identified in the existing literature. While the concepts of social structure and agency are ubiquitous in much of the sociological literature (Hays, 1994), their definitions are frequently varied and conflicting (Sewell, 1992). For example, structure can be defined in terms of constraint, in relation to available opportunities for action (Healy, 1998); in terms of the 'rules and resources' that enable actors to operate (Giddens, 1986); or, quite simply, as the broader context within which individuals act (Bates, 2006). While agency has become more prominent in some accounts of desistance (Giordano *et al.*, 2002; Maruna, 2001), there has been a lack of attention towards this aspect of the process and this may be, in part, because of the preponderance to try and identify social factors that can facilitate desistance transitions. The lack of attention may also be the result of inadequate conceptualisations of the term, and although there has been greater attention paid towards the concept, usage of the term in a desistance context remains somewhat vague (Bottoms *et al.*, 2004; Healy, 2010).

What is agency?

In the broader sociological literature agency is frequently defined in juxtaposition to structure, and this contrast is often taken to mean 'that structure is systematic and patterned, while agency is contingent and random; that structure is constraint, while agency is freedom; that structure is static, while agency is active; that structure is collective, while agency is individual' (Hays, 1994: 57). However, such a contrast is unhelpful in exploring the interaction between structure and agency, as there is no consideration of how individuals are able to actively reproduce or transform their social contexts. This is required if research is to be able to explore the 'black box' of desistance – that is, *how* and *why* individuals desist under certain social circumstances (Farrall, 2002).

Sen (1999) suggested that human agency involves the ability of an individual to act in order to achieve certain goals or objectives, and of the ability of that individual to choose the goals or objectives that they value. Sen distinguished between human agency and human wellbeing because certain decisions made by individuals may not lead to experiences of wellbeing, but are made in order to achieve what the individual personally values. For Bandura (2001: 1), a notion of agency as being in control of actions, goals and values is central to human existence: 'To be an agent is to intentionally make things happen by one's own actions....The capacity to exercise control over the nature and quality of one's life is the essence of humanness'. Therefore, one might argue that agency entails having the freedom to set personal goals and decide upon courses of action to realise them. From a life-course perspective this entails that agency can influence patterns of goal-setting and achievement over longer periods of time. As Hitlin and Elder Jr. (2007) have argued, agency entails 'attempts to exert influence to shape one's life trajectory' (2007: 183). Moreover, agency can be conceived as the ability to choose particular courses of action, such that action itself becomes planned and purposive. However, agency is sometimes conceptualised simply as individual choice or human action in more general terms, yet this ignores the possibility that there are certain social forces that can impact upon human action or the range of opportunities that individuals may be faced with. These forces may be structural (Archer, 2000) or cultural (Hernandez and Iyengar, 2001), and they may enable or constrain what the individual is able to do or how they can act in their everyday lives.

Over the life-course these forces may have differential effects upon the individual concerned, enabling or constraining their actions in different ways and expanding or limiting the possibilities of their actions accordingly. As such, choices are temporally and spatially contingent and will alter depending on the situational context that the individual lives within (Elder, 1994), and individuals are more-or-less aware of their situational context and their ability to act within it at different points in their life (Metcalf *et al.*, 2010). Consequently, two important aspects of agency are the processes of maturation and rationality, and this can have an impact upon an individual's motivation to act in certain ways. For individuals to be able to understand their situational contexts with some degree of coherency, they construct narratives throughout their life-course. This allows individuals to account for how and why they acted in particular ways, and enables them to see alternative possibilities for the future. Therefore, it can be argued that agency, structure and culture are interconnected and mutable, and just as social structures can enable or constrain agency, so too agency can influence social structures. There is an assumption within this that agency has some degree of 'transformational power' (Simmonds, 1989: 187), which allows individuals to create, reproduce or transform their personal and social environments (Hays, 1994). More recent research has developed integrated theories of desistance which focus upon the ways in which similar social factors can be mediated in different ways by different individuals, and how this can lead to different desistance outcomes. For example, Giordano *et al.* (2002) have argued that 'agentic moves' (2002: 992) are the most influential aspect of the desistance process, and that an individual's commitment to change, openness to change, and ability to identify 'hooks for change' are the factors which are most likely to facilitate desistance. Similarly, Maruna and Roy (2007) have suggested that desistance is more likely to result from changes in an individual's 'self-identity and worldview' such as their commitments, concerns and needs (2007: 115), and the ways in which social and environmental factors are likely to be interpreted differently depending upon these changing outlooks.

Maturation, rational choice and reflexivity

Within the existing desistance literature, agency theories have been primarily concerned with the role that the individual plays in the process of desistance. There are two distinct agency explanations, those which emphasise maturation and those which focus on the rationality of the individual (Barry, 2009). Maturation theories suggest that the individual inevitably grows out of crime, but they do not account for the influence of external factors. Rational choice theories, on the other hand, essentially explain desistance in terms of alterations in the individual's decision-making. Indeed, some have argued that 'if you believe in agency you need to adopt a rational choice perspective' (Paternoster and Bushway, 2004, cited in Sampson and Laub, 2005a: 38). Within this position, individuals are presumed to be rational actors who make rational calculations about their situations in order to make decisions about those situations (Kim, 2009: 316–17). For Clarke and Cornish (1985) the driving force behind desistance is the individual's role in making a decision to give up crime, and individuals will base this decision upon wider social factors in their lives.[1] Explanations of desistance which emphasise personal agency, therefore, highlight that individuals reassess and re-evaluate their personal and social contexts and the implications that this has on the decisions that they make about offending (Cromwell *et al.*, 1991; Cusson and Pinsonneault, 1986; Leibrich, 1993; Shover, 1983). A re-evaluation could be prompted, for example, by the deterrent effect of a possible lengthier sentence, or the reduced likelihood of obtaining material goods through crime; in other words 'the probability of desistance from criminal participation increases as expectations for achieving friends, money, autonomy and happiness *via* crime decrease' (Shover and Thompson, 1992: 97, emphasis in original). Agency can often be assumed to suggest that individuals are able to make decisions free from the constraints of the social environment. However, the above quote would suggest that interactions with the social context are central to agentic actions. It can also be argued that the rational aspect of agency implies that individuals will make decisions which are in the best interests of their own wellbeing. However, an alternative view of rationality could suggest that it refers to choices which are made to achieve the decision-maker's goals, even if these are not always related to their wellbeing. Adolescents are likely to make decisions which maximise immediate goals or short-term pleasures, and certain decisions such as committing crime or other antisocial behaviours could, in this context, be considered to be rational (Reyna and Farley, 2006). Adolescents are also more likely to make risky decisions, such as those relating to alcohol or drug use and antisocial or criminal behaviour, than adults. In a study of 306 individuals across three age groups (13–16, 18–22, 24 and older), Gardner and Steinberg (2005) found that there was a chronological decline in risky behaviour, and that during the transition from 'adolescence to adulthood there is a significant decline in both risk taking and risky decision making' (2005: 632). From a desistance perspective, it could be argued that individuals who persistently offend during adolescence and into adulthood may retain the risky decision-making characteristics that are more common among adolescents, whereas those who cease offending are less likely to make risky decisions or engage in risk-taking behaviour.

Cauffman and Steinberg (2000) measured decision-making against a range of factors associated with ageing and maturity among a sample of 1,015 individuals across five age groups. They measured decision-making against age and psychosocial measures of maturity, including *responsibility* (measured as self-reliance, self-esteem and clarity of the self, and work orientation), *perspective* (measured as the ability to see short- and long-term consequences, and the ability to consider others), and *temperance* (measured as impulse control and self-restraint). They found that decision-making was correlated with chronological age and psychosocial measures. Individuals who were more responsible, had more perspective, and were more temperate, were less likely to make antisocial decisions. Cauffman and Steinberg also found that when they conducted hierarchical regressions with age and psychosocial maturity, the effect of age became insignificant when psychosocial measures were introduced. In other words, psychosocial measures were stronger indicators of decision-making than age. This may suggest that individuals who persistently offend during adulthood are less responsible, have less perspective, and are less temperate than individuals who have desisted from crime.

In a similar vein, Paternoster and Pogarsky (2009) developed the concept of thoughtfully reflective decision making (TRDM) to assess how individuals make good decisions in the short- and long-term. For them:

> TRDM refers to the tendency of persons to collect information relevant to a problem or decision they must make, to think deliberately, carefully, and thoughtfully about possible solutions to the problem, apply reason to the examination of alternative solutions, and reflect back upon both the process and the outcome of the choice in order to assess what went right and what went wrong. It is thoughtful decision making because persons who have these characteristics are deliberate, careful, and mindful in how they go about collecting and using information about a problem/issue they are confronted with. It is reflective because individuals can step out of themselves and examine how well they have made a decision and learn from it. TRDM, then, describes the process of good decision making.
>
> (2009: 104–5)

They argued that TRDM is an essential aspect of human agency, because agency is not merely free will or personal freedom, but rather it is an intentional action towards either an immediate or a long-term goal, and an important part of goal realisation is effective decision-making. As goals are realised (or not), or as goals can change over time, human agency also entails that individuals reflect on themselves and their actions; they need to 'self-regulate' (2009: 113). The authors analysed data from the National Longitudinal Study of Adolescent Health over three waves and found that measures of TRDM were predictive of positive outcomes in both the short- and the long-term. At wave 1 respondents were adolescents, wave 2 was conducted 6–18 months later, and wave 3 was conducted when respondents were making the transition from adolescence to adulthood (ages 19–26), some five to seven years after wave 1. Individuals who made less thoughtfully reflective decisions at wave 1 were more likely to be involved in delinquency and other antisocial behaviours at wave 2, and at wave 3 were more likely to be involved in delinquency, heavy drinking and drug use. Respondents whose decision-making was less thoughtfully reflective at wave 1 were also less likely to have conventional and prosocial attachments when they had become young adults in wave 3.

In a development of this work, Paternoster, Pogarsky and Zimmerman (2011) found that TRDM was also closely related to investments in social, human and cultural capital, such that individuals who made more thoughtfully reflective decisions more likely to have invested in their own personal development, established attachments with significant others, and invested in hobbies and other cultural pursuits. The authors found that individuals who were less reflective in their decision-making during adolescence were less likely to accumulate different forms of capital, which could compromise life outcomes in early adulthood. As discussed earlier in this book, human and social capital have been identified as crucial dimensions of the desistance process, strongly related to the development of social bonds (Farrall, 2002; McNeill, 2006).

Motivation, moral agency and the perceived opportunity to change

The existing literature suggests that motivation can be highly influential in the desistance process, despite the sometimes inverse relationship between motivation and actual outcomes (Burnett, 2000; Farrall, 2002). This has prompted some to develop concepts which are related to motivation, but which might account for the apparent discrepancy in its relation to actual desistance. Burnett and Maruna (2004) developed the concept of 'hope', which they define as both the willingness and the perceived ability to change and, therefore, it is intrinsically related to the individual's motivation to desist (Maguire and Raynor, 2006). The absence of the perceived ability to change may account for why some individuals who indicate that they are motivated to desist actually do not act in ways which conform to this. A positive indication that an individual is motivated to desist may also be found in changes to their moral agency.

Moral agency can be considered to be the capacity of individuals to utilise moral reasoning, or moral judgements, to make decisions about particular courses of action in order to achieve a particular goal or objective. Changes to an individual's moral agency can be related to the desistance process, and this can occur in two distinct ways. Leibrich (1996) argued that shame about one's behaviour could act as a trigger to begin the process of desistance, whereas Giordano *et al.* (2002) suggested that shame and remorse about past behaviour is more likely to occur later in the change process as individuals seek to distance themselves from their criminal past. In the first scenario, if an individual's morality changes such that it becomes discordant with offending behaviour, then this may lead to alternative decision-making processes and non-offending courses of action which begin the process of desistance. In the second, changes to patterns of behaviour and decision-making could lead to a change in moral agency which could cement the transition towards desistance. In either case, there would appear to be a relationship between decision-making and moral agency.

Tittle *et al.* (2010) analysed data from random sample household surveys in major cities in Greece and Russia to assess attributes and characteristics which could mediate decision-making skills among the general population. They found that morality had the most significant impact upon decision-making. They also found that morality could work independently of perceived self-control or self-efficacy. The relationship between moral agency and decision-making has also been found within empirical studies of offenders and non-offenders. Palmer (2003) argued that non-offenders have more developed moral agency than offenders. For Palmer, it is the ability to make decisions through a process of moral reasoning which distinguishes offenders from non-offenders, and not merely the presence of knowledge about 'right or wrong'. The capacity to make judgements based on moral reasoning is influenced by a complex array of factors relating to upbringing, family relations, social contexts and social cognitions.

Moral reasoning could also vary across the life-course, and the development of more prosocial moral judgements can be associated with broader processes of maturation. However, the capacity to make moral judgements might be best considered as occurring developmentally, with some offenders having moral agency, and some who lack it not offending (Prior *et al.*, 2011). Sapouna *et al.* (2011) have also suggested that decisions to desist could vary according to gender. For Jamieson *et al.* (1999) this is due to differences in moral reasoning. In their study of young people in Scotland, they found that female offenders were more likely to attribute a decision to desist to moral reasoning, while male offenders were more likely to offer a utilitarian rationale. They explained that differences in moral reasoning between genders could be the result of females having a more general ethic of care and responsibility, and also due to experiences of victimisation. The boys in their study were more likely to have been the victim of physical assault outside the home, and were consequently more likely to blame the victims of their own crimes, indicating an individualistic approach to moral reasoning. The girls, on the other hand, were more likely to consider the effects of offending on other people.

Shapland and Bottoms (2011) identified moral judgements as part of the desistance process among the young men in the Sheffield Desistance Study. They found that the men in their study, generally, held conformist views and held conventional social aspirations. However, the authors found that morality was contextual, and that recidivist offenders could identify some criminal acts which were more acceptable than others. This could account for why almost 80 per cent of the sample were reconvicted within a three-year period during the study. However, Shapland and Bottoms argued that the dissonance between moral judgements and reoffending could be explained partly by individuals resorting to the habitual nature of criminal behaviour in times of increased tension or pressure, and also in part by the spontaneity of offending behaviour. In other words, a combination of obstacles to desistance and temptation (for example, invitations to offend from delinquent peers) could overcome moral agency and lead to reoffending. Therefore, moral agency is highly contextual and can vary both between individuals and across the life-course. On its own, moral agency is not sufficient to initiate and sustain desistance, and while some successful desisters may utilise feelings of shame and remorse about past actions to positive effect, there is also the possibility that, for others, 'the deep internalisation of shame may trigger feelings of depression and powerlessness' (LeBel *et al.*, 2008: 137), which could lead to further offending. For individuals to be able to utilise moral agency to positive effect, opportunities to desist are required and the individual needs to perceive them as readily available.

As an individual's outlook changes they may become more open to the possibility of change and, in a propitious social context, they may be more likely to identify possible opportunities to change. Openness to change and the availability of opportunities to change are regarded as the first two stages of the desistance process by Giordano *et al.* (2002) and Rumgay (2004). For an opportunity to be regarded as having the potential to lead to change it needs to be both readily available and relevant to the individual's personal and social contexts (Giordano *et al.*, 2002). For Rumgay (2004), recognising new social roles as an opportunity to change one's identity 'marks the beginning of active attempts at personal change' (2004: 408). New social roles offer a 'skeleton script' (2004: 409), providing the individual with behavioural cues as to how to act appropriately within the social role and how to act in accordance with the new identity. Giordano *et al.* (2002) refer to these scripts as 'a detailed plan of action or fairly elaborate *cognitive blueprint*' (2002: 1055). While it is most likely the case that certain identities or social roles offer behavioural 'cues' or 'roadmaps' for how to act, the approaches referred to above do not adequately account for how individuals' strategies for desistance develop during times of institutional or structural uncertainty, or in light of the challenging social contexts that have been well documented in previous research (Mair and May, 1997; Rex, 1999; Harper *et al.*, 2004).

Narrative and identity

The ability to alter one's identity is regarded as a crucial aspect of living in late-modernity (May and Cooper, 1995). Individuals must live more reflectively, in order to continuously develop new possibilities of thought and action (Giddens, 1998). New forms of action, or social activity, can be achieved by resituating one's identity in order to establish an alternative social role. Such an argument would suggest that individuals are responsible for their own destiny and their own futures. Individuals can change the social world around them if they choose to do so (Greener, 2002). For Giddens (1998: 37): 'We have to make our lives in a more active way than was true of previous generations, and we need more actively to accept responsibilities for the consequences of what we do and the lifestyle habits we adopt.' Indeed, 'modern guidelines actually compel the self-organization and self-thematization of people's biographies' (Beck and Beck-Gernsheim, 2002: 31). As such, the construction of identities is continuous as individuals engage in processes of identity re-evaluation and revision (Archer, 2007). Individuals may construct their identities to suit new social roles, either that they wish to adopt, or which they have acquired unwittingly, or in response to other actors in their social context. Identities, therefore, are never permanently fixed and can change according to interactions with social contexts and responses to social challenges (Archer, 2000, 2003). Identity also requires the construction and maintenance of an ongoing narrative which 'conjoins, in a personally (and probably socially) acceptable and plausible way, the disparate elements of one's life and the past to the present' (Stevens, 2012). Meaningful life-course events, therefore, can be internalised by the individual and then reconstructed so as to provide coherence and understanding of the life-course. As late-modern society is characterised by risk and uncertainty, the autobiographical narrative becomes more important for individuals to obtain a sense of control and order in their lives (Giddens, 1991).

Narrative, behaviour and social context can, therefore, be regarded as co-conspirators in the production of one another. Future behaviours can be conditioned by narratives, as individuals will often seek to align their actions and interactions with the narratives that they construct. Likewise, narratives may be conditioned by social contexts and the interactions which take place within them. Narratives may be evaluated and possibly revised if unexpected events or interactions occur. In turn, this can have a subsequent impact on future actions, behaviour and identities. Life-course events can, therefore, perform two important functions. First, they can consolidate the narrative. If particular events or interactions confirm that the narrative is 'working' then the individual is likely to continue on that particular pathway. Second, if life-course events occur which prompt re-evaluation of a chosen pathway then the narrative may alter and the individual may change their identity to fit with the new narrative (McAdams, 1985). Such re-evaluation is likely to occur when existing narratives and identities come under scrutiny, often in the aftermath of particular life-course events (Pals, 2006).

The existing desistance literature has situated narrative and identity change as crucial elements of the overall process, largely in terms of changing values, morals and beliefs, which can lead individuals away from offending. The development of alternative pro-social identities is regarded as being a crucial aspect of individual change. This is likely to entail a new identity which is incongruent with offending behaviour (Giordano *et al.*, 2002; Rumgay, 2004), and may also entail an identity of 'generativity' which is driven to 'give something back' to the community (Maruna, 2001; McNeill and Maruna, 2007). The notion that successful desisters envisage future identities and formulate plans to achieve them is also explored by Paternoster and Bushway (2009). They argued that would-be desisters need to 'cast off' old identities in favour of alternative versions of the self (2009: 1107–8). These authors argued that this process provides both a motivational and deterrent effect which can facilitate desistance. Individuals may envision two versions of the self: a 'possible self' and a 'feared self'. The former is the person that they could become if they make changes in their lives, and this is the identity that they are motivated towards. The latter, by contrast, is the person that they could become if they continue to offend, and this identity deters the individual from persistent offending behaviour. Consequently, successful desisters need to reconstruct their autobiographical narratives in order to work towards the 'possible self', and avoid the 'feared self'.

While Maruna (2001) argued that desisters 'rewrite a shameful past into a necessary prelude to a productive and worthy life' (2001: 87), Paternoster and Bushway's (2009) argument is premised on the notion that the would-be desister needs to 'cast off' old identities and replace them with an alternative version of the self (2009: 1107–8). For Paternoster and Bushway (2009) the 'feared self' acts as a deterrent, someone that the would-be desister would want to avoid becoming. The 'possible self', on the other hand, provides the initial motivation to change as the individual is able to perceive an alternative future self. It is this combination of deterrence and motivation which encourages the individual to alter their social preferences in a way which would be more concomitant with an emerging new identity. According to these authors, human agency provides the 'upfront work' (2009: 1152) which begins the process of desistance. The next stage in the process is an alteration to 'structural supports' (2009:1129), which include social roles and networks with other people. These facilitate desistance as they offer more conventional ties and pro-social supports, which creates further opportunities for the individual to act in ways which are more suited to the 'possible self' and the person that they want to become.

The role of narratives is important within the desistance process as they serve three crucial functions. First, they can allow the individual to distance themselves from past behaviours and events. As such, the narrative can enable the individual to have greater recognition of the harm caused by particular actions. Second, they can provide meaning to particular life-course events or 'turning points' (Sampson and Laub, 2005). This is important because life-course events are more likely to be influential if they have some subjective meaning to the person concerned (Farrall, 2002). Third, the narrative-building process can enable the individual to develop a new non-offending identity. Moreover, the influence of narrative and identity change can often facilitate desistance despite the significant structural barriers faced by many offenders (Barry, 2006; Presser, 2009; Marsh, 2011). In Maruna's (2001) Liverpool Desistance Study, the narratives of 30 desisting offenders and those of 20 active offenders were com-pared. The two groups shared similar backgrounds and criminogenic characteris-tics, but the narrative accounts from the two groups differed in important respects. Both groups contended that past behaviour had been the result of cir-cumstance – in other words, both groups suggested that they were victims of their own situation, and that this had led to them offending. However, while the desisters were able to reconstruct their identities in order to accomplish 'what he or she was "always meant to do"' (2001: 87), the persisters instead lived by what Maruna (2001) referred to as a 'condemnation script'. These individuals regarded their future outlooks as dire; as Maruna wrote 'they claim to have a clear picture of the "good life" but do not feel they have the ability to get there using their own volition' (2001: 83).

In a similar vein, Vaughan (2007) argued that successful desisters will con-struct a narrative which directs them towards a new 'non-offender' identity, while simultaneously distancing themselves from their past 'offender' identity. He suggested that desistance could be explained according to three interrelated processes, drawing upon Archer's (2000, 2003) notion of the internal conversa-tion. First, the individual reviews a range of possible choices that they could make in relation to their lifestyle. Second, the individual considers the possible courses of action that they could take to achieve this lifestyle. This includes a comparison of who they were, who they currently are, and who they would like to be. Third, the individual commits to a new non-criminal identity (Vaughan, 2007). For Vaughan (2007), desistance narratives cannot be a simplistic recon-struction of the past. The individual's narrative needs to include some repudi-ation of past events so that the narrative can establish a new identity which allows for the continuation of non-offending behaviour. As such, the narrative needs to enable the individual to make sense of past events, and pass judgement on them accordingly (Vaughan, 2007: 398).

As such, the nature of change in this context is one whereby individuals come to regard their past actions in a different way, such that for the would-be desister there is an 'acquisition of an altered perspective on their youthful self and activ-ities' (Shover, 1996: 131). This externalisation of the past, and the emotional responses elicited as a consequence, allow for the narrative construction of a possible future. Harris (2011) has similarly noted that desisters may draw upon negative accounts of the past self to inform the potential future self that the indi-vidual could become, given the propitious structural and cultural environments required. Thus, desistance is more likely to result from changes in an individu-al's 'self-identity and worldview', which may include alterations to their com-mitments, concerns and needs such that they are incompatible with their past identity (Maruna and Roy, 2007: 115). Therefore, it is this distinction between past, present and a future identity which, for many, is at the heart of desistance journeys, and it is the building of a desistance narrative which underpins the development of new identities.

There is much empirical evidence to support the argument that narratives and identity change are highly significant to the overall desistance process, primarily through helping individuals to account for past criminal behaviour, and in explaining how individuals have become a reformed character with a new pro-social identity (see for example: Burnett, 2004; Gadd and Farrall, 2004; Giordano *et al.*, 2002; Laub and Sampson, 2003; Maruna, 2001; Vaughan, 2007). However, existing accounts tend to approach the analysis of desistance narratives retrospectively, which may present a distorted account of the nature of human agency in the desistance process. Individuals may be more likely to rationalise events or add coherence to their narratives. As such, existing accounts may present desistance narratives in a structured and coherent manner, with a certain degree of consistency in the ordering of life-course events and life-scripts to which would-be desisters might adhere. Retrospective accounts are also less likely to account for how some individuals are able to make the initial transition towards desistance in the face of social and structural challenges, while others are not.

Agency and social context

Structural theories explain desistance in relation to particular life-course events, such as employment, marriage or parenthood. These changes to the life-course alter the individual's socio-structural context to the extent that reoffending becomes incompatible with the new role that the individual occupies. The personal and social challenges faced by offenders have been well documented (Burnett, 2000; Farrall, 2002; SEU, 2002). A significant number of offenders experience homelessness or face barriers to housing (Niven and Olagundaye, 2002; Niven and Stewart, 2005; Petersilia, 2003), and many face problems with employment and education (Fletcher *et al.*, 1998; Sarno *et al.*, 1999). It is perhaps, then, little surprise that many offenders experience financial difficulties and debt, particularly those offenders who have served custodial sentences (Hagell *et al.*, 1995). Many experience mental health problems (Ditton, 1999), and for many offenders alcohol/drug misuse is a factor in their offending (Rumgay, 2004; Ferguson *et al.*, 2006; Schroeder *et al.*, 2007). These structural factors may have a compounding effect, whereby individual offenders become increasingly socially excluded and segregated. For example, incarceration can 'knife off' opportunities to participate in mainstream society (Sampson and Laub, 1995), while increasing opportunities to commit crime.

However, 'the structuring aspects of society are not merely *constraining* – they are at the same time, *enabling*' (Farrall and Bowling, 1999: 256, emphasis in original), and changes to the social context during the life-course can, therefore, lead towards desistance. The work of Sampson and Laub (1993, discussed in the previous chapter) identified a series of turning points which can lead to such changes, and the subsequent establishment of a stake in society which would preclude offending behaviour. A central aspect of the structural explanation of desistance would suggest that such changes can occur irrespective of the individual's own actions or volition. Indeed, Laub *et al.* (1998: 225) argued:

[T]hat turning points are 'triggering events' that are, in part, exogenous – that is, they are chance events. If these events were entirely the result of conscious calculations or enduring patterns of behaviour, we could not argue for the independent role of social bonds in shaping behaviour.

Therefore, if structural changes can be 'chance events' then it must be presumed that they can occur without any impetus from the individual agent. This position would overlook the possibility that individuals can shape their own lives, instead painting a picture of human beings as passive agents whose lives are determined by the wider social structural environment. Instead, they characterise the individual as a 'super-dupe', or someone whose behaviour is determined by the social context (Farrall and Bowling, 1999). While Sampson and Laub (1993, 2005) acknowledged the influence of human agency, the role of structural turning points takes primacy in their explanatory account. Their argument stated that desistance occurs as a result of a series of side-bets which do not require any lasting commitment from the individual concerned. Taking this argument further, desistance would be regarded as the outcome of various life-course turning points which would remove criminal opportunities and enhance pro-social opportunities without the knowledge of the would-be desister (Vaughan, 2007). Laub and Sampson (2003) refer to this as 'desistance by default' (2003: 278–9), absent of meaningful intention on behalf of the individual or the narrative processes described above. According to this account, therefore, agency is conceptualised as being reactive, rather than purposive. There are similarities here with Turner's (1976) theory of the impulse self. This theory suggests that individuals react impulsively to the situations that they encounter and, therefore, do not create any institutional commitments. As a result of this lack of commitment, individuals only establish weak social bonds, so if more alluring opportunities are presented then the individual may be likely to alter their course of action accordingly. However, as behavioural intention and actual behaviour can be related (Ajzen, 1991; Serin and Lloyd, 2009; Forste *et al.*, 2010), it is unlikely that would-be desisters act in such passive and structurally submissive ways. Giordano *et al.* (2003), observing the interplay between marriage, peer association and persistent criminality, found that in the absence of motivation and commitment to a new 'self', individuals were more likely to ignore their spouse or leave the relationship altogether. Indeed, it is argued that desistance involves at least some form of conscious deliberation about future goals, and some evaluation of present contexts to determine how these could be achieved. As Maruna (2001) stated, successful desisters 'had a plan and were optimistic that they could make it work' (2001: 147).

In their account of identity and desistance, Paternoster and Bushway (2009) did not discount the effect of social contexts on the transition towards desistance, and its subsequent maintenance. However, they explicitly stated that the decision to desist and acquire a new identity is intentionally and actively made by the individual. Indeed, they described human agency as 'intentional self change', that individuals create their own futures and that they are not coerced by external social contexts (2009: 1149–50). Therefore, desistance identities are acquired through the wilful decisions of the individual themselves; they decide that they no longer want to be identified as an offender and choose an alternative identity as a non-offender for the future. Envisaging this future identity provides the individual with a strategy to realise their goals:

> The possible self of a non-offender provides a current offender with a specific and realistic route, roadmap, or strategy to take in order to realize that self, and steps that can be deliberately taken to change one's life in a way consistent with that self.
>
> (Paternoster and Bushway, 2009: 1149)

This suggests that the transition towards desistance is to a significant extent dependent upon the wilfulness of human agency. Indeed, it has been suggested that choice is 'implied in all definitions of agency: alternative courses of action are available, and the agent could have therefore acted otherwise' (Hays, 1994: 64). This line of argument would cohere to the depiction of Probationers in recent policy and practice outlined earlier in this book, which is to suggest that individuals are active decision-makers in the process of desistance and that they are responsible for actively and reflexively determining their own rehabilitation.

Others have placed greater emphasis upon the social context in enabling human agency in the transition towards desistance (Giordano *et al.*, 2002; Rumgay, 2004), but it is most likely that individuals who are embedded in criminal contexts are less likely to be presented with opportunities to acquire desisting identities, and this could have a negative effect upon motivation, confidence and, ultimately, the successful transition to desistance. The social context may provide strategies for desistance in the form of 'skeleton scripts' (Rumgay, 2004: 409) or a 'cognitive blueprint' (Giordano *et al.*, 2002: 1055), but this does not account for how individuals' strategies develop during early transitions towards desistance, or how they change in response to challenging social contexts. Such conditions may have deleterious effects upon the likelihood of desistance (Farrall *et al.*, 2010), and could negatively affect the strategies that individuals develop in the early stages of desistance. Therefore, the desistance literature suggests that individuals need to have an availability of choices in order to make the transition towards desistance, yet the suggestion that the life-course provides an array of opportunities for individuals may be overly optimistic (Jamieson, 1999; Skeggs, 2004). Would-be desisters are likely to face numerous personal and social problems, and this may adversely affect motivation, moral agency, narrative and identity construction and, ultimately, desistance itself (King, 2012).

This is where a greater emphasis upon human agency becomes more pertinent to understandings of desistance. LeBel *et al.* (2008) have argued that the primary concern in existing desistance research has been with uncovering the social factors that impact upon desistance by controlling for individual differences (2008: 139–40). Such views of desistance emphasise the role of the social environment in conditioning (if not determining) humans' activity, to the neglect of the complicity of the individual agent in the occurrence of life events. In other words, a 'strong social' understanding of desistance 'omits consideration of how the agent originally submitted to these [structural] forces and why they remain enthralled by them' (Vaughan, 2007: 390). Laub and Sampson (2001, 2003), in their follow-up study of the life-history narratives of 52 offenders and ex-offenders, argued that they would integrate structure and agency in their explanation of desistance (2001: 4). However, theirs is essentially a structuralist approach, and they suggested that desistance occurs through a series of 'side-bets'. Attachment to marriage and employment inhibits involvement in offending in the short-term and, over time, as individuals invest more in these institutions long-term conformity is secured (2001: 50–1). They argued that individuals do not need to develop 'deep and lasting interests' to alter their behaviour and sense of self, but rather that various structurally induced turning points 'knife off' criminal opportunities and ensure a commitment to desistance without the individual realising it (Vaughan, 2007: 391). Indeed, structural turning points dominate the 'strong social' models of desistance which contend that changes in an individual's social context coerce the individual towards moving away from crime. As LeBel *et al.* (2008: 139) argued:

> It is the arrival of these events, which are largely outside of an individual's control, that will best predict success after prison (see Lin, 2000). From this viewpoint, the subjective mindset of the released prisoner is not important for going straight.

Such an approach adheres to the notion of determinism, and advocates would claim that outcomes could be predicted given a specific set of circumstances that operate as variables within their explanatory frameworks. The transition towards desistance cannot be fully explained by such structuralist accounts, as there is no elaboration in respect of why people choose to submit themselves to certain structural institutions or why they remain committed to them during periods of ambivalence. In the short-term it could be argued that individuals seek to satisfy their immediate preferences, but this does not explain why this is so during challenging times in the absence of 'deep and lasting interests' to sustain their commitment (Vaughan, 2007: 392). Alternatively, they could argue that structural institutions provide the individual with a particular role and an associated set of behaviours and obligations to which members of that role adhere to (Farrall and Bowling, 1999: 256–7). However, individuals do not always have full knowledge of their social contexts (Archer, 2000: 90) and, thus, may be unaware of how to conform to particular roles. This may be particularly the case for offenders, who have spent much of their lives marginalised and excluded from mainstream society. Individuals can only fulfil certain roles through reflecting on their situational context in relation to their long-term interests, and the range of possible courses of action available to realise them (Vaughan, 2007: 392).

The importance of agency to the desistance process is that it allows for an exploration of how individuals actively consider who they want to become, how they want to act in the future, and how they decide upon the structural turning points necessary to achieve these objectives. This is because the life-course events that Laub and Sampson (and the wider desistance literature) refer to need to be 'relevant' to the individual in order to facilitate a move away from criminal activity (Haigh, 2009). In the absence of this relevance individuals are unlikely to be able to reorient their preoccupations with the factors that maintain criminal activity towards those factors which are likely to sustain desistance (Serin and Lloyd, 2009: 352). In order to explore the relevance of structural factors for individuals engaging in the desistance process, it is necessary to explore how they receive such structures and how this influences their decisions and strategies for future action.

However, just as it cannot be argued that desistance can occur given propitious structural conditions, regardless of individual cognition or intent, it also cannot be argued that desistance can be achieved in the face of challenging structural barriers by individual willpower alone. Adopting such an approach would be a concession to voluntarism, or a 'strong subjective' model of desistance, whereby 'one need only decide to change and envision a new identity for oneself in order to go straight' (LeBel *et al.*, 2008: 138). This would imply that individuals are capable of transforming or reproducing their environment with free will, which is not the case (Elder-Vass, 2007a: 26). Rather 'it is precisely because such elaboration is co-determined by the conditional influence exerted by antecedent structures together with the autonomous causal powers of current agents, that society can develop in unpredictable ways' (Archer, 1995: 75). In this respect, 'players make their own history, in part creating their own rules, but they do not do it in conditions entirely of their own choosing' (Hollis, 1994: 19). In other words, properties in the social environment condition the possibilities of action available to individuals, and the manner by which individuals respond to, utilise, subjugate or circumvent these properties will, in turn, condition the possible outcomes of their actions. This is why attempts to examine the process of desistance require an approach which gives proper consideration to agency and action but also accounts for structural constraint (Marshall, 2005: 69).

Agency and desistance transitions

LeBel *et al.* (2008) argued that subjective changes within the individual's mindset could lead to turning points in the social environment which could initiate desistance. Indeed, they stated that individuals could 'act as agents of their own change', and that a positive approach to desistance could help 'to triumph over problems and make the best of situations' (2008: 155). By contrast, others have argued that individual change is preceded by structural turning points, either in the form of pro-social events (Laub and Sampson, 2003), or negative experiences (Cusson and Pinsonneault, 1986). Unravelling the 'chicken and egg' debate in desistance is fraught with difficulties, and it is likely that each scenario may be true for different individuals. Commonality is more likely to be found in the way in which early transitions towards desistance are almost certain to be characterised by obstacles, change and uncertainty. Some individuals who are in the transitional phase may have recently been released from prison, perhaps with very limited funds or burdened with debt, and with no or only insecure accommodation or employment (see for example Ross and Richards, 2009). Others may be contemplating attempts to fulfil strongly conventional pro-social goals, having spent many years living within the habitual routines of offending behaviour, and the dissonance between goals and habits may lead to ambivalence and relapse (Shapland and Bottoms, 2011).

Maruna and Roy (2007) referred to the process of 'knifing off' to explain how desisters need to cut ties with old peer networks in order to fashion a new, non-offending lifestyle. In a similar way, Shapland and Bottoms (2011) described the process of 'diachronic self-control', where individuals deliberately avoid particular activities to ensure that they are not tempted into criminal activity when this contradicts their moral perceptions. However, it is likely to take time to make pro-social contacts, networks and opportunities; social bonds will develop gradually; and non-offending identities will be modified and adapted before they become an established part of the 'new person'. During the transitional phase of desistance, therefore, individuals may find that they lack their old networks and social contexts, but do not yet have replacements to align themselves with. They are, at the same time, neither 'offender' nor 'desister', as they may avoid engaging in 'old' criminal networks or environments, but do not yet have alternative networks or environments to otherwise engage in.

Healy (2010) described this as the 'liminal' phase of desistance, where individuals operate between two social worlds. Drawing upon the work of Victor Turner (1970), she described the liminal phase as one which is 'characterised by introspection, ambiguity and social withdrawal' (Healy, 2010: 35), as individuals begin the process of rejecting their past and distancing themselves from it as they forge alternative future identities. Prior to liminality, individuals experience the 'separation' phase, which involves the individual withdrawing from old patterns of behaviour and previous social roles. After the liminal phase, individuals experience 'aggregation', where their transition is consolidated and changes may be symbolically recognised (Healy, 2010: 35–6). Throughout the desistance literature various explanations can be found which suggest that there are a series of sequential phases that individuals progress through on their journey to becoming a 'desister'. Weaver and McNeill (2010: 43) identified three desistance models which articulate this. Each of the models explains desistance as involving an interaction between the social environment and the individual, which leads to changes to the individual's social roles and self-identity (as shown in Table 4.1). Similar phases can also be identified in Rumgay's (2004) theory of female desistance, and the work of Sommers *et al.* (1994) who argued that desistance occurs following: a catalyst – a triggering event or re-evaluation of crime which leads to the decision to desist; discontinuance – the public announcement that the individual has decided to desist; and maintenance – the renegotiation of social roles and self-identity.

Table 4.1 Explanatory models of desistance

Giordano et al. (2002)	Vaughan (2007)	Sheffield Pathways Out of Crime Study (SPOOCS)
General cognitive openness to change	Discernment: reviews possible choices	Triggering event
Exposure and reaction to 'hooks for change'	Deliberation: about possible courses of action	Decision to try to change
Availability of an appealing conventional self	Dedication: commitment to non-criminal identity	Thinking differently about oneself
Transformation in attitudes to deviant behaviour		Taking action to desist
		Maintaining change – offender looks for reinforcers, but may encounter obstacles

Source: Weaver and McNeill, 2010: 43.

There is resonance here with DiClemente and Prochaska's (1982; Prochaska and DiClemente, 1992) work on change processes. The first stage of the change process, *precontemplation*, involves little, if any, understanding on behalf of the individual that change is necessary. Rather, any change that does take place may be coerced by significant others, and it is likely that for some individuals it will be temporary until the pressure to change is alleviated. The second stage, *contemplation*, is where individuals become aware that a problem exists which requires change, but they may not yet be committed to take action. Individuals may contemplate change for relatively long durations before they commit to take action. The third stage, *action*, is where individuals modify their behaviour or environment in order to achieve change. This is the most overt and visible stage of the change process, and the one which is most likely to prompt external recognition that change has occurred. The final stage in their cycle of change is *maintenance*. Within this stage individuals seek to concretise changes made to their behaviour. Individuals within this stage will work to prevent relapse, and this is a continuous and ongoing activity which individuals will engage with.

Prochaska *et al.* (1992) included a fifth stage, between *contemplation* and *action*, which they referred to as *preparation*. Within this stage individuals are seeking to link intentions with actual behaviour. Individuals may have made some small behavioural changes, but full behavioural change is not yet complete. During this stage individuals are in the process of planning to commit to behavioural change in the near future. Prochaska and DiClemente's work has been incorporated into approaches to working with offenders to try to facilitate change (for example: Harper and Hardy, 2000; Prochaska and Levesque, 2003). Their work has also been referred to within the existing desistance literature. The model of change proposed by Prochaska and DiClemente offers a useful way of conceptualising the dynamic nature of desistance, and of accounting for the complex interplay between changes within the social environment and the internal reorientations which individuals undergo throughout the process of moving away from crime (Mulvey and LaRosa, 1986; Fagan, 1989; Horney, Osgood and Marshall, 1995; Shover, 1996; Laub and Sampson, 2001; Maruna, 2001; Piquero, 2004).

Indeed, it is possible to see aspects of Prochaska and DiClemente's approach within some of the broad models of desistance which have been constructed to explain these complex change processes. The 'general openness to change' phase outlined in the work of Giordano *et al.* (2002) and Rumgay (2004) may be regarded as comparable to the contemplation phase of Prochaska and DiClemente's model. The decisions to desist which were discussed in the previous chapter may be regarded as examples of Prochaska and DiClemente's contemplation phase. The men in the study spoke about their decisions to move away from crime, and they clearly articulated that they recognised the problematic nature of their behaviour. They also spoke about how they wanted to change the direction of their lives, and make alterations to their lifestyles and behaviours.

The last two stages of the desistance process outlined in the Sheffield Desistance Study entail the individual taking action to desist and seek reinforcers to maintain positive changes which have been made, and these two stages clearly mirror the final two elements of Prochaska and DiClemente's work. However, relatively little attention has been paid towards the stage which Prochaska and DiClemente refer to as the 'preparation' phase. Instead, where this model has been referred to in the existing literature, the focus has tended to be upon the individual's readiness to change (Mulvey *et al.*, 2001; Maguire and Raynor, 2006; Burrowes and Needs, 2009). Relatively little attention has been paid to the preparations that individuals may make as they embark on desistance journeys. It has been recognised in the literature that successful desisters often make plans, but there has been little research conducted which explicitly examines these plans, and how and why individuals construct them. It is argued here that individuals are likely to begin making such plans and preparing for change during the transitional phase of desistance.

Within the subjective-social model outlined by LeBel *et al.* (2008) it is argued that while it is the interplay between social and individual factors that leads to desistance, subjective changes are likely to lead to particular structural turning points that can facilitate desistance:

> The findings suggest that subjective changes may precede life-changing structural events and, to that extent, individuals can act as agents of their own change. This prior influence of internal logic, or cognitive scripts, works in both positive and negative directions: positive 'mind over matter' helps the individual to triumph over problems and make the best of situations, while a negative frame of mind leads to drift and defeatism in response to the same events.

(LeBel *et al.*, 2008: 155)

Thus, it is reasonable to assume that individuals making the transition towards desistance would display agency, as they occupy the initial stages of desistance that may precede structural turning points that could lead to longer-term desistance.

Explanatory models of desistance, therefore, suggest that there are numerous stages that individuals need to navigate in order to desist from crime. These models may operate more as heuristic devices than actual representations of reality, as the sequences are unlikely to occur in a linear fashion and some individuals may be likely to 'skip' certain phases. However, it can still be argued that such models illustrate the complexity and time-intensive nature of desistance, and that the transitional phase of desistance is one which might be characterised in particular by ambivalence, difficulty and change. However, the transitional phase may also be characterised in terms of opportunities to change. It is a time where individuals may reflexively consider their social contexts and the goals that they want to realise within them. Archer's (2000, 2003, 2007) arguments are relevant here, as individuals' capacity for exercising agency that can challenge social contexts and routinised actions can be enhanced by particular forms of reflexivity. Reflexive deliberations which are concerned with generating alternative future possibilities are more likely to lead to the individual exercising transformative agency. This is because, in undertaking these reflexive deliberations, the individual wishes to distance themselves from their present context. However, individuals may wish to maintain their contexts, to retain a sense of ontological security, and will therefore act to achieve this by undertaking habitual action.

Thus, reflexivity can lead to a 'strong' form of agency, whereby the potential for transformative action is heightened, or it can lead to a 'weak' form of agency, whereby individuals will accept their structural surroundings as they are and will seek to reproduce them. In other words, what is argued here is that desistance can be achieved through the exercising of particular forms of agency, which will lead to structurally transformative action. Particular forms of reflexivity undertaken by individuals in certain social contexts can enable such agency, while other forms of reflexivity may lead to the reproduction of habits and structures. Reflexivity operates as an underpinning characteristic of each of the agentic factors outlined earlier. Individuals may reflexively consider their life aims, what they want to be, and how they intend to get there; they may reflexively consider their moral agency, and whether this is incongruent with the goals they set; identities may become the subject of reflexive deliberations, as individuals consider how they perceive themselves, how they are perceived by others, and how they would like to be perceived; and individuals may reflexively consider their social contexts, identifying possibilities, obstacles and pathways towards achieving certain goals.

Human agency is, therefore, likely to be of particular importance in the transitional phase in order to develop the motivation and moral agency required to identify possible opportunities for change, and to be able to construct new narratives and identities which will allow the individual to take advantage of those opportunities. It is also likely that significant levels of human agency will help to maintain the resolve to desist in the face of adverse conditions in the individual's social environment. However, while the social context of the transitional phase may present many difficulties and constraints, for some it will also present opportunities and it will enable them to undertake the transition towards desistance. In part, this is because agency and structure are interconnected and so it stands to reason that a particular configuration of agentic factors will allow different individuals in similar situations to act (or react) in different ways. Likewise, it is also logical to conclude from this that structural conditions will condition the agentic capacity of particular individuals.

5 Obtaining accounts of probation

This study aimed to contribute to the existing knowledge on desistance from crime in three predominant ways. First, the study was designed to explore the strategies formulated to sustain desistance. While it is acknowledged that desisters tend to construct plans for the future (Maruna, 2001), little attention has been paid to the content or scope of these. In part, this may be a consequence of the methodological implications of retrospective research designs, which may be limited by instances of cognitive dissonance or rationalisation as research subjects seek to construct a coherent narrative. Indeed, the validity of retrospective research depends upon the memory recall of participants (Hegney *et al.*, 2007: 1184), and cognition can lead to retrospective justifications or rationalisations for particular actions (Thakker *et al.*, 2007: 15). Second, this study was designed to explore the role of human agency in the early stages of desistance. Desistance from crime is now widely acknowledged to be the product of an interaction between structural and agentic factors (Barry, 2009). However, there is little detailed understanding of how meaningful social attachments and agentic orientation interact and, in particular, how this interaction might be temporally contingent (Bottoms *et al.*, 2004: 382). Third, the study was designed to explore the impact of probation on the early stages of desistance. A body of literature exists which examines the interface between desistance and probation (Rex, 1999; Farrall, 2002; McCulloch, 2005; Farrall and Calverley, 2006), but there is considerable room for more research in this area. The central theme within this study, therefore, is based upon the proposition that individuals act in an agential manner throughout the desistance process, but that the capacity to exercise agency is conditioned by the social context that the individual resides in.

Capturing the essence of this agentic capacity in empirical research poses several difficulties. First, the various characteristics which constitute human agency in the desistance process are, in reality, difficult to separate from one another and are likely to interact in a complex and multilayered manner. Second, in order to understand how human agency operates in the desistance process it is important to understand how individuals mediate the effect of various structural properties, and how this impacts upon subsequent decisions, attitudes and behaviours. Third, if the study of desistance transitions is concerned with how individuals respond in the immediate aftermath of making a decision to desist and, therefore, with the goals and projects in relation to this which individuals commit to, then an account of how would-be desisters decide upon these is required. It is also necessary to employ a methodological approach which is capable of distinguishing between reflexivity at the time that decisions are made, and reflexivity which is rationalised after the event. This is necessary, in part, as reflexivity in the present tense will reflect the influence of structural inequalities and barriers in the social context, as well as those which may contain enabling properties. There is also considerable value in exploring agentic considerations contemporaneously as this is more likely to unearth a more accurate picture of individuals' strategies for desistance.

Exploring transitions to desistance

In order to achieve the study aims, three main research questions were constructed. The first two were based upon the assumption that desistance involves an interaction of social and subjective factors, and that individuals, to a greater or lesser extent, are instrumental in the desistance process – in other words, they decide to desist and they construct plans to achieve this. Social factors shape individuals and their future trajectories, such that particular factors may enable or constrain desistance. However, the influence of social factors may be mediated by the individual and their capacity to exercise agency. For example, the prospect of marriage will only have a meaningful effect on an individual's transition to desistance if they hold a subjective attachment to the concept of marriage and regard that particular prospect as being viable and attainable. In other words, would-be desisters must possess a certain arrangement of subjective factors that are congruent with their structural circumstances in determining that desistance is both possible and desirable. The study, therefore, aimed to explore (1) what social and subjective factors are relevant to would-be desisters when making the transition towards desistance, and; (2) how would-be desisters understand desistance prospectively, and how this influences their strategies for desistance.

The third research question was based on the assumption that there exist aspects within the probation experience which can either enable or constrain the pursuit of desistance. New Labour's approach to reducing reoffending, it is argued here, was underpinned by a discourse of agency that presents the individual as responsible for their own desistance. Policy developments under New Labour acknowledged the influence of a number of structural disadvantages that many offenders are likely to face, and there was a concern for risk assessing individuals in relation to a range of 'criminogenic needs'. However, assessing individuals in this manner assumes that individuals with similar needs will share the same motivation and willingness to challenge them as those who are doing the assessing (Maguire and Raynor, 2006a). Further, interventions which target these needs are located within a framework of individualism as they are often directed at improving individual capacities, such as skills and qualifications. An example of this is the primary objective of the Offenders' Learning and Skills Service (OLASS), which is to 'increase employability and thereby reducing re-offending' (National Audit Office, 2008b: 5), whereby the emphasis is clearly upon the manipulation of agency as opposed to addressing structural factors. Thus, while approaches have been introduced aimed at exerting an influence over agency, the mediation between an individual's agency and the impact upon their structural context has been neglected. New Labour consistently exclaimed a commitment to evidence-based policy, but the focus was upon clearly measurable performance indicators (Hale and Fitzgerald, 2007), and the demonstration of the outcome effects of interventions (Hollin, 1999). Various meta-analytic studies have also sought to identify particular interventions that reduce reoffending (Antonowicz and Ross, 1994; Dowden and Andrews, 2004; Lipsey, 1992, 1995; McGuire and Priestley, 1995), yet the conclusions from these analyses tend to focus upon the intervention content, rather than exploring how individuals receive them.

Thus, New Labour's approach to reducing reoffending had been premised upon the manipulation of agency, but with little concern for how such manipulation impacts upon how individuals then act within their social contexts. This is, in part at least, a corollary of New Labour's emphasis upon a 'weak' discourse of social exclusion, where 'solutions lie in altering these excluded people's handicapping characteristics and enhancing their integration into dominant society' (Veit-Wilson, 1998: 45), and 'it is the weak thesis which has by far the widest political currency' (Young, 2002: 459). This claim is evident in the focus within probation upon reducing levels of risk, predominantly through altering cognitions, attitudes and behaviour, in order to provide offenders with the opportunity to become 'homo prudens' (Kemshall, 2003: 6) – that is, the aim is to inculcate the marginalised into society by encouraging them to become mainstream, rather than challenging the structural factors that marginalise them in the first instance.

This study, therefore, builds upon the work of Farrall (2002) and McNeill (2009). It is argued here that New Labour's approach to probation and reducing reoffending was focused upon manipulating agency (or, as they argue, 'human capital'), to the neglect of challenging structural barriers (or, 'enhancing social capital'). This is the case for two predominant reasons. The first is the emphasis upon the responsibilisation of individual offenders, which is evidenced by tougher community penalties, risk assessment which targets 'criminogenic factors', and the premium attached to cognitive behavioural programmes designed to realign individuals' attitudes and thinking to fit with dominant society. The second is the rise of 'bureaucratic positivism' (Whitehead, 2007) within the Probation Service, which has led to practitioners becoming detached from much of the face-to-face work which characterised more traditional forms of probation, and which is widely recognised as being central to supporting desistance (Barry 2000, 2007; Burnett and McNeill, 2005). Probation will perhaps, albeit temporarily, constitute a relatively significant aspect of an individual's 'objective circumstances', and it is, therefore, reasonable to assume that the courses of action that individuals decide are appropriate to achieve their goals will be influenced by the probation that they receive. For some, probation may initiate a transition towards desistance, while for others it may contribute to their prospective strategies for sustaining desistance. Therefore, this study aimed to explore: how probation, with an emphasis upon the manipulation of agency, influences would-be desisters' strategies for sustaining their moves away from crime.

Researching probation and desistance

The first stage was to decide upon the most effective and practical approach to obtain narrative accounts of the early stages of desistance from individuals under probation supervision. The interface between probation and desistance is a relatively under-explored area of research, and the nature of one-to-one supervision in a probation context similarly suffers from a lack of understanding. As Farrall (2002) highlighted, despite the fact that very few individuals will complete a sentence within the Probation Service without experiencing one-to-one supervision, very few studies have gone beyond a rudimentary account. Indeed, as Hedderman (1998) wrote: 'we know little about the *content* of one-to-one supervision' (1998: 1, emphasis added). As a result, little is known about the nuances of probation supervision in individual cases (Farrall, 2002: 25). To rectify this, direct observation could be undertaken to explore the content and nature of one-to-one supervision in situ, complemented by follow-up interviews to explore the impact of supervision sessions or to discuss in greater detail issues raised from the observation. However, this could influence the interaction between officer and offender during the period of observation, and could also, more importantly, harm future work. Therefore, while a combination of direct supervision and one-to-one follow-up interviews may be highly appropriate in terms of answering the research questions, such methods are unsuitable when the research situation and likely participants are considered.

Desistance research has, generally, been conducted within one of three research designs. According to Brame *et al.* (2003), the dominant method of studying desistance is to employ approximate desistance models, which measure offence frequencies and use single measures (such as number of arrests). As a result, desistance is often measured in relation to changes in arrest and reconviction patterns over time (Le Blanc and Frechette, 1989; Le Blanc and Loeber, 1998; Nagin and Paternoster, 1991; Nagin and Farrington, 1992; Tracy and Kempf-Leonard, 1996). There is also a tendency for researchers operating within this tradition to examine the relationship between official offending data and demographic variables, such as age, gender or class (e.g. Wikstrom, 1987), or against social processes, such as marriage or employment (e.g. Kruttschnitt *et al.*, 2000). Research of this type utilises official data on rates of arrest and reconviction, which, as argued earlier, are somewhat unreliable given the nature of crime reporting, recording, and criminal justice priorities. Indeed, official datasets may reveal more about the organisations collating statistics than about the actual reality of crime. As Francis *et al.* (2004) argued:

official rates of crime are produced according to *the actions actually taken by persons in the social system*, actions that define, classify and record certain behaviour as a crime. For example, if the police are very active then there will appear to be more crime – even though the actual amount of criminal behaviour may remain the same.

(2004: 53, emphasis in original)

A second approach to desistance research has been to employ survey methodology, examining self-reported changes in offending (e.g. Warr, 1998). Similarly to those which study official data, self-report surveys often measure changes to offending behaviour over time. These methodologies are capable of modelling offending in relation to a greater number of types of criminal behaviour than the dichotomous variables used in other studies (e.g. Farrington and Hawkins, 1991; Loeber *et al.*, 1991), as well as in official datasets (Massoglia, 2006). Although self-report surveys avoid the biases and methodological difficulties associated with using official reconviction data, they do not capture the subjective experiences of individuals who are attempting to desist from crime.

The third approach does capture these subjective accounts, often through the use of narratives or in-depth interviews to capture individuals' accounts in their own words. This approach to desistance research has become more common in recent years (Farrall, 2002; Farrall and Calverley, 2006; Giordano *et al.*, 2002; Maruna, 2001), and the rich data collected has provided a detailed insight into the processes and challenges associated with desistance. Research within this paradigm has been criticised for its lack of generalisability beyond the sample of interviewees (Massoglia and Uggen, 2007), yet its suitability is often when situated within exploratory studies, as Marshall and Rossman (2006: 55, emphasis in original) argued:

> The most compelling argument [for qualitative research] emphasizes the unique strengths of the genre for research that is exploratory or descriptive, that accepts the value of context and setting, and that searches for a deeper understanding of the participants' lived experiences of the phenomenon under study....A study focusing on individual lived experience typically relies on an *in-depth interview strategy*.

The overall aim of this study was to examine individual subjective experiences of probation. The study was also concerned with identifying the role of human agency in the transitional phase of desistance. In-depth, semi-structured interviews were undertaken with men who had been required to undertake a probation element as part of their sentence. In-depth, and particularly face-to-face, interviews, have developed as the most common type of method used to explore peoples' experiences in particular contexts, both within desistance research and the wider social research agendas. This has largely been in response to alternative approaches which have employed survey-based methodologies or research which has 'relied predominantly on data derived from official sources' (Farrall, 2002: 4).

This is not to argue that in-depth interviews are not problematic. Indeed, there exist a range of issues in relation to *interviewing* as a method in the social sciences that can impact upon the gathering of data, the analysis of data, and the reliability and validity of data (Potter and Hepburn, 2005). There remains a largely unchallenged assumption that interviewees will be willing and able to 'tell it like it is' in much qualitative, interview-based, research (Holloway and Jefferson, 2001: 105). Thus, where in-depth interviews are regarded as providing an insight into authentic experiences, there is an assumption that the participant is both willing and able to convey these experiences (Silverman, 2001). Further, interviews rely on self-report data, and so the researcher must concede that for participants there may be a 'gap between word and deed' (Bryman, 1984: 81). However, this issue can be resolved (in part, at least) by triangulating self-report data with responses from others discussing the same events or processes. There may, of course, be disagreement between two parties, as different individuals have different perspectives on certain issues. If there is significant variation at the aggregate level, however, then this could be seen as a threat to the validity of the study (Farrall, 2002: 56).

Constructing the interview

These limitations aside, it is argued here that in-depth, face-to-face semi-structured interviews were the most appropriate method for this study. This is because a reliance on the, generally, quantitative methods employed in collecting most current (particularly official) data conceals the interaction effect between Probationer, supervising officer and wider circumstances (Farrall, 2002: 19–20). Further, the qualitative method employed here is most appropriate for a study which considers agency as the capacity to make choices (albeit constrained by social structure), and which is manifested in action (as the previous chapter discussed). In order to explore the interactions described above and in the previous chapter, the study must be able to elucidate how individuals understand and perceive the various factors involved in such interactions.

An initial interview schedule was produced which highlighted the key issues for exploration, based upon the research questions, and existing empirical and theoretical knowledge. The schedule was designed so that the interviews would be open-ended, to encourage participants to discuss issues in a manner which was most meaningful to them, and also following two pragmatic concerns raised by Farrall (2002). First, the interviews would need to be flexible enough to accommodate a range of offence types, offender characteristics, obstacles and challenges, and desires, goals and objectives. Second, the interviews would need to be adaptable to suit a range of abilities with respect to literacy (2002: 55). Before interviewing began, meetings were held with the three probation teams who participated in the study, to recruit participants for the study and to discuss the various issues that had arisen from the literature review and the design of the research questions. These meetings acted as pseudo focus groups and were used as an approximation of 'interview trialling' (Gillham, 2000), in order to highlight key issues and to make alterations to the interview schedule as necessary. The meetings were also an opportunity to ratify the issues in the interview schedule as appropriate for further discussion with Probationers. The meetings were particularly insightful in relation to sampling and recruitment issues, which will be discussed later.

The issues covered in the interview schedule related to particular stages of the prototypical desistance models, discussed in the previous chapter, and are highlighted in Table 5.1. The content of the interviews would need to reflect existing knowledge about the desistance process. As such, interview themes were grouped around three central propositions, which were informed by the existing desistance literature. First, there are various structural factors which are related to the likelihood of desistance taking place. Various contextual factors may increase the availability of criminal opportunities, while also decreasing the range of opportunities to pursue desistance. Part of this context includes probation, and the effect that various aspects of probation may have upon the individual's wider personal and social contexts. Second, would-be desisters determine objectives (however tenuous) for the future, and will aim to fulfil them. Third, would-be desisters reflect upon their personal and social contexts in relation to the objectives that they have determined to be appropriate to achieve desistance. The outcome of these reflexive deliberations will inform the individual's desistance strategy.

Practitioners were asked about similar issues to those outlined in Table 5.1, and also about their role and their understandings and experiences of probation. While practitioners were asked questions about the Probationers who were interviewed, they were encouraged to draw upon experiences or examples from other cases wherever appropriate. In part, practitioners were interviewed to triangulate the validity of the data (as discussed above), but also to provide an insight into the role of probation from the practitioners' perspective.

Selecting participants for interview

Sample criteria were formulated from the research questions and existing empirical and theoretical knowledge. Participants had to be considered to be in the transitional phase of desistance, and this entailed a conceptualisation of early desistance in relation to the measurement of reoffending and the duration of non-offending. Uggen and Kruttschnitt (1998) distinguished between 'official desistance' and 'behavioural desistance' – the former is measured by officially recorded reconviction data and the latter by self-report data. To mitigate some of the methodological issues associated with officially recorded data, participants were selected on the basis that they had not reoffended according to both official and self-report data. The timeframe for desistance is an issue of much debate in the existing literature. Moreover, as the transitional phase of desistance is a relatively unexplored phenomenon there are few guidelines as to the duration of time required to have passed for an individual to be considered as an early desister. Suffice to say that the duration of time in question will be significantly

Table 5.1 Interview themes in a desistance model

Desistance framework	Interview themes
1) Structural properties	Overall experiences of probation: • supervision sessions • relationship with supervising officer • additional requirements • previous experiences of probation • why previous sentences had not resulted in desistance Details of the current offence: • circumstances that had surrounded the offence • brief details of previous offending The personal and social circumstances of the probationer: • at the time of interview • whether these had altered since beginning the current sentence
2) Subjectively defined objectives	The Probationer's motivation and capabilities to stop offending: • people or events that might assist. Future plans or ambitions: • employment • education • family and relationships • drug/alcohol use • finances • attitudes and behaviour
3) Reflexively determined courses of action	How the individual planned to sustain their moves away from crime, and why they thought this was the most appropriate strategy. Particular problems or difficulties that the Probationer was experiencing at the time of interview: • whether these had changed at all since beginning the current sentence • extent to which the Probationer believed these would need to be overcome in order to stop offending • whether the Probationer had made plans for overcoming them

less than many other studies of desistance, such as Mischkowitz (1994), who stated that for desistance to have occurred the individual concerned needed to have committed their last offence prior to age 31, and be free from conviction or incarceration for at least ten years. Healy and O'Donnell (2008) suggest that a one month period of non-offending should be used as a measure of primary desistance. This study expands on this by suggesting that an individual should be crime-free (either officially recorded or self-reported) for a period of at least one month, but not more than one year. This ensures that a significant time has elapsed since the last offence, such that a period of non-offending has been measured, while retaining a prospective outlook, such that the timeframe under observation can be considered to be a period of transition.

An upper age limit was not imposed, but participants had to be 18 or over for a number of reasons. First, at this point of the age-crime curve, many individuals have either ceased, or have significantly reduced, offending (see also Bottoms *et al.*, 2004). Second, it is from this age that individuals begin to make the transition into adulthood, and it is reasonable to assume that transitions to desistance may accompany transitions into adulthood. Third, as most adolescent offenders do not continue to offend in adulthood, it is argued here that data from youth offenders is of little theoretical interest to this particular thesis. Indeed, many studies have focused upon youth transitions and much policy has been directed towards youth offenders. In order to address this imbalance this study retained a central focus upon desistance transitions among adult offenders.

Participants had to have been under probation supervision at the time of interview, predominantly because the research design was prospective rather than retrospective. Indeed, data were required from individuals discussing their current experiences and future outlooks, and the impact of probation upon transitions. The meetings with probation teams mentioned above provided an additional aspect to this sampling criterion. Discussions revealed that many practitioners believed Probationers were considerably more enthusiastic during the first or second supervision, and that these sessions usually entailed the practitioner outlining obligations in relation to the sentence. Thus, it was decided that a better reflection of peoples' experiences might be achieved if the sample had experienced at least one month of probation.

Most commentators have argued that desistance can only be studied with individuals who have a history of multiple acts of offending (e.g. Laub and Sampson, 2001; Serin and Lloyd, 2009). The rationale for this in terms of sampling is to eliminate one-off or occasional offenders. It is argued that these individuals are likely to have higher self- or social control (Kazemian, 2007: 12), as well as fewer criminogenic needs and less risk of future offending. This study followed Bottoms *et al.* (2004), whose sample includes individuals who have at least two convictions on their criminal record. This would allow for a broader sample of individuals, while omitting first-time offenders and those who had committed only minor offences which resulted in warnings or fines. Finally, while some studies have explored particular offence types (for example, Shover, 1983), the sampling criteria for this study allowed for the inclusion of all offence types. Following the formulation of these sampling criteria, a recruitment algorithm (see Figure 5.1) was constructed which would serve as an easy reference tool for probation practitioners to use when considering potential research participants.

In total, five practitioners (including Probation Officers and Probation Service Officers) volunteered to participate in the study. Other than being employed within the probation area that was the site of the research, no criteria were imposed on the participation of practitioners. This was primarily to ensure a sufficient number of individuals participated in the research, and also to ensure that Probationers would be recruited from a variety of sources. It was agreed with Senior Probation Officers that practitioners would recruit participants from their own caseloads, and practitioners were asked to follow the criteria from the recruitment algorithm when considering potential participants, but were also encouraged to ask a variety of cases to participate. They were also provided with an information sheet about the research that they could share with potential recruits, so that individuals had some prior

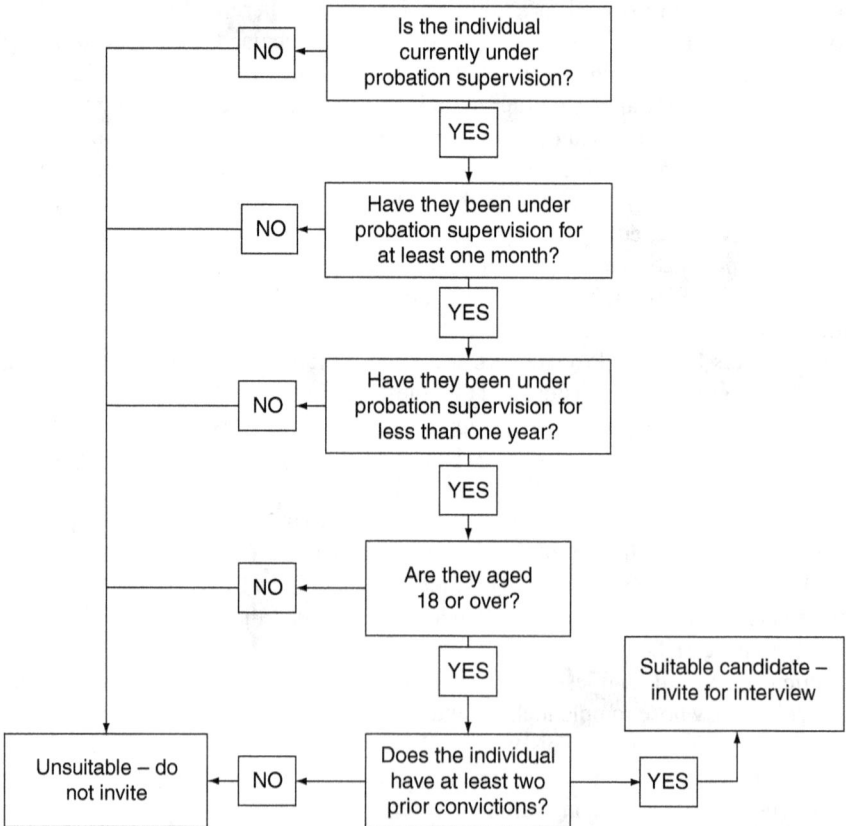

Figure 5.1 Participant recruitment algorithm.

knowledge of the research focus and what the interview would entail before they were interviewed. No payment or inducement was offered to individuals for their participation.

It is acknowledged here that the recruitment process involved some degree of selection bias, particularly by virtue of the fact that the only practitioners involved were those who volunteered, and the potential group of Probationers involved was, therefore, limited to those who were supervised by these practitioners. However, it is suggested that this is a largely unavoidable facet of this research, insofar as 'gatekeepers' were required to recruit Probationers for the study. As a result, selection of participants necessarily involved a certain degree of choice on behalf of the supervising officer. Moreover, it is argued that the absence of any payment being offered, and the use of the recruitment algorithm, minimised the impact of the selection bias within the sampling process.

In total, 25 Probationers and five practitioners agreed to participate in the research. All of the practitioners were interviewed, but five of the Probationers either withdrew or were not used in the analysis stage. Two withdrew prior to interview and two after interview. The recruitment process only resulted in one female Probationer agreeing to participate in the research, so it was decided to proceed with a male-only sample. Participants were asked a number of structured questions at the beginning of the interview, which provided some data on the sample characteristics (as shown in Table 5.2). Consistent with much previous research (Farrall, 2002; Maruna, 2001; Rex, 1999), responses suggested that participants experienced a range of personal and social problems, with many ($n=13$) experiencing multiple (three or more) problems. Most ($n=14$) were unemployed, and two of those who were working were doing so within informal labour markets. Participants ranged from 18 to over 50 years of age, with a mean age of 32.8 years. More than half ($n=12$) were white, two identified themselves as dual heritage, three as black, and two as Asian. The most common offences involved violence, drugs and theft. All 20 had a supervision requirement as part of their order. Collectively, interviewees had experience of seven of the 12 requirements available to sentencers at the time of interview (see Ministry of Justice, 2007a: 14).

More than half ($n=12$) had to complete an accredited programme, and 18 of the participants had experience of supervision plus at least one other requirement. The majority of interviewees were originally sentenced to orders of 24 months or longer ($n=14$), only one interviewee was sentenced to less than 12 months, and four had had their orders extended while under probation supervision. Almost half ($n=8$) of the interviewees had been in custody prior to interview, and durations ranged from three weeks to three-and-a-half years. Of the remaining 12 interviewees, nine received Community Orders (CO) and three were given Suspended Sentence Orders (SSO).

Given that the sample was recruited through a third party (in this case, the supervising officer), there is a risk of bias or misrepresentation in the study. It could be argued, for example, that practitioners could 'cherry pick' the most

Table 5.2 Sample profile at time of interview

Age	18–24 6 (30%)	25–29 4 (20%)	30–39 5 (25%)	40–49 3 (15%)	50+ 2 (10%)			
Employment	Unemployed 14 (70%)	Informal 2 (10%)	Formal 4 (20%)					
Accommodation	Private rent 4 (20%)	Social housing 6 (30%)	Owner-occupier 2 (10%)	Living with others 4 (20%)	Residence (part of order) 2 (10%)			
Self-reported problems	Employment 14 (70%)	Housing 3 (15%)	Finance/debt/money 12 (60%)	Drugs/alcohol 4 (20%)	Relationships 6 (30%)	Attitudes/decision-making 9 (45%)	Health 4 (20%)	Three or more problems 13 (65%)
Sentence requirement	Supervision 20 (100%)	Accredited programme 12 (60%)	Unpaid work 4 (20%)	Residence 2 (10%)	Prohibited activity 1 (5%)	Exclusion 4 (20%)	Curfew 3 (15%)	
Time on probation at interview	1–3 Months 6 (30%)	4–8 Months 4 (20%)	9–12 Months 10 (50%)					
Current offences	Violence 9 (45%)	Theft 4 (20%)	Drugs 3 (15%)	Sexual 2 (10%)	Robbery 1 (5%)	Criminal damage 1 (5%)		
Most common previous offences	Assault 12 (60%)	Theft 5 (25%)	GBH 4 (20%)	Criminal damage 4 (20%)	Affray 3 (15%)	Motoring 3 (15%)	Drugs 3 (15%)	

cooperative Probationers in order to try to obtain a positive representation of probation practice. Also, it is possible that the most amenable Probationers might naturally be selected given their proclivity towards compliance. It could be argued that this could bring the validity of the study under scrutiny, as it is possible that those individuals who participated could provide more positive responses to particular questions about probation practice. Finally, it is also possible that those practitioners who volunteered could be more dedicated to the humanistic core principles of probation, and may be more likely to offer desistance-focused practice. If this is the case then this may be reflected in Probationers' responses, thereby offering an overly optimistic account of probation practice. This has obvious implications for the data analysis, as it could be suggested that the possible selection bias in the method of participant recruitment employed here could lead to skewed interview data. It should be acknowledged that the possible issues involved in the recruitment of participants, described above, could influence the data that is obtained and, in this case, that this could entail a more positive portrayal of probation.

However, the means by which individuals were recruited was an unavoidable aspect of the sampling process. Characteristics of the sample profile were compared to national data (where available), and there is broad consistency between the two (see Table 5.3), which suggests that the sample obtained was reasonably representative. It is argued here that the possibility for selection bias in this study is largely unavoidable, given the nature of the recruitment process, but that the checks implemented during recruitment (through the use of the algorithm), and after (through comparison with national data) ensure a broadly representative sample and help to uphold the validity of the study. Furthermore, as the following chapters will illustrate, if the sample did provide an overly optimistic account of probation and desistance then the reality for the majority of individuals would, unfortunately, appear to be somewhat underwhelming.

Table 5.3 Sample characteristics and national data

	Sample	National*
Community Order (as % of all court orders)	80	71
Suspended Sentence Order (as % of all court orders)	20	29
Average length of Community Order (months)	21.6	15.4
Average length of Suspended Sentence Order (months)	22.5	18.5
Age groups (%)		
18–24	30	36.2
25–29	20	18.3
30–39	25	25.5
40–49	15	14.8
50+	10	5

Note
* National data from Ministry of Justice, 2009e.

Understanding accounts of probation and desistance

Interviews were fully transcribed, manually coded, and analysed in relation to the desistance model outlined in the previous chapter – individuals are open to the possibility of change; they survey the social landscape; they consider future trajectories of action; actions are executed. The analysis design was based upon the use of 'thematic networks', which were used to organise, structure, illustrate and represent the themes within the data (Attride-Sterling, 2001: 387–8). As such, transcriptions were coded to identify events, thoughts and biographies of the decision-making process and initial transitions towards desistance.

Some have argued that thematic analysis is essentially an inductive approach, allowing both dominant and minor themes to emerge from the data (Sanders, 2007: 80). However, analysis (like all aspects of research) cannot take place in a theoretical or epistemological vacuum (Braun and Clarke, 2006: 84), and accounts which describe themes as 'emerging' from the data are inherently flawed as they deny the active role played by the researcher in the identification of such themes. Such accounts suggest that themes already exist in the data, and that analysis is simply a process of unearthing them. However, 'if themes

Table 5.4 Analysis coding framework

Desistance framework stage	Coding categories	
	Agency	Structure
1) Structural properties		Employment/education/ training Family/relationships Alcohol/drug misuse Finance/money/debt Accommodation Probation experience
2) Subjectively defined concerns	Future identities Motivation to change	Employment/education/ training Family/relationships Alcohol/drug misuse Finance/money/debt Accommodation
3) Reflexively determined courses of action	Hope/self-efficacy Shame/remorse Internalising stigma Alternative identities Self-mastery Status/victory Achievement/ responsibility Empowerment Generativity	

"reside" anywhere, they reside in our heads from our thinking about our data and creating links as we understand them' (Ely *et al.*, 1997: 205–6).

This echoes Miles and Huberman's (1994) recommended method of coding data. They advise that researchers create a provisional list of codes before fieldwork. This may be generated from the literature, conceptual and theoretical frameworks, research questions, and so forth. Such coding categories were formulated prior to data collection, and were supplemented and amended during and after this phase of the fieldwork. These categories provided a coding framework from which the analysis could take place (Schmidt, 2004: 255). The interview data were coded in accordance with two sets of thematic categories which had been discerned from prior theoretical and empirical knowledge. The first of these related to agentic themes, and the second to structural themes. It was important, in this stage, to not simply identify topics based upon the questions asked, but to explore: whether the participants actually discussed the terms of these questions; what meaning they ascribed to the terms; whether there was any elaboration; which ones they denied or omitted; and, what new topics occurred in the data, which were not anticipated from the prior empirical and theoretical knowledge (Schmidt, 2004: 254). Agentic themes were drawn from the work of McAdams (1992, 2001), Maruna (2001) and LeBel *et al.* (2008). Structural themes were drawn from the existing desistance literature and findings from official government reports (Farrall, 2002; National Audit Office, 2002; SEU, 2002; Raynor, 2007a). The coding framework is represented in Table 5.4, and was refined as themes were sub-categorised primarily using *in vivo* codes, reflecting interviewees' own expressions (Flick, 1998: 180). This was intended to retain the contextuality of the data, and to allow the individuals' 'voices' to be heard through the interview data.

6 First steps

The transition to desistance

Research into pathways to desistance from crime has emerged as a criminological field in its own right in recent years, and several commentators have shed light on the processes associated with this journey. Knowledge around these processes has become more comprehensive and detailed, and there is now significant breadth in our understandings of how and why individuals move away from crime. It is now widely accepted that desistance is a process whereby individuals gradually move away from a previous criminal lifestyle towards one characterised by pro-social attitudes and behaviours, and cemented with a new 'non-offender' identity. This gradual process is usually explained as entailing an initial decision, which may be prompted by a particular event or set of circumstances; an alteration in the way that the individual perceives themselves and their lifestyles; dedicated action to desist, and; the acquisition of a new, alternative, identity.

Various social factors have been identified which may initiate or support the desistance process, with employment and family formation being particularly prominent in the existing literature. There are also a variety of subjective factors which have been shown to facilitate the process, such as motivation, determination, a positive outlook, confidence and a sense of 'hope', and the acquisition of an altered perspective of the self. Within the desistance literature these subjective factors are often taken to be indicative of human agency at work in the process of moving away from crime, yet this provides an incomplete and vague understanding of the role of agency. There remains a lack of an adequate conceptualisation of agency. Vaughan (2007) has suggested that Archer's work on the 'internal conversation'[1] could provide an explanatory framework of agency in the desistance process, yet there has been limited empirical research which explicitly accounts for the role of agency.

Where the desistance process has been examined the tendency has been to delineate between the two categorical phases of primary and secondary desistance, and to focus upon the latter. This distinction draws upon the work of Edwin Lemert (1951, 1967). Lemert (1951) argued that an 'initial flirtation and experimentation with deviant behaviours' could be identified as primary deviance, whereas secondary deviance would involve deviant acts becoming 'incorporated as part of the "me" of the individual' (1951: 11). Within the desistance literature this has been adapted to suggest that a 'flirtation' with desistance, signalled by a lull in offending behaviour, could be defined as primary desistance. Secondary desistance, on the other hand, would follow that the assumption of a non-offending role would become incorporated as part of the 'me' of the individual, thereby indicating that the person had changed (Maruna *et al.*, 2004: 19).

This has meant that there has been relatively little attention paid towards the transitional phase of desistance, which means that our knowledge of the cognitions and understandings of individuals at the moment where they are between crime and conformity is necessarily limited. There is also a lack of focus on any adequate conceptualisation of agency, which entails that our understandings of how and why individuals make particular decisions about how they will act, of how they set goals and objectives, and of how they set out to achieve them, is also restricted. The work of Emirbayer and Mische (1998) offers a framework for understanding how individuals utilise agency within particular social contexts in order to identify certain goals or objectives, and to determine particular courses of action in order to achieve them.

This chapter begins to examine the early transitions towards desistance by exploring the participants' reflective accounts of their decisions to desist. In doing so it draws attention towards the social and personal factors associated with the onset of desistance, and the psychological impact of making a decision to desist. The accounts are examined in order to determine the relevance of human agency to these early decisions to desist, and the nature of agency is examined by considering the temporal orientation demonstrated by individuals within these reflective accounts.

Instigating desistance – human agency and making a decision to desist

It is commonly accepted that desistance is a process which is characterised by periods of ambivalence and vacillation. The initial transition towards desistance is one such period, as individuals are prompted to take a leap of faith as they move from a habitual lifestyle involving offending-related behaviour, to one which is characterised by conformity to pro-social behaviours. Consequently, factors which can provide reassurance at this time are likely to facilitate the first steps towards desistance.

'I've made my mind up and nothing's going to change that'

Previous research has often begun by asking individuals if they want to desist from crime (Burnett, 1992; Farrall, 2002), and while desire to move away from crime is not a precursor to actual desistance it was deemed to be necessary to unearth each individual's motivations in relation to desistance. All participants stated that they wanted to move away from crime, and the majority indicated that they felt confident in their capabilities to desist, which corresponded with previous research (Farrall, 2002; Healy and O'Donnell, 2008):

I know I won't offend again. I've made my mind up and nothing's going to change that. Erm, I've been involved with criminals for quite a long time, but now I just want to live my own life, get on with things. I won't offend again. Definitely.

(Dean)

Dean's quote above is illustrative of the high levels of self-confidence suggested by a number of participants. Generally, individuals believed that they were capable of moving away from crime on their own, and individuals also suggested that desistance would be achieved by simply the avoidance of potentially criminal situations:

I'm just not going to let myself get into those situations again. In the past, I let myself get into the kind of situation where something bad could go down. Now, I'm not going to let myself get into that kind of situation, I just won't let it happen. If it looks like something might happen, or could happen, I'll walk away from it. I won't have anything to do with that no more.

(Brian)

In this respect, individuals showed both the desire to desist, and the perceived ability to achieve desistance. This echoes Burnett and Maruna's (2004) conceptualisation of the term 'hope' as an agentic phenomenon, which they found to be correlated with successful desistance. Individuals contrasted this confidence and motivation with earlier experiences of reoffending:

SK: So what do you think happened that led to you offending again?
ALAN: Apathy. Pure apathy. I could be wrong, but I've never done well at trying to give up crime.

Therefore, the findings from the interviews suggest that individuals believe that they are in control of their own desistance, and that making a decision to actively engage in the desistance process will increase the likelihood of successful desistance. This echoes Burnett's (1992) finding that individuals who demonstrated greater motivation were more likely to desist successfully. The relationship between motivation, confidence and self-efficacy is unclear from the interview data, but it is reasonable to assume that greater levels of self-confidence and self-efficacy will help to maintain motivation, particularly during challenging times, setbacks or relapse. Furthermore, while confidence and motivation might not necessarily be precursors to making the initial transition towards desistance, making a decision to move from a previous lifestyle characterised by offending-related behaviours to one characterised by prosocial behaviours is likely to be easier if confidence and motivation are present.

'Some people are just born to always get into trouble'

The concept of 'othering' has been explored elsewhere in criminological ana-lyses (Hudson and Bramhall, 2005: 737) and has emerged in some recent accounts of desistance (Murray, 2008, 2009).The concept of othering within the wider process of desistance can be understood as a means by which individuals are able to distance themselves from current offenders, and typical responses in the interviews included: 'I'm not like them.' Furthermore, individuals also othered their past selves with responses such as: 'I'm not like that anymore', and: 'That's not me anymore.' In this respect, othering influenced the decision to desist as individuals reinterpreted their past selves as being different to the people who they wanted to become:

> I've decided I'm not going to [offend again]. I've made my mind up, I don't want to be like how I used to be, do you know what I mean? I just don't want to be like that no more. I want the normal life now, you know? What I used to be like, I want to be totally different to that now. I don't like who I was, I'm not proud of what I done, so I want to be different from now on.
>
> (Charlie)

The concept of othering within desistance is not new. Indeed, the assumption of a 'non-offender' role as qualitatively different from an offender identity is at the heart of the notion of secondary desistance (Maruna and Farrall, 2004). However, within my research, the process of othering needs to be considered within the context of individuals' descriptions of making the transition towards desistance. In turn, this needs to be seen within the context of the individual's attempts to disassociate themselves from offenders, particularly peer groups who continued to undertake offending or antisocial behaviour. Past offending was frequently associated with a particular group of friends or acquaintances, and individuals often referred to specific peers with whom they had associated in the past, in relation to offending:

> SK: Why do you think you weren't able to stop [offending] at that time?
> RYAN: Just the crowd I was with. I know the people I'm with now wouldn't get me into any trouble. But back then, it was just everyone I was with was up for it, and you couldn't not go along. When I did this offence, I was with the same crowd.

Similarly, much of Dean's offending history was related to relationships forged through the use and supply of drugs. He associated his offending in large part to these associations and was keen to distance himself from this peer group, which he referred to as 'them criminals':

> They're ruthless, heartless people....They tried to get to me and get me involved, with, 'When we get out, we're going to do this and we're going to

do that Deano. Are you interested?' And I says, 'Look, I've had my day. You do what you wanna do, but I've had my day and I want nothing part of criminal activities in the future'....Rob places, sell cocaine, sell crack, sell heroin....Or break into places, whatever they've done in the past that's what they're talking about. Laughing about it, bragging about it. I don't want that. I ain't going to be no part of their silly little laughs.

(Dean)

Interviewees were, thus, keen to distance themselves from the actions of offenders, and offending or offending-related behaviour was frequently described as 'daft' or 'stupid'. Furthermore, interviewees often spoke about offenders in somewhat derogatory terms, as the following passage illustrates:

And [I want to stop because], it's just fucking daft, ain't it? There's one guy, he's a bit younger than me but I've known him for years. A couple of weeks ago he'd been up town shoplifting, he does that a lot. Anyway, he's telling me how he'd took it round [acquaintance] to flog it, and [he'd] offered him like 30 quid the lot. This guy says, 'fuck off pal, this is worth at least 50', and then he's telling me how he started punching him and kicking fuck out of him, like it's something to be dead proud of. I'm just thinking, 'you're a twat, why would you be saying that like it's something special?' And that's happening all the time, and I don't want no part of that.

(Kurt)

In constructing such narratives individuals establish a clear distinction between what it means to be an 'offender' in contrast to a 'non-offender'. In doing so, individuals affirm that they want to desist, and that they are willing to commit to that goal. Sometimes individuals othered particular types of criminal, distancing themselves from who they perceived to be more serious offenders. Individuals who made these assertions were not trying to disassociate themselves from peer groups, rather they suggested that they wanted to disassociate themselves from people whose offending had escalated towards serious crimes. Furthermore, the othering of more serious criminals involved identifying such individuals as lacking the personal agency necessary to desist from crime, insofar as they were 'born' to be in trouble:

The people in there [prison], there's people in there who are serious criminals, people who are robbing or shooting or killing, and I'm in there just for fighting, just for doing what I like doing. I was listening to people in there, and people were like: 'I'm looking at seven years for having a loaded gun in the house.' Another guy was looking at 12 years. There was one guy on a murder charge. I'm looking around thinking: 'I ain't like that.' I don't want to go around shooting people, why would I want to shoot someone for? Why would I want a loaded gun in the house? And people who are talking about robbing a post office, and that ain't me. There was part of me that was thinking: 'I shouldn't even be here, this place is for people who do big crimes.' Mine was just a stupid little fight. It ain't for me. Some people are just born to go in and out of prison, just born to always get into trouble.

(John)

For these individuals, othering did not represent an *in toto* identity change as delineated in the concept of secondary desistance, which would suggest that the individual would distance themselves from their own past identity. Rather, these individuals appeared to divorce their present identities from what their future identity could potentially become if they did not desist – that is, that they did not want to become a more serious offender.

For those individuals who othered criminals, including their past selves and past peer groups, the personal transformations that they envisaged often involved reference to non-criminal social contacts, which were either prior, or subsequent to, offending. These included friends (known prior to offending), religious contacts and partners. Moreover, this involved individuals becoming allied to the values and behaviours of these social contacts, and this, in turn, led to a series of perceived rewards to be gained from sustaining desistance.

'If I hadn't have done it then I wouldn't be here now'

The data showed correspondence with the themes of 'regret', 'shame' and 'remorse' from the existing desistance literature, and also in relation to the delineation of 'offenders' as 'others'. Interviewees expressed high levels of regret, most often reflecting a perception that past offending had not been worth the trouble they experienced as a consequence. Typically, individuals described experiences of 'loss' as a result of their offending, such as losing contact with, or missing the birth of, a child:

I love my kids to bits and I've missed out on no end of stuff. I've missed birthdays and Christmas, I couldn't even send them a Christmas card. I've got stuff, clothes and toys, for my son and I can't even give it to him. I don't want no-one else to give it to him, cos I want to be there to see him when he opens it, but I can't so it's just sitting there. They're just down the road, but I can't see them, I'm not allowed near them and it's heartbreaking really, to think of them growing up and I'm not there to see it, it's horrible....And it's all cos of this that I've lost out on seeing my kids, if I hadn't have done it then I wouldn't be here now, I wouldn't've missed all this.

(Ken)

Interviewees also explained that their involvement with offending had entailed their foregoing of alternative opportunities, which suggests that individuals are aware that criminal behaviour may incrementally 'mortgage' future life chances through the negative effects of offending (Sampson and Laub, 1995: 147).

Dean's offending history had revolved around his involvement in the drugs scene, and he was a drug addict himself for many years:

> I never thought I'd see the day when I packed the dope. But it's just another burden i'nt it? That £30 or £40 or £50 you'd spend on dope every week, if you didn't spend that you could've had a totally different life. You're spending that every week, and it's gone for good. It's a mortgage ain't it? I've lost all them chances I have.
>
> (Dean)

Interviewees also stated that they felt ashamed of their past actions. For younger participants this was often related to a belief that they had 'let down' a parent. Interestingly, many individuals were also keen not to apportion any blame to others for their actions: 'I'm ashamed at myself....There's no excuse for what I done' (Kev). Feeling ashamed was less apparent than feelings of regret, but such sentiments were evident among participants of all age groups, offence types, and lengths of criminal career. Where interviewees expressed feeling ashamed at their past actions, this appeared to follow a period of personal reflection: 'Obviously looking back now it was not the best thing to have done' (Chris).

Decisions to desist were also influenced by expressions of remorse for the victims and others who had been affected by past offending. Often this entailed feeling sorry for individuals who had been physically, emotionally or financially hurt by the individual's actions:

> I felt very remorseful for the people that I caused injuries to. Obviously I can't talk to the people, but if I could see them I'd say sorry to them.
>
> (Josh)

> I've hurt a lot of people in the past, robbing off 'em, beating 'em up, whatever, and, when you understand that, it's a good feeling knowing that people aren't being hurt by you no more.
>
> (Kurt)

The importance of remorse in influencing an individual's decision to desist is that an individual reflects upon their past actions, and reinterprets these actions as an affront to their morality. As discussed in Chapter 4, Paternoster (1989) found that changes in morality had an effect upon desistance for certain types of offence, and Shover (1996) also argued that desistance followed the 'acquisition of an altered perspective on their youthful self and activities' (1996: 131). In Liebrich's (1993, 1996) study, remorse was found to be 'the primary reason' behind making a decision to desist. By contrast, Giordano *et al.* (2002) suggest that remorse is associated with a repudiation of past actions, and that this forms the final stage in making a decision to desist, with its importance realised only after an offender is presented with an opportunity to change and has a subjective attachment to that opportunity. The findings from my interview data suggest that the decision to desist from crime is influenced by a reorientation of moral agency, 'triggered by an individual offending against their personal morality – coming to think that their offending was wrong' (Weaver, 2009: 18), and prior to any perceived opportunity to change.

Finally, it should be noted that guilt, shame and remorse should not necessarily be considered in isolation from one another. Rather, these agentic feelings are likely to interact to produce a particular form of personal agency that both acts as a deterrent from future offending and a motivation to make the transition towards desistance. As Chris stated:

> I don't want to go prison, I don't want to do anything like this again. For a few weeks I just didn't want to admit to myself that I'd done it. I don't want to be in that situation again, I don't want to hurt my partner, I hate what I did, I don't know why it happened, I'm not a violent person and I don't want to be in that situation again.

'If you're going to be a dad then you can't afford to be mucking about'

Some individuals envisaged new, general, non-offender identities that they wanted to assume – 'I don't want to be known as a troublemaker no more' (Leroy) – while others were more specific about 'who' they wanted to become – 'I just want to be a family man' (Robert). Indeed, typically, future identities involved becoming a 'good father' or 'good partner', by making statements such as, 'I want to look after my kids', or 'I want what's best for my girlfriend', and individuals regarded these identities as incongruent with offending behaviour. This finding echoes that of Giordano *et al.* (2002): that desisters adopt a new, pro-social identity that is 'fundamentally incompatible with continued deviation' (2002: 1001). They argue that such identity change is prompted by the process of reassessment of one's life and the presence of opportunities to change within the social environment.

The conceptual definition of secondary desistance is that desistance occurs over time as individuals develop a new identity as non-offenders. However, it is argued here that desisters are agentic in the early stages of the process in envisioning a new identity that they aspire to adopt. This was particularly the case for Brian, Chris and Josh, who were expectant fathers, who all explained that the primary reason for their decision to desist had been the desire to be a good father and a good provider for their children. They had determined that offending was incompatible with the identities that they wanted to commit to:

> Obviously I don't want to be in prison with a kid. Also with a kid on the way you have to be a lot more mature, you have to think I've got a kid on the way, I have to think about my partner, making sure she's going to be okay. I have to make decisions that will be good for them as well. You have to look after your finances a lot more. If you're going to be a dad then you

can't afford to be mucking about making stupid decisions, you've got to act more responsibly. Cos what you do will affect your kid, so that's what I want to do, to be a good dad and look after my family.

(Chris)

'She's helped me to think about my life in a different way'

The interview data suggested that primary desisters are empowered in both making a decision to desist and in the early transition towards desistance. Empowerment here follows McAdams (2001) conceptualisation of empowerment as an agency theme. For McAdams (2001) empowerment occurs where an individual (including their agency) is enhanced by someone or something larger than the self. In this respect, this does not necessarily suggest that individuals gained more power than they had before, but rather that perceptions or orientations had been enhanced by someone or something else to the extent that desistance appeared to be a more feasible objective.

Most instances of empowerment occurred when a supervising officer helped the individual to gain a new insight into their life, and typical responses included: '[My Probation Officer/PO] has helped me to think about my life in a different way.' Moreover, supervising officers were often identified as enabling an individual to reflect on their lives to a greater degree, and to adopt a more future-oriented perspective:

They [PO] have made me see things differently, and I will do, that won't change. A lot of people do it for five minutes and then go back to their old ways. Just cos I won't be in probation after August doesn't mean that I won't look at life the same as when [PO] sat me down and spoke to me and thought things through. I'm going to be thinking, am I doing the right thing here? And I'll think to myself, nah. If I don't feel right, I'll turn around and go home. It happened before my birthday. We were up town as couples and a bunch of them wanted to party, and I said to the missus: 'I don't want to, I'd rather go for a meal.'

(Josh)

Indeed, most interviewees cited their supervising officer in relation to empowerment, but for two individuals in particular (Dean and Raj) empowerment resulted from religion:

Becoming a Christian as well, that's changed me as well, see? I know what it's like to be on the receiving end of this hurt. Whether it's something to do with stealing off somebody, if I stole off somebody, what would it be like if someone stole off me? You then put yourself in these positions. And it's like the drugs, you've gotta kinda think: 'What about the mam and dad of a son who's thirty years of age, and you're selling the dope to him, or speed?' If I was a father, would I want my son to go through what I was putting him through? He might've been stealing to pay for his habit, so I've learnt a lot, you know? And to be on the receiving end, I've thought, put myself in that position and it's made me think a lot about what I've done wrong in the past. And that's why I intend never to go back there.

(Dean)

It's helped me so much. I've totally cut down on intoxications, I've totally cut down on going out. I was a violent person before, I used to do boxing, kickboxing, weightlifting, I used to work on doors, and it was just in my nature to be aggressive. But, in the last six months it's totally changed. Because I've become religious.

(Raj)

'Once you get to understand that it was quite easy for me to stop'

Most often, enhanced self-control entailed overcoming or managing a drink or drug habit, while some described taking control of anger issues that had previously contributed to offending. Individuals related drink and/or drugs to prior offending, and thus identified overcoming these issues as a key factor in primary desistance. Some suggested that they had been able to completely refrain from drinking or drug taking:

SK: Do you still do drugs now?
LEROY: No I don't. I've been off them for about 17 months, from being in there [prison]....I'm not bothered about doing 'em anymore, I'm over all that. Obviously when I was doing them I was getting into trouble, and like I say I was high when I done this offence, so coming off 'em has to be a good thing really. And like I say, I'm done with 'em and I'm not really interested in going back to 'em.

Other individuals explained that they had significantly reduced their alcohol or drug intake, and they suggested that the level that they had reduced their usage to was negligible in impacting upon the potential for reoffending (an assessment that was supported by the supervising officer). Individuals who had taken greater control described how they had first come to realise that their drinking or drug taking was problematic:

That's the type of thing that you do, when you're under the influence, whether it's driving or fighting or thieving or whatever it might be. It's about a careless attitude, and once you get to understand that it was quite easy for me to stop drinking, virtually.

(Tom)

In some cases the data suggested that, while individuals stated that they had been able to take control of a drink or drug habit, they also lacked confidence in their ability to sustain this. Words like 'hopefully' were common in participants' explanations of increased self-control, which suggests that individuals did not feel entirely in control at the time of interview. Most likely, for these individuals, they would need to experience further successes during the desistance process to be more confident in their actions and to commit further to desistance:

> That's been a problem throughout my life, yeah. Like I say, I genuinely can't think of a case where I've been in trouble with the police without it being me drinking. So that's the root of it all I think. Hence, stopping and not drinking no more, so hopefully I won't get in trouble again. Never say never, but I'm hopeful.
>
> (Nath)

For many individuals the decision to desist followed the realisation that there existed a problem, and the initial transition towards desistance was accompanied by enhanced self-control. It is likely that enhanced self-control will increase the likelihood of greater success in the early transition towards desistance, and this success, in turn, will secure greater commitment to the longer-term desistance process. The references to self-control from the individuals in the present study resonate with McAdams (2001) conceptualisation of 'self-mastery' as a component of agency, which can be expressed by the individual through increases in self-awareness and understanding, and an enhanced sense of control.

'I've got all what I need, you know, for the outside world'

This theme is distinct from self-control, where the achievements were more personal accomplishments such as overcoming a drug habit. For some individuals, achievements involved enhancing their education or skills, and this was often undertaken during time in prison:

> I trained up for agricultural mechanics; light vehicle body repairs; gardening; computer maintenance and building; and art, I've got certificates in art. I've got all what I need, you know, for the outside world, you know?
>
> (Dean)

Others identified the completion of particular requirements of their sentence as a personal achievement, and this most often involved the successful completion of an accredited programme:

> At the moment actually I've just finished a course on IDAP, which is an Integrated Domestic Abuse Programme. I finished that four months ago. I completed that successfully, which is good, and that's helped me, so I'm pleased with that.
>
> (Robert)

What might be considered 'lesser' accomplishments were also identified by interviewees as achievements, including completing the sentence without breach at the time of interview, and maintaining all appointments that were required of the individual. As I have already mentioned, these may be considered to be 'lesser' achievements, but in a context where desistance is conceptualised to be an ongoing process characterised by incremental success and accomplishment, such smaller events are likely to be influential. Moreover, it is important to consider the importance of 'lesser' achievements for individuals who are, perhaps, unaccustomed to performing relatively routine activities:

> Well there's actually quite a lot to do for probation, it does take up a lot of your time. It's hard, cos even though you might only be here for 30 minutes or whatever, less sometimes, it might take you an hour, hour and half to get here, same to get back, that's your morning done. I've been going to the Job Centre, I'm just trying to keep my appointments....So far I haven't missed one, touch wood. But I do find it hard cos I've never had to do it before, do you get me?
>
> (Kurt)

Nath described how he had started his own business, running a garage, while he had been under probation supervision. This is not only an example of personal achievement, but also shows increased levels of self-efficacy, self-control and responsibility in a man who identified himself as an alcoholic, and who had lost two previous jobs through drinking:

> NATH: The chance of getting the garage came up and at the time it came up I was really positive. There was a time when a similar garage came up and I couldn't be bothered.
>
> SK: Prior to the garage becoming available were you in employment?
>
> NATH: No, I wasn't in employment, but I was doing bits and bobs, but nothing you could actually call 'in employment'. I was in employment about a year previous, which ended through drink. But then I sort of fell a bit, I went through a rough patch with my partner, we split up once, separated, and just became a bit of a sort of recluse I suppose, a bit down, and I didn't bother doing anything, just wasting my life.

Indeed, in a similar respect to 'self-control', as described above, personal achievements were identified as being influential in the early transitions towards desistance. The importance of achievements would be realised after a decision to desist had been made, as it is unlikely that personal achievements would prompt a decision to desist. It is not necessarily the case that personal achievements correspond with goals or objectives set by the individual concerned, but it is likely that achievements will be more influential if there is correspondence with specific goals.

Instigating desistance – social cues and making a decision to desist

The argument presented so far in this chapter has suggested that a range of agentic factors indicate when an individual 'feels ready' to make an initial commitment to desistance. This may resonate with the 'strong subjective model' outlined by LeBel *et al.* (2008), wherein the individual only has to decide to commit to desistance in order for the transition to take place. Within such a model of desistance, life events would either be irrelevant, in as much as desistance would take place whether they happened or not, or they would occur only as a consequence of the subjective mindset of the individual. However, various social factors were identified in the interviews which suggested that agentic factors did not operate independently of social factors during the initial transition towards desistance.

This is not to suggest that such social factors would have an influence independent of the individual's mindset, as indicated in the 'strong social model' (LeBel *et al.*, 2008), or by Farrall and Bowling's (1999) 'super dupes'. Rather, this to argue that particular social cues may prompt an alternative agentic orientation, enabling the individual to consider that the possibility of desistance is both desirable and viable. Alternatively, the development of such an agentic orientation may lead the individual to determine that particular life events (such as employment or family formation) are accessible.

'It's nice to have family around'

The negative impact of past offending on relationships was a prominent theme in the interview data. Past offending had often led to the breakdown of relationships with family members:

> Cos of the way I've been, I ain't known my mum since I was about 15....My mum threw me out when she found crack in my bedroom. A lot of crack in my bedroom. I got thrown out. We spoke on the street, but I didn't call or nothing, and cos of that my other sister didn't talk to me, and cos of the other one's old man I never spoke to them.
>
> (Martin)

In a number of cases, family members had offered the individual a 'second chance' to restore these relationships. Furthermore, this second chance had entailed family members offering the individual support in the form of practical assistance and encouragement, with the proviso that the individual would complete their probation requirements and attempt to desist. Thus, structural changes to the individual's relationships had led to the decision to desist:

> I come out of jail and they're all helping me....It's nice to have family around, but not just because they're helping me, it shows they care. I've always

worked for myself, and lived with my girlfriend and that. I've done what I wanted to do myself, I've never listened to no-one. I wish I had done now.

(Martin)

I'm chuffed right now. My mum and dad are my best mates. They've done so much for me they have. So much....My nana's done a lot for me. And my mam's been a main one as well. If I've been in debt, or if I've been in trouble, she's been there to help me out. She's lovely ... it's helped. Since I've done this crime, I'm back with my dad, back with all the others, and it's great. I'm not doing anymore [offending].

(Charlie)

For some, however, experiences of probation had prompted certain aspects of agency, notably regret, shame or remorse, and these had led the individual to make changes to their relationships. This was the case for Dean who, following a period of reflection, had decided to desist and had determined that this could be facilitated by severing ties with former associates in the drugs scene and re-establishing older peer groups that he had associated with prior to his involvement in offending. Demonstrations of support from these older networks had also engendered feelings of confidence and motivation:

I can beat it. With the help of my friends what want to help me. You know, my friends what I met out of the drug scene, years ago. I've never had so many people show support for me. It's amazing really.

(Dean)

There were a minority of cases where unexpected positive outcomes had resulted from behavioural changes, as Nath described it: '[I]t turns out me changing some of my ways has made her [his wife] happier and made our relationship better.' For most, however, a decision to desist was undertaken with the expectation of particular rewards, including the restoration or development of relationships with significant others. This appeared to be particularly the case for those individuals who had young children. For example, Martin's son had been born while he was in prison, and at the time of interview he had still not met him as a result of the prohibitive requirements of his sentence. He explained that he wanted to prove to others that he had changed, and that the reward would be being allowed to develop a relationship with his son:

I'm not allowed [to see his son] until I can prove I've sorted myself out....That's my aim, to show everyone else I'm sorted out, and then they'll think yeah he's changed let's give me a chance. Unless you try it ... you're not going to sort it out for him. Everything I'm doing at the minute is geared towards that. That's why I'm trying to get probation behind me saying, 'Yeah he's done well, he's changed', and that, they'll look differently at me, not just think, 'Oh, he's violent, he's done this'....They'll think, 'He's changed it'. They're all good people to have behind you if you're going to try and get your son for custody, they're genuine people like.

(Martin)

Underpinning this was a perception that sustaining desistance would earn the trust of others, and this was particularly the case for a number of interviewees who suggested that, by desisting, their supervising officer would trust them and that this would be reciprocated by the issuing of rewards, such as: the removal of certain sentence requirements; or help with particular issues, including employment, housing and debt. Interviewees stated that the prospect of such rewards made attempts to desist more worthwhile, as one person said: 'I feel, if they're going to go out of their way for me, I'll go out of my way for them' (Raj).

'I don't want to spend my life in and out of jail'

Previous research has highlighted the impact that the perceived or real consequences of offending can have on making the decision to desist from crime (Cusson and Pinsonneault, 1986: 74; Maruna, 1997: 78; Hughes, 1998: 147). It has also been suggested that individuals can make the decision to desist if the possibility of longer or more punitive sentences becomes more likely, which has been referred to as criminal justice system 'burn out' (Shover, 1983; Burnett, 1992). Some of the men in my sample had been given either a Community Order or a Suspended Sentence Order, but the possibility of a custodial sentence had prompted some degree of reflexivity. For these individuals, the potential costs involved with going to prison were clear, and they appeared to significantly contribute to the decision to desist:

> Obviously I've got a criminal record for the rest of my life, probation for two years, and if I do anything wrong in the next two years I go straight to prison for ten months....I thought when he said ten months imprisonment I thought the rest of my life's over now, and when he said suspended over two years I was relieved. If I'd gone to prison I'd have lost my job and everything. Luckily I didn't go prison. I feel quite good about that, that I didn't go jail.
>
> (Chris)

It could be argued that receiving a community, instead of a custodial, sentence, could inhibit the transition towards desistance. Indeed, from a classicist perspective the argument would follow that the individual would be more likely to reoffend as the deterrent effect of a custodial sentence has been nullified. However, it is argued here that it is the possibility of a custodial sentence that prompts a re-evaluation on the part of the individual. Yet, this is not a reification to rational choice, but rather an illustration of the reflexive deliberations that individuals engage in during the transition towards desistance. Among those in the sample who had served a custodial sentence, the experience of prison was a reminder of the costs associated with offending. Prison had prompted a reassessment of the costs of crime, and the choice between prison and desistance had become an easier decision to make:

> It's not much of a choice. Being in a cell 23 hours a day, trapped behind a steel door with some stupid bloke in there, shitting and pissing at the end of the bed, it's horrible.
>
> (Josh)

Leroy's case highlights how an individual can make a decision to desist while they remain in custody, and develop a growing awareness of the probable consequences of continued offending:

> SK: Was there any point when you thought, I don't want to do this anymore?
> LEROY: Only when I ended up inside. I just started thinking, it's not worth coming in and out of here all your life. It's just a one-way street if you carry on like that.
> SK: Are you confident that you won't offend again?
> LEROY: Yeah....Well, like I say, I don't want to spend my life in and out of jail. I know that if I carry on then that's what my life'll be like. Just in and out.

However, it was often not the case that the actual lived experience of prison was particularly deleterious, as a number of those who had served custodial sentences described how 'prison's easy'. Indeed, Ryan suggested that he would not be deterred by prison, provided he felt the offence was justified:

> If I do it for no reason I'll be gutted, cos I'll be thinking, what have I done that for, why did I do that? But, if I done it for a reason, like if someone started it, or someone said something to me or whatever, then I'd think fuck it, send me prison, I don't care. Cos I'd've done it for a reason.
>
> (Ryan)

Rather, it was the realisation that further offending would cause the individual to become ensnared in the 'revolving door of prison and probation' that prompted a reassessment of the costs of crime. Furthermore, the threat of longer sentences also initiated such a reassessment:

> Last time I was in there [court] he said to me, I'm getting sick of seeing you in here, next time I see you in here you're going down for a long time. That did shit me up a bit, I must admit. I don't want to waste my life inside.
>
> (Kurt)

'*It's a good feeling knowing that people aren't being hurt by you no more*'

Often individuals described how offending had become more commonplace, or more serious, and this had influenced their decision to desist from crime:

'Up town, you've only got to look at someone the wrong way and you get a glass in the side of the face. My mate got stabbed, up town, for nothing' (Josh), or: 'You don't know what someone's going to be carrying now' (John). Whether or not the seriousness or dangerousness of offending in the local area had actually increased is unknown, but it is not the factual accuracy of these statements that is important. Rather, it is the perceived structural change in the seriousness of offending that encouraged individuals to desist.

In some cases, changes to the nature of risk followed the initial decision to desist. Often this involved risks, to the wellbeing of the individual concerned, that were associated with offending. Following his decision to desist, Dean remarked that he was 'glad to be ... free of not having to look over my shoulder every day', as had been the case previously when he had been involved in violent offending. For others, changes to the nature of risk entailed a reduction in the risks posed to others as a result of the individual offending. An awareness of the impact of offending upon victims, and knowing that cessation of offending meant that they were no longer victimising others, appeared to offer the individual encouragement and motivation:

> SK: What else do you talk about with [PO]?
> KURT: Just about victims and that kind of stuff really. It's good to be aware of the people you've hurt, and it's nice to know I'm not doing that no more. I've hurt a lot of people in the past, robbing off 'em, beating 'em up, whatever, and, when you understand that, it's a good feeling knowing that people aren't being hurt by you no more.

Thus, structural changes in the form of reduced risk following a decision to desist appeared to support that decision, encouraging the individual to sustain the transition towards desistance.

'Getting back on my feet'

For two of the individuals in the sample, accommodation was a prominent example of structural change influencing the early transition to desistance. Dean and Ken had both found new accommodation since being under probation supervision. Both reflected that finding accommodation was an important part of their initial moves towards desistance, and that probation had helped them to facilitate this:

> SK: How has getting a flat helped?
> KEN: It's been great, getting a place of my own, helping me start getting back on my feet. That's what I want to do, I don't want to get in trouble again, but I know I need to get back on my feet if I'm going to have a chance of doing that. [PO] helped me get that sorted, and she says she'll carry on helping me with it, and, erm, I can't complain. She's been 100 per cent and it's made me positive about things, so I'm going to keep going and see what else I can get out of it [probation supervision]. And all this has been after a few months really, imagine what I could achieve in two years.

Dean had been living in a probation hostel for the first two months after his release from prison, and he described how probation had helped him to move into a council flat and that this was helping him in the early stages of desistance. He explained how getting a flat of his own would help by allowing him to cut ties with delinquent peers and also by giving him a sense of self-worth. He described how he felt that the help he received from his supervising officer and the local authority in obtaining his flat in terms of someone taking an interest in his wellbeing:

> When I applied for me flat, I told the council how sorry I was for what I'd done, and the actual woman who I spoke with on the phone said 'Look, Mr. Robinson. You've done your time, you've paid for your crime. So don't keep putting yourself down for it, feeling sorry or whatever. You've done your time, you've paid for it. You've lost everything you'd got. Why should you keep on losing? Or paying for it?' And that's a nice feeling, I thought when I come out [of prison] everyone'd be against me, so.
>
> (Dean)

Later he described how having a sense of self-worth and a positive attitude was helping him to abstain from drink and drugs, and that he believed that enhancing these feelings would help him to make further progress. Ken was homeless when he began probation, and similarly explained how probation had helped him to find a council flat and that this too was helping him to desist. Ken described obtaining accommodation as helping to get his 'life back on track', and Dean stated that it had given him 'a boost'. They both stated that finding accommodation had improved their confidence and given them a positive sense of wellbeing. Thus, while both of these participants demonstrated personal agency in their decisions to desist, structural changes appeared to be instrumental in helping them to act upon these decisions, and also appeared to further enhance their personal agency.

7   Strategies for desistance

Although there may be some individuals for whom desistance occurs by 'default', or as a result of a series of 'side bets' (Laub and Sampson, 2001), in most cases individuals who have successfully desisted from crime had a plan for how they would be able to refrain from offending behaviour in the future (Maruna, 2001). Although the relationship between intentions to desist and reoffending outcomes lacks robust empirical support within the existing literature, there are some authors who have argued that 'desistance intentions predict reoffending' (Porporino, 2010: 72). Giordano *et al.* (2003) identify the future envisioning of an alternative 'new' self as central to the change process. Others have also argued that intentions and actual behaviour are closely correlated (Ajzen, 1991; Serin and Lloyd, 2009; Forste *et al.*, 2010).

During the transitional phase of desistance individuals may begin to construct strategies for future action. In part, this may be in response to individuals' perceived need to change, and in part due to the process of reflecting on the personal and social circumstances which they find themselves in. As such, the transitional phase of desistance may be considered to be part of the overall change process, and the sequence of phases in this process may be similar to that outlined by DiClemente and Prochaska (1982; Prochaska and DiClemente, 1992). In particular, the *preparation* phase, which occurs between *contemplation* and *action*, may be the most similar to the transitional phase as it is conceptualised here. During the preparation phase individuals are making the transition from intended to actual behaviour. Small changes may have begun to take place, but full behavioural change has not yet occurred and individuals are not fully committed to change (although they may commit in the near future) (Prochaska *et al.*, 1992). The desistance literature has paid close attention to several of the phases outlined by Prochaska and DiClemente, in particular the contemplation, action and maintenance phases. However, relatively little attention has been paid to the preparations that individuals make as they embark on the process of desisting from crime. It has been recognised in the literature that successful desisters often make plans, but there has been little research conducted which explicitly examines these plans, and how and why individuals construct them. This chapter offers an examination of the strategies that individuals devise in order to achieve desistance.

The chapter offers an account of the objectives that the men in the study held, and it explores the means which had been identified in order to achieve them. There was general correspondence between the areas of improvement that individuals related to their strategies and the key areas highlighted in the literature (SEU, 2002; NOMS, 2005; Raynor, 2007a), perhaps unsurprisingly given the extent of personal and social problems experienced by the interviewees. In particular, the men spoke about relationships, accommodation difficulties, alcohol and drug taking, finance and debt problems, and, mental and physical wellbeing. The identification of overcoming such issues as necessary for sustaining desistance has been highlighted within the literature (Farrall, 2002; Farrall and Calverley, 2006; Byrne and Trew, 2008). For several of the men familial relationships were identified as being central to their desistance efforts, while for others the place of residence was more important. A common theme for all of the men, however, was the need to obtain or retain employment. Indeed, within all of the interviews, employment was held either as an objective in its own right, or as necessary to achieving other objectives.

Constructing strategies – the importance of employment

More than half of the sample (n = 14) reported that they were unemployed at the time of interview. This is a slightly lower unemployment figure than that reported by the Ministry of Justice and Department for Work and Pensions (MoJ/DWP, 2011). These figures suggest that 75 per cent of offenders make a claim for out-of-work benefits during a two-year period following release. It is likely that the unemployment rate among the individuals in the present study was slightly lower as several of the men had not received custodial sentences and, therefore, would have had a better chance of retaining existing employment. Individuals who are sent into custody are more likely to lose their jobs while in prison. That aside, it is perhaps unsurprising that many of the men suggested that gaining employment would help them to desist from crime.

'You get a job and everything else follows that'

It is difficult to underestimate the value that the men in the study placed on gaining employment, and it was typical to hear statements such as, 'I'll be sorted if I can get a job', or, 'work is the number one priority'. Most of the men did not specify a particular type of work that they would seek, and some suggested that the type of work was insignificant. It is possible that individuals did not specify a particular type of work because they felt that the type of work that they would undertake would be implied. Particular forms of work have been associated with traditional working class male identities (Nixon, 2006; Fletcher, 2007), and it may be the case that these identities implicitly inform individuals' employment objectives. However, it could also be argued that in the face of multiple adversities, and in the context of economic recession, the men in this study were simply more concerned with obtaining employment of any kind:

SK: What kind of job would you look for?

CHARLIE: I'm not bothered. Not bothered. I just want to do the norm from now. That's what I want.

During the interview Charlie did not elaborate on what he meant by 'the norm', but in the context of discussing types of employment it implies that he regarded any type of legitimate employment as being appropriate. Bottoms *et al.* (2004) suggested that individuals' future concerns may be fairly conventional, and this has been supported by findings from subsequent studies (Shapland and Bottoms, 2011). Indeed, in the Sheffield Desistance Study it was found that going straight, being drug/alcohol free, and living a normal/regular life, were the most common future goals (2011: 262). Therefore, it is likely that 'the norm' may refer to a preconception of a law-abiding lifestyle simply entailing any kind of regular, secure employment. Others made similar suggestions about the relationship between employment and 'normal' behaviour:

If you ain't got a job you'll get into trouble, if you've got a job you won't get into trouble, I see it like that.

(John)

Some of the men in the study identified more specific benefits to be gained, in relation to desistance, from having employment. Employment was often related to income, and income was in turn regarded as being synonymous with the availability of a greater range of life opportunities:

When you've got a job and you've got money, you can do what you want, sort of thing.

(Leroy)

Others related employment with 'keeping busy', offering a routine which would preclude many opportunities to offend. Indeed, later in his interview, Charlie suggested that employment would help him to desist due to the structuring effect employment could have on his routine activities:

SK: Do you think that a job and a house would change your life?

CHARLIE: Yeah, cos I'd be doing something all day and I'd just come home, have my dinner, chill out and go bed. I wouldn't get into no trouble then. I wouldn't get into no trouble. Like when I was working in them two years I didn't get into no trouble at all. When I work I work, I graft my arse off.

It is argued here that individuals approach a particular situational context, that of becoming a desister, with a pre-existing definition of employment as being both pro-social and normative – that is, that the condition of employment is fundamentally incongruent with offending behaviour, and that sustained desistance is dependent upon sustainable employment. Of course, this is a fallible definition, not least because this would preclude all manner of white collar crimes, but also because a substantial number of crimes are committed by individuals who hold legitimate forms of employment, and because many unemployed individuals lead law-abiding lifestyles. However, such a definition would explain why employment is of such significance here, and why the individuals in this study regarded gaining employment as a necessary event for the accomplishment of other objectives.

This is further supported by responses which included references to friends and family members, their employment status, and their tendencies towards offending-related behaviour:

> As it happens, within two days of me getting done, he was done – a mate of mine. And, you know … he lost his job … and now he's still around, moping around town without a job, and doing nothing except drinking and getting up to no good.
>
> (Tom)

Indeed, employment was held to be of such significance that individuals remarked that all other concerns could be achieved if employment was gained. Aside from the specific concerns that individuals held (to be discussed below), interviewees stated that employment would enable them to accomplish goals more generally, and that the absence of employment would preclude all other efforts to desist:

> If I can't get a job then I'm, basically, I'm fucked. Cos what else can I do for money. Forget about buying drugs, how am I going to buy a fucking cup of tea? I need a job, cos that's what you do ain't it? You get a job and everything else follows that.
>
> (Kurt)

'It's down to me to make my family normal again'

Individuals suggested that developing new relationships, maintaining relationships, and restoring relationships, would help them to sustain desistance. Several authors have suggested that marriage or family formation can facilitate desistance. First, this may be because marriage creates and strengthens social bonds as individuals invest more of themselves in the relationship (Laub and Sampson, 2003). Second, the relationship between marriage and desistance may be explained in terms of the individual's routine activities and the manner by which marriage constrains criminal opportunities while simultaneously providing prosocial opportunities (Osgood and Lee, 1993; Warr, 1998; Farrall, 2002). A third explanation may be that marriage enhances levels of self-control, such that through the experience of marriage individuals are more capable of self-regulating their own behaviour (Forrest and Hay, 2011). Finally, a fourth explanation for the relationship between marriage and desistance may be that marriage mediates the changes that an individual makes to their own identity and cognitions (Giordano *et al.*, 2002), individual biographies (Maruna, 2001), and emotional regulation (Giordano *et al.*, 2007).

For many of the interviewees in the study, relationship concerns were identified as long-term, ongoing objectives, the achievement of which was dependent upon gaining and sustaining employment. Individuals stated that the objective of improving relationships would instil motivation and an incentive to stay away from crime. Individuals also identified relationships as a means of altering their routines, providing the impetus for attitudinal change, developing a support network, and offering them a stake in society. Fundamentally, relationships were regarded as a means of moving away from crime as they offered a different perspective on the future, encouraging the individual to 'settle down' rather than lead a chaotic lifestyle involving offending:

> All my mates, they're my family, cos none of my mates have got family either. All of us are like a tight bunch, obviously I want my own family though. I want a big family. Cos when you've got kids all you think is, I want the easy life now, I don't want no more of this mayhem and messing around. So even though I'm only 20 I wouldn't mind settling down now.
>
> (John)

Individuals sometimes made reference to friends' relationships, and spoke about the perceived positive impact that this had had on their lives. The men in the study suggested that developing relationships with girlfriends or wives appeared to help their friends to live in a more pro-social manner:

> Yeah, I'd like to meet someone, a nice bird, someone I could maybe settle down with. I see some of my mates and they've got wives, girlfriends, kids and whatever else, and they're doing alright now. Maybe something like that's what I need, give me a push. Get me moving in the right direction, instead of messing about and that.
>
> (Kurt)

Interestingly, far fewer references were made to other people's children as having a pro-social influence. Rather, the perception that having children could have a positive impact upon an individual's life appeared to emanate predominantly from those individuals who had children of their own. Indeed, in those cases where the men in the study either already had children of their own, or where they were expectant fathers, developing these relationships further was a prominent theme. In this respect it could be concluded that it is the actual experience of parenthood, rather than the perceived benefits of it or a desire to experience it, which is related to desistance.

Although the desistance literature has paid relatively little attention to the influence of fatherhood on desistance, becoming a father has been identified as a possible correlate for desistance (Shannon and Abrams, 2007). Kreager *et al.*

(2010) also found that motherhood had a significant effect on reducing delinquency, alcohol and marijuana behaviours. They found that motherhood had a stronger effect on reducing delinquent behaviours than marriage. While some have suggested that having children has a negligible effect upon transitions in and out of crime (Warr, 1998; Blokland and Nieuwbeerta, 2005), it has been argued that fatherhood enhances motivation and offers a 'hook for change' (Helyar-Caldwell, 2012). Although the rebuilding of father-child relationships can positively influence desistance, becoming a father can have an even more dramatic effect on the process of moving away from crime. As discussed earlier in this book, some accounts have suggested that ex-offenders' stories of becoming fathers are akin to religious testimonies, where individuals clearly distinguish between 'before and after fatherhood' scenarios, and herald fatherhood as fundamentally changing behaviours and attitudes (Eden *et al.* 2004).

Sometimes individuals may already have children, and the motivating factor behind efforts to desist is to become a good parent or 'family man' (Farrall *et al.*, 2010; Farrall *et al.*, 2011). Indeed, the very act of fathering can be generative, insofar as ex-offender fathers feel as though they are engaged in productive activities for the good of others (Walker, 2010). The men in this study stated that they wanted to be 'good fathers', and that they wanted to ensure that their own children did not enter into the criminal lifestyles that they had been part of:

> I don't want my kid having my sort of lifestyle, I want the kid to have the sort of lifestyle I always wanted but that my dad couldn't provide for me. I want my kid to have the life I wanted, not the life I was in....Basically I want him to be a success, but I want him to do it properly, you know what I mean?
>
> (Brian)

During the interview, Brian spoke about how he wanted to ensure that his own son would be able to achieve material success without resorting to criminal activity. He suggested that he would be able to ensure this by acting as a positive role model and by ensuring that he would be present in his child's life. He stated that this would help him to desist because the desire to have a presence in his son's upbringing enabled him to resist the temptations or opportunities to engage in criminal activity. At the time of interview he was experiencing some animosity with a group of drug dealers who lived on the same estate. He explained that previously he would have resorted to violence in order to resolve such an issue, but that he no longer wanted to resort to such actions in order to preserve his relationship with his son:

> right now there's crackheads and smackheads, coke dealers and whatever all over. I can't take them on, cos at the end of the day I don't want my kid growing up without a dad. You know what I mean? It could be jail for me if I did, or it could be worse. You get me? It could be a lot worse. So I ain't getting involved with that.
>
> (Brian)

Similar sentiments were expressed by other men in the study. Josh, for example, explained how he would be motivated to refrain from further offending because of the risk of imprisonment and the consequences that this would have for his relationships with his daughter and unborn son. Interestingly, he also explained how his girlfriend had given him an ultimatum to either stop offending or risk losing his family:

> If I offend again, I will lose everything that I've got. I'll lose my girlfriend, my daughter, I've got a son on the way. I've already been in prison once when my daughter was born, I can't let that happen again. Plus, if I go inside again it's going to be for a lot longer and I can't have my kids growing up with a dad in jail. I'll lose all of that, cos women can only take so much. If I go back in prison again she's off, I've been warned. She's said if I go back in prison again she won't hang around again.
>
> (Josh)

For several of the men in the study, therefore, attempts to develop, restore or maintain relationships with partners/wives and children were central objectives for the future. In order to achieve this, the men recognised that they would need to desist from crime, or else risk jeopardising these relationships. However, the men in the study also identified employment as being necessary in order to help them to develop and maintain relationships with their partners and families. For some this was due to the financial security offered by full-time employment. Individuals felt that being able to provide for others was a fundamental aspect of being a good 'family man':

> I need a job, I've got nothing coming in right now really, and I've got the house to pay for, plus bills and all that. I've also got to make sure my kids are looked after, you know? I need to be able to provide for them, I'm a good dad, I've always looked after them and I'm determined to carry it on like that.
>
> (Kev)

Economic motivations may not be sufficient on their own to maintain desistance, and in the absence of legitimate employment the temptation of a criminal opportunity may prove difficult to resist. For some of the men, however, employment was regarded as an opportunity to demonstrate to others that they were making changes in their lives, and that they were able to live a crime-free life. In this respect, developing or restoring relationships appeared to be dependent upon the individual being able to show that they were capable of desisting, as merely asserting that they had changed would be insufficient to convince significant others. This is one of the conundrums of desistance, insofar as a desister needs to prove that they are no longer offending by abstaining from a particular activity (Maruna, 2001). In this respect, the demonstrations of change that my participants sought through employment appear to mirror the 'certification' from others, reported by Meisenhelder as the final stage in desisting from a criminal career

(1989: 784) – that is, that primary desisters may need to 'certify' to others that they have changed, in order to receive the benefits that those individuals can offer:

SK: How important is work to you at the moment?

KEN: Very. If I can get a job then I can start getting back on my feet. Erm, like I said, I'm only on the social so I ain't earning much, so it'd help me out no end there. But also, it'd help me to look after my kids, and if I can get a job and hold it down it's all going towards showing people that I've changed and that I want to become a better person.

Martin described how sustained employment would help him to see his son:

But this'll all help as well with seeing my son, if I can start this job working with my sister and her old man, and if I can stick it out, make a go of it, then that's going to help me cos they'll say, 'he's doing alright now', and that's when people start trusting you, so that'd be good.

(Martin)

Individuals also suggested that increased 'self-efficacy' and 'self-control' were required in order for relationships to be improved, often suggesting that changes would be dependent upon individual change:

It'd be better for them [the children] to see me more, to see me laugh. I've got to make changes to make things better between me and my kids, I know that, it's just about being able to put it into practice, do you know what I mean?...They're getting older, and I'm missing out on so much. If I carry on the way I am then I'm going to miss out on them for good, so I need to take control of things. It's down to me to make life better, to get back normal, make my family normal again.

(Terry)

'I just can't hang around with them'

Some of the men in the study stated that in order to desist they would need to make alterations to the peer groups that they associated with. In some instances this would entail severing ties with friends and acquaintances. A number of men identified a range of criminogenic factors associated with particular peer groups, including alcohol or drug use, and unemployment. Some of the men in the study had suggested that previous attempts to desist had been frustrated by the maintenance of ties with certain peers:

SK: Why do you think you weren't able to stop [offending] at that time?

RYAN: Just the crowd I was with. I know the people I'm with now wouldn't get me into any trouble. But back then, it was just everyone I was with was up for it, and you couldn't not go along. When I did this offence, I was with the same crowd.

Later in the interview, Ryan went further to state that without severing ties with particular individuals he would not be able to move away from crime:

> I want to stay away [from previous peers]. I do like them, but I just can't hang around with them without fighting....I know if I get mixed up with the wrong crowd I'll be straight back into trouble again.
>
> (Ryan)

Awareness of the connection between peer group association and offending behaviour was often instigated by the supervising officer, who suggested that the individual would be less likely to reoffend if they severed contact with delinquent peers:

> SK: Do you think that your relationship with your Probation Officer has had a direct impact on your attitudes and behaviour?
>
> TOM: Yeah. Particularly drinking. And realising the associations I had with other people, sometimes of less than reputable character. That was caused through just pubbing it all the time. I remember, years ago, my dad saying to me 'Never take work out of a pub'. And it's true. I mean someone'll offer you a job in a pub and you either don't get paid or you only get half of what you should've got. They're schisters. You shouldn't do it. But I was doing it, and therefore, you put yourself in a position of 'I want that money I'm owed', but how are you going to get it?...If you go and knock on their door, that might bring you all kind of trouble. That's the cycle. That's what happens. You either have to back down, or do something you shouldn't do, and still not get your money. So is it better to keep out of that sphere or not? I think it's better to keep out of it. I think it's better to do a job for a reputable person.

Tom's interview illustrates how formal, legitimate employment was considered to be necessary in order to cut ties with delinquent peers. He had spent almost his entire working life engaged in what he called 'pub jobs', whereby he would accept work from individuals who drank in the pubs that he would frequent. Thus, Tom's working history was located within the informal labour market, predominantly as a labourer undertaking cash-in-hand jobs. The nature of his work was directly related to certain offences, notably violent crimes that he had committed in an attempt to recoup the earnings that he had been promised but which had not been delivered. These types of job had also allowed Tom to sustain his drinking habit, which had led to other offences, such as drink-driving:

> I mean, I used to go to the shop myself, it opens at half past six, used to leave the door about seven o'clock, get baccy stuff like that, he'd [a friend] bowl up in the van half a dozen cans of beer to take to work with him. Then he'd be out [at the pub] at dinnertime, or work through dinner and leave at two o'clock, and start boozing again until 11 at night. I used to be the same, start drinking

early, while you're on the job almost, and then finish early so you can get in the pub. You can get away with it, see, cos no-one's keeping an eye on you, no-one's going to discipline you, yeah you might get a bollocking, but everyone's in the same boat so most often you'd just carry on as you are.

(Tom)

With respect to cutting ties, employment was regarded as necessary due to the impact working would have upon routine activities. The interview data suggested that a number of offences (notably: theft, shoplifting and drug-taking) were related to the routine activities of time spent with a peer group who were largely unemployed. Many interviewees made reference to time spent with friends 'hanging around' in the town centre or on street corners:

SK: Where do you spend your time, if you're never at home?
RYAN: Like I said, a lot of the time I'd just be round my mate's house smoking weed, but we can't always do that so we just hang around the estate or go up town. There ain't much to do up town, it's shit, but it makes a change from hanging round the estate, so. I prefer to go round my mate's house, but we'd be hanging round the estate quite a bit as well, there ain't nothing else to do.

Interviewees suggested that if they were able to find employment then they would not be able to participate in these activities:

SK: Are the people you're referring to there criminals?
BRIAN: Yeah, obviously. They still are now. I mean, I was once like that, but my life's changed. They just want to hang about town, see what girls are about. People like that don't have ambition, they just want to meet up and smoke weed outside McDonalds till six o'clock then go home. I don't want that lifestyle, I can't do that no more so I just have to keep myself to myself. Get myself a new place to live for my girlfriend and the baby, get a job. I've changed anyway, but if I had that then I wouldn't be able to do that anyway cos I'd just be at work all day then home to my family, spend time with them.

Furthermore, individuals supported these claims by suggesting that periods of time where they had not offended had coincided with time spent in employment, as indicated by Charlie (see earlier in this chapter) when he stated that work precluded the opportunity to associate with delinquent peers. However, it was also apparent that individuals believed that peer group association was something that they could control, demonstrating 'self-efficacy':

SK: Do you still hang around with the same people now?
LEROY: A mixture, sort of thing. I've got quite a few different mates. I don't hang around with the same people all the time, you know? At the end

of the day, it's up to me who I hang around with, ain't it? If I thought that hanging around with them would get me in trouble then I'd stay away from them, but I'll hang around with whoever I want.

It was clear that for some individuals, peer group association had empowered them to implement strategies for desistance. Such associations had generated feelings of confidence and motivation, which are key aspects of the desistance process. Crucially, these positive feelings came from establishing or re-establishing, relationships with non-offending peers.

'Round my way there's a lot of people up to no good'

For some individuals, peer groups associations were not regarded as being of particular importance in terms of refraining from offending. Rather, the area or neighbourhood that they lived in was perceived to be more important, in relation to both past offending and the likelihood of sustained desistance. Many of the men spoke about their 'neighbourhoods', 'estates' or 'areas', and often they associated their offending with the area that they lived in. The men described the area that they lived in in terms of high unemployment, a lack of legitimate employment opportunities, prolific drug use, poverty and high crime. Some of the men in the study stated that they wanted to move away from their area, in part to reduce opportunities for offending and in part to demonstrate to others that they had been able to transcend the perceived normative trajectories of individuals living in their area:

> Where I'm living now it ain't the best of places to bring up kids, and it's a council estate, that says it all really don't it? Don't get me wrong, I ain't ashamed of where I live, put it this way I'd rather live there than anywhere else, but when I'm older, when I move out of there I want to tell my kids what it was like and how I got out of there....I can't complain where I come from, but it's just people around me, all drug dealers and that....Like I say, it ain't the best of areas, but it's like everyone who lives round my way is in the same position, you know? Hardly no-one's working, there's a lot of people up to no good, and everyone pretty much is either taking drugs or selling drugs.
>
> (John)

John clearly regarded the area that he lived in as being a contributing factor in his previous offending behaviour, and he was willing to sever the ties between himself and the neighbourhood that he had grown up in as part of his strategy for achieving desistance. However, when asked whether he had considered cutting the ties with his friends who were also involved in deviant behaviour, John was adamant that he would not incorporate this as part of his wider strategy:

> The people I hang around with I've known for years, I've known since I was like nine years old so obviously I'm going to be with them and listen to

them rather than [PO]. They're all close friends....I've been through a lot of things with them so I ain't going to change for no-one.

(John)

This is indicative of the complex nature of desistance strategies. While individuals may seek to make changes in their lives and develop new pro-social networks, it is likely that they will also try to retain some degree of continuity in their lives. This may be to retain some 'ontological security' (Giddens, 1990) in a fast-paced and ever-changing world. Conversely, it could be to maintain an element of excitement and risqué behaviour in their lives. Shapland and Bottoms (2011) have argued that for individuals to be able to desist they may need to resist various invitations to offend. In order to do this, individuals may need to use 'diachronic self-control' as a technique to avoid the temptation and opportunity to offend in the future. This entails taking a particular course of action so that during the routine patterns of the day individuals will be able to avoid the temptation and opportunity to commit crime, even though this may involve quite boring and monotonous behaviour. One of the participants in the Sheffield Desistance Study described how they had limited their behaviour to just watching TV and playing video games all day (Shapland and Bottoms, 2011: 274). While this might be necessary for some individuals so that they are not faced with opportunities which they are unable to resist, others may be unwilling to engage in less exciting behaviour even if it means that they are likely to face greater temptations to offend. Interestingly, John's supervising officer had identified his peer group as having a negative effect upon the progress that John had made towards desistance in the past, and had made efforts to try to influence his peer associations in the future:

I know what he's like when he hangs around with them. He can be doing so well, but with them he just gets carried away or caught up in it, and he just seems to forget everything that we've worked on and all the progress he's made. I try to encourage him not to see them so much, but I don't think he takes much notice.

(PO4)

Other men in the study demonstrated that they were more willing to sacrifice certain aspects of their lives as part of their desistance strategies. For example, one of the men, Martin, spoke about the neighbourhood that he had grown up in and how it had influenced his involvement in deviant behaviour. He had become a drug dealer as a teenager, which he explained was easy to do as it was possible to acquire drugs from other men in the area and then sell them on before paying back the initial debt owed. He described how, over time, he began to buy and sell larger quantities of Class A drugs, and that his involvement in violent crimes escalated simultaneously. Martin explained that he had begun to store reasonably large quantities of Class A drugs at his mother's house (where he was living at the time), but that she had thrown him out when she discovered that this was taking place, and for a period of time they had stopped talking to one another.

He also stated that many of his friends were involved in similar activities. Since being sent to prison, Martin had regained a relationship with his mother, who still lived in the same neighbourhood that Martin had grown up in. Martin had moved in with another family member and, at the time of interview, was living in a different area. Martin explained how he would like to be able to see his friends and his mother on a more regular basis, but that he was willing to forego that in order to live away from his old neighbourhood:

> Well, I'm not too bothered [about returning to my old neighbourhood]. I am because, obviously, I have got my mum down there, and all my mates are there and everything. But in another aspect I'm not because I was selling drugs before I went down anyway and that's all I need, to get back down there. I ain't got no money, do you know what I mean? I work for family, so I don't get paid a lot, I'm always skint, so I'd end up getting some [drugs], cos you'd end up getting it on the tick and selling it, and that's all I need isn't it? Just bomb out and end up back in jail for a few more years, I can't be doing with that.
>
> (Martin)

Martin's desistance strategy, therefore, may be more indicative of the use of dia-chronic self-control as a technique to avoid future offending opportunities. Interestingly, Martin was one of two men in the sample who had been required to reside in a probation hostel for a period of time after being released from prison. Both men stated that being forced to live away from their old neighbourhoods had helped them to develop a stronger resolve to desist from crime, and that being away from their old neighbourhoods had helped them to cut ties with their previous lifestyles and friends.

Other men in the study also stated that moving away from their local area would help them to desist, but this was often qualified with a statement that they had few opportunities to move elsewhere, and that anywhere that they could move to would be similarly rife with drugs and unemployment. Ryan had explained earlier in his interview that he had cut ties with previous peer groups in an attempt to move away from crime. Later, he stated that moving away from his neighbourhood would also help him to desist, but that this was not possible given his financial circumstances at the time of interview. Instead, he had adopted a strategy of avoiding criminal opportunities by staying indoors:

SK: Do you still hang around with this crowd?

RYAN: No, I ain't been with that crowd for about two years now. Which is a good thing.

SK: So who do you hang around with now?

RYAN: Just a couple of new mates.

SK: What do you spend your time doing?

RYAN: They like smoking weed and that. But they just do it in their own house, not in the streets like. They ain't into trouble.

From his interview, it can be seen that Ryan had contextualised deviant behaviour, such that staying indoors smoking marijuana was regarded as being acceptable. In part this was because it enabled him to avoid violent encounters on the streets, which is what had led to him being convicted of assault on several occasions in the past. It might also be seen that Ryan regarded this as his only course of action to achieve this level of avoidance, as he did not perceive moving away from his area to be a viable option. Indeed, Ryan appeared to be quite fatalistic when he was asked about his future strategy for maintaining desistance:

> I don't plan cos it just fucks up. So I just take it day by day. Everyone says that, 'if you plan it fucks up'.
>
> (Ryan)

Here, Ryan can be seen to have adopted an approach which reflects not only the influence of the social structures which surround him, but also the attitudes and beliefs of those closest to him. Ryan had few job prospects, and lacked the resources to be able to move away from his neighbourhood. However, he also identified informal work with someone in his local area as being the most likely source of employment opportunity:

> SK: Do you have any ideas about how you might get into that [line of work]?
>
> RYAN: Probably just ask people around my way. Someone'll probably have some work going and if I can show that I'm a hard worker then I should be alright.

This suggests that Ryan had reflexively deliberated on his circumstances and what he wanted to achieve, and had determined that the sporadic informal work that he might find in his local area offered the most realistic opportunity to make a living. He simultaneously identified his local area as being a source of criminal opportunities and temptation, and a realistic means of earning money in a quasi-legitimate manner. This presents a complex and challenging conundrum for would-be desisters. The extent to which certain deviant behaviours (such as working cash-in-hand) are regarded as 'acceptable' may impact upon the likelihood that the individual will be able to sustain desistance. Longer-term desistance may be more likely for individuals who regard most deviant behaviour in negative terms under any circumstances (Shapland and Bottoms, 2011), yet the maintenance of such views may not be possible at all times. Individuals, such as Ryan, may find themselves in a situation where they have clear ideas about what conventional behaviour entails, but may have to alter their perceptions of what is acceptable within certain contexts. In Ryan's case this can be seen in the way that he described moving away from his local area. He said that this was a factor which would help him to desist, and that to do this he would require a job. However, he also stated that his job prospects were poor and that informal contacts in his local area were his most realistic source of opportunities for work. Ryan was more accepting of certain deviant behaviours, and this clearly impacted upon his strategies for desistance.

Like Ryan, many of the men in the study identified gaining employment with being able to move away from the neighbourhoods that they associated with criminal behaviour. Most of the men suggested that this would reduce the number of criminal opportunities presented to them. Typical responses included: 'Getting a job means I can get out of here', and 'If I have a job I can move somewhere nicer'. Individuals were keen to stress the reality of what could happen if they were unable to secure employment that would enable them to move away, and stay away, from the area that was associated with past offending:

> SK: Is there anything that could lead you to reoffend again?
>
> MARTIN: Well, as long as I can get work up here, a proper job I mean, and keep working then I should be okay cos it'd keep me busy, I'd be making money and everyone'd be happy. If I can't get work then I don't know what I'll do. I'll probably end up moving back down there [to his old neighbourhood], and there's a good chance I'd get back into my old ways.

'It becomes a vicious circle if you're not careful'

For some of the men in the study, moving away from their local area was not only associated with an attempt to reduce criminal opportunities, but they also saw moving away as being in the best interests of others who were close to them. As discussed earlier, a number of the men held concerns about being a 'good father', and several men suggested that they wanted to live in an area that would offer an alternative lifestyle for their children. In this regard it is possible to interpret the interview data as suggesting that individuals regarded their local area as a socio-structural barrier to being able to adopt the identity of a 'good father'. Indeed, some men stated that they would be less capable fathers if they remained living in their neighbourhood:

> It becomes a vicious circle if you're not careful. I mean, my mum done the best she could, I can't complain at all, we always had food on the table, roof over our heads, but it's just being round there you're bound to get up to no good. It would've been a lot easier for my mum if we lived somewhere nicer, I can guarantee that. That's what I want for my kids, somewhere nice where there's no chance of them getting into trouble. If I stay where I am, I'm more likely to get into trouble, and if you've got kids what see you getting into trouble, they're just going to copy you, ain't they? And that's what I mean, it's a vicious circle.
>
> (John)

Again, for many men employment was identified as being central to this aspect of being a good parent. Josh described how he was considering moving to another country with his family:

> I just want to start a new life, start fresh, and give the kids somewhere better to grow up....I'd've done it before, but being on probation stopped me. That's my main goal in life, to get my family out there. Other than that, if it don't work out, buy a nice house here. I'm on a good wage, I can afford it. I'm lucky I'm in work the way things are at the minute [referring to the recession] so I can't complain. If it [the move] don't work out then at least I've got a job here and we can set up somewhere fresh in this country instead....My main goal is to look after my family, keep out of trouble.
>
> (Josh)

Many of the men, therefore, had identified their locality as problematic and a barrier to desistance, but a significant number had not formulated strategies to alter this. Often this was because individuals perceived few employment opportunities away from their locality and, therefore, possible courses of action were limited. By contrast, individuals (such as Josh) whose employment was not linked to the locality perceived a greater range of possibilities.

'I want to move out, have a bit of independence'

For some of the men the area that they lived in did not appear to be of much significance to their plans for desistance. Rather, they suggested that securing accommodation of their own, or more secure accommodation, would help them to refrain from further offending. Some were living in temporary accommodation at the time of interview, either through social housing or with friends or family. Only three individuals identified their housing circumstances as being a personal problem, yet the interviews revealed that many more would like to find more suitable accommodation, or more long-term arrangements (many of the interviewees either had experienced, or were experiencing, temporary living arrangements; spending short periods of time living with various family members or friends). The existing desistance literature has indicated that poor or unstable housing can have a negative effect upon the likelihood of an individual desisting from crime (Farrall, 2002; McNeill, 2006; LeBel et al., 2008), and certain groups of would-be desisters, for example those from particular ethnic backgrounds, are likely to find housing to be even more problematic (Calverley, 2013). Having stable accommodation can reduce the likelihood of reoffending by as much as one-fifth, yet a third of prisoners lose their home while in prison (SEU, 2002). The individuals in the Sheffield Desistance Study were more likely to have experienced a 'volatile recent housing history', often in the public sector or in probation hostels or approved premises. Moreover, they were more likely to experience non-sequential accommodation, whereby they would not live at one address for the entire week (Bottoms et al., 2004: 377).

A number of the men in the study indicated that they wanted to 'settle down', and that they wanted to become more independent of the friends and family who provided them with assistance. This is an interesting finding, as there is evidence to suggest a general tendency among released prisoners to rely upon friends and family for assistance in finding employment and housing (Niven and Olagundaye, 2002; Niven and Stewart, 2005). It could be that part of the process of desistance involves the individual gradually increasing their levels of independence and personal responsibility. In other words, while individuals may draw upon the assistance of friends and family in the early stages of desistance, as they progress they may actively seek to enhance their independence. Arguably it would be expected that individuals would rely less upon assistance from others as they progress throughout the desistance process, but the interview data indicated that individuals were agentic in actively trying to initiate this. Some of the men suggested that finding accommodation of their own would instil greater responsibility, independence and stability in otherwise chaotic lives:

> I'm second on the list for a council flat, so that's great. So I just want to sort my head out, and get some responsibility. I am sick of counting on other people to help me out all the while. So I want to start helping myself out.
>
> (Charlie)

Others wanted to obtain more suitable accommodation, and this was often related to providing a better home for partners and children. Moreover, some individuals equated dissatisfactory accommodation with anger management issues, stating that frustration with current circumstances contributed to the perpetuation of these personal difficulties. Such individuals explained that anger and frustration had contributed to their offending in the past, and thus felt that improvements in their housing situations would help to alleviate these issues:

> No-one's coming to me saying, 'oh I heard you're looking for a place'. None of that. No-one's telling me anything, no-one's even said any of that. And, this place [probation] expects me to come down here all the time expecting everything to be fine. But I've got to go back to that place [flat]. [PO] has even come down and said it's not nice, it's not right. She's even said that. It's not nice for my girlfriend, or for myself. It's not suitable.
>
> (Brian)

Two of the men, Dean and Ken, had found new accommodation since being under probation supervision, and both explained that this change had helped them to make the initial move towards desistance. For these individuals, further improvements to their accommodation were regarded as influential in helping them to be able to sustain desistance:

> She's [PO] helping me out with some forms to try and get some furniture, cos I moved into a flat in December with absolutely nothing. I'm hoping to

get something out of that, cos I've moved in there now but it's absolutely horrible not having anything to sleep on or sit on, so I just need a bit of help and that's what she's going to give me. I'm grateful for that cos, erm, I'm sure that that's going to help me, it'll make me a better person as well.

(Ken)

Most individuals, however, were less optimistic about their accommodation prospects, partly because of a lack of housing opportunities in the local area and partly due to a lack of income. Lack of income was a result of individuals' employment circumstances, which situated accommodation as a second-order concern that could only be achieved once employment had been gained:

SK: Whereabouts are you living at the moment?

RAJ: I'm living with my parents at the moment. But when this business kicks off, I'll move out. I'm ready for it now. I want to move out, have a bit of independence. I just need to get the money together and then I can get my own place.

SK: Have you got any plans for this?

RAJ: Just rent to begin with. Once the business is up and running, and money starts coming in, then I'll be able to do it. It should be fairly straightforward, doesn't need much planning.

While individuals suggested that improved accommodation circumstances would follow employment, many were pessimistic about the likelihood of this occurring, in the near future at least, and the reality of future living arrangements was perceived to be both temporary and unstable:

SK: Have you thought about where you might live after probation?

KURT: Once I get out the hostel I'll probably stay with some friends, I haven't got anything set up but, erm. I don't think I'd get another council flat cos of what happened before [Kurt wouldn't say what had happened, but he had been evicted from his flat]. If I could get a job then I could probably find my own place after a while, but I don't think that'd happen anytime soon, so yeah, it'd probably be mates' places for a bit. Back on the sofa! I don't mind though, it's better than sleeping rough.

Improving accommodation circumstances, therefore, was regarded as an event which would both facilitate relationship concerns and help to develop an individual's agency, in terms of improving self-confidence, independence, responsibility and self-efficacy. However, individuals were structurally constrained, most notably by poverty and a lack of income, and employment was regarded as a necessary objective for accommodation concerns to be realised. Not all interviewees held employment as a concern which needed to be achieved before improvements to accommodation circumstances could be made. Rather, these individuals described being similarly constrained by socio-structural factors (including income), but they suggested that they were dependent upon the actions of others to overcome these:

> SK: Is there anything you can do to improve your living arrangements?
> BRIAN: Not really, no. Cos I've just got to wait for [PO] or the council or whoever to sort something out. Obviously I'm not working so there's nothing I can do about that, so I just keep asking them to help. They say they're trying to sort something out, but so far nothing.

Barriers to strategies

As discussed so far in this chapter, the men in the study had constructed their own strategies for desistance, generally involving changes to relationships, living arrangements, peer associations and employment. Employment was identified by some of the men as being the most important factor in their future strategies, while for others accommodation or restoring relationships were clearly regarded as having the highest priority. That said, in those cases where employment was not considered to be the most important aspect of the future strategy, it was still regarded as being a necessary element of that strategy. In other words, employment was seen to be necessary for the achievement of all other goals. This was, perhaps, unsurprising, given the level of unemployment among the group of men at the time of interview (n = 14). With this in mind it was, again, perhaps not unusual for the men to have identified barriers to employment as being the biggest difficulty in relation to the fulfilment of their strategies.

'Someone might need a carpenter for a week and they'll ask me'

While many of the men spoke about employment in quite general terms, it was not uncommon for some of the men to talk about specific occupations or indus- tries within which they would seek, or were seeking, work. For some of the men this corresponded with previous work experience, and the jobs that were dis- cussed were often of a low-skilled and low-paid nature. Interestingly, some of the men had never had a job before, yet some of these individuals also identified the same type of low-skilled, low-paid jobs as being suitable for their desistance strategies. This may reflect individuals' perceptions of 'traditional' masculine identities in relation to employment expectations (McDowell, 2003; Nayak, 2006; Nixon, 2009).[1] Many of the men had also experienced most of their previous employment in 'informal' occupations. Fletcher (2007) defines this type of employment as ' "cash-in-hand" jobs secured through friends [or family] and acquaintances' (2007: 83). Again, the men who had no previous work experience also suggested that their best course of action would be to find work within informal labour markets. Some of the men were clearly accustomed to finding work through informal channels, and this was reflected in how they anticipated finding work in the future:

In the [construction] trade there's always someone to help you out giving you work. You give it each other. Someone might need a carpenter for a week and they'll ask me....Jobs on the side are good, cos you're getting cash-in-hand, there's normally plenty of it going around, not at the minute there ain't, but, erm. So, that's what I'm hopeful of, once some of my mates get work then there'll be someone what can pass something my way. Like I say, I got offered that one job from a mate but I couldn't take it, but I'm sure there'll be something else before too long.

(Kev)

In part, this may explain why many participants were unwilling to engage in programmes which were intended to improve job prospects and create greater opportunities for employment:

LEROY: Like they said, 'if you want help getting a job we'll help you'. But I just said, 'no I don't want your help thanks, don't worry about it'.
SK: Why did you say that?
LEROY: I'd just rather do it my way.

Only a minority of participants stated that they would seek work in the formal labour market, and employment objectives tended to follow past experience, insofar as those who wanted to gain formal employment generally had worked in formal labour markets previously. Only six men were in employment at the time of interview, and four of these were in formal occupations. The two other men who were working at the time of interview were employed in informal occupations. For those individuals who had past experience of informal work, their employment history could be characterised as sporadic and temporary. Labouring or work in the construction trade was the type of employment most often undertaken, and interviewees described how work in the informal market was of an insecure nature:

I've been floating around [between various jobs]. I'm working for a firm now, but before I'd just pick up work on sites through friends, or a friend of a friend. It's good money doing that cos obviously it's cash in your pocket, and you just hope that a job'll last long enough 'til the next one comes round. I've been lucky, I've never really been without work, but you know plenty of people who can work for a bit and then get nothing for weeks at a time.

(Josh)

Josh had since found work in a formal occupation, and contrasted his past experiences of working in informal jobs with the security afforded by formal occupations:

It's better now cos I know I've got work, alright I pay a bit more to the taxman but at least I know I've always got money coming in.

(Josh)

However, it was clear that most individuals believed that their only employment opportunities existed within informal labour markets, and that they were dependent upon family and friends for work. This may suggest that many of the individuals in the study felt marginalised from the formal labour market:

SK: What type of work will you look for?

KURT: For now I'm going to have to ask around, you know, my mates and that, see if anyone's got any work going. Like I say, I've done painting and decorating for mates before so I might be able to get back to that. You've got to be honest, who's going to give me a job? Criminal record, on probation, fuck all education, I can't really expect too much.

This resonates with Fletcher's (2007) contention that offenders are often marginalised from contemporary formal labour markets, leading them towards a cycle of sporadic informal employment 'interspersed with spells of criminal activity and imprisonment' (2007: 81), and also with Niven and Stewart's (2005) finding that offenders most often obtain work through networks of family and friends. Only seven of the men in the study indicated that they had past experience of working in formal labour markets, but four of these men were in employment at the time of interview. The other three men who had formal employment experience stated that they would seek formal work again in the future. Men who had formal work experience were noticeably more confident about how to undertake the task of looking for work, and about the prospects of finding work. Those who had past experience of formal employment were also more self-assured by comparison to those individuals whose past experience was in informal labour markets:

SK: How will you go about getting a job?

BRIAN: You've just got to go out and ask. If you ask enough people eventually you'll get a job, if you're willing to do it.

It also appeared to be the case that those who had formal work experience, and those who were seeking formal work, were more active in their pursuit of employment. Those who were seeking informal work were more passive, waiting for an opportunity to be offered to them as opposed to applying or asking for work:

I'm unemployed at the moment. I thought I had a job when I come out, but I didn't....I had a job as a scaffolder for a few months with a mate, and then I worked with my dad for a few months and then I went inside. I thought I'd be able to go back to that, and he did as well. But obviously there just isn't any work at the moment so he can't take me on. Hard times isn't it? .. he's said as soon as there's work I'll be the first one to know.

(Leroy)

Thus, employment was recognised as a fundamental aspect of most strategies for desistance. However, most participants' work experience could be located within informal labour markets, and this influenced the type of work that they would pursue in the future.

'I left school with nothing and you can't really get a job without it'

The strategies for employment discussed by individuals were also often related to educational experiences. Perhaps unsurprisingly, educational attainment among the participants was relatively limited, experiences of school were often characterised in terms of truancy and exclusion, and these early experiences were often related to the onset of offending behaviour:

> [School was] [s]hit. I hated it. I wasn't that good, like I didn't want to con-centrate or nothing. So the teachers'd tell me off for not paying attention, or distracting other people or whatever. After a while I just thought, fuck it, I'll act bad. I'm not getting anywhere anyway, so I might as well do what I want. It just got to the point where I thought, I can't be done with this no more, and that's when I'd do something [antisocial/illegal].
>
> (Leroy)

Individuals were aware of the impact of their educational experiences upon their employment opportunities. For most of the men poor educational experiences had the effect of pushing them towards working in informal labour markets. A lack of formal work experience then compounded future opportunities, whether perceived or real, which maintained the individual's position at the margins of the labour market:

> SK: So you left without any qualifications?
> RYAN: Yeah, I left before all that.
> SK: Did you start work at that point?
> RYAN: No. I've never had a proper job. Just cash in hand. Removals, house clearing. If someone's been evicted or whatever, we go in clear the house and do a bit of cleaning. Obviously, like I say, I left school with nothing and you can't really get a job without it, so, erm, I'm a bit stuck with that really.

'There's no jobs for people who want one'

Many of the men in the sample did not appear to be particularly confident with regard to seeking or obtaining employment. However, it was not just the effect of past experiences of employment or education which had an influence upon individuals' levels of confidence; many of the men were also able to identify factors in their present personal and social contexts which would act as barriers to them fulfilling their strategies. The men were fully cognisant of the economic recession, and they articulated their fears about the impact that this would likely have on limiting their employment opportunities. This clearly affected individuals' confidence, and made them less assured about the prospects of fulfilling their desistance strategies:

> I'm not [confident] at the moment. I'd like to be, but I'm not at all. You've only got to read the paper every day [to see why]. So I'm not. It's everywhere you look, there's no jobs for people who want one, and people who've got one are being laid off every day.
>
> (Alan)

Many of the men suggested that, given the current economic conditions, they would seek employment through informal channels. As discussed so far, this was partly due to the effect of past experiences of employment and education, but partly also because of the present social conditions that the men found themselves in. It is possible that these men would seek work in informal labour markets regardless of the economic conditions, but it is reasonable to assume that concerns about the recession would condition individuals further towards seeking employment informally. Leroy, for example, had only ever worked with his dad or a friend, always cash-in-hand, and he explained that this would be the type of work he would seek in the future. In part, this was as a result of his past experience, but also partly because of the economic circumstances of the time:

> SK: Are you looking for work?
> LEROY: No. No point. I'll go work with my dad as soon as things pick up, so that's that.

Others seemed less relaxed about their future employment prospects, and recognised that economic conditions would also negatively affect informal labour markets:

> There's not much in the building [trade]. If you look in the papers for jobs, there's nothing in the construction trade. All my mates who work for [name of company] they're just not building houses. A lot of my friends have been working all their life, they're on the dole. Hopefully, if mortgage rates come down people'll buy and then there'll be work and a mate can send something my way.
>
> (Kev)

This is likely due to the range or type of factors incorporated within an individual's desistance strategy. Kev, for example, had indicated that he wanted to be a good father to his children, and continue to pay for and live in his own home. Leroy, by contrast, had fewer factors of concern within his desistance strategy. He wanted to avoid further prison sentences, and he wanted to get a job at some point in the future. This may be because he was not as committed to the notion of desistance as some of the other men in the study, or perhaps because he was more uncertain about the possibility of change and how he would be able to achieve it. Such ambivalence may itself act as a barrier to fulfilling desistance strategies.

'If they're asking for a CRB check they're not going to employ people with a criminal record'

Some of the men also suggested that their criminal record would deter them from seeking formal employment. Often this was because there was a perception that employers would not consider individuals with a history of offending, but it was also suggested that past experiences of disclosing criminal record information had been negative. This had a deleterious effect upon individuals' self-confidence, and this appeared to have conditioned them to seek informal work in the future as they had dismissed the possibility of seeking work which entailed the employer asking for criminal record information:

> You've got a lot of jobs around, quite a few that ask for CRB checks, which I wouldn't apply for anyway because I've got a criminal record, they'll see I've got a criminal record – I don't know whether it'd be worth applying to be honest. But I tend to have the mindset that if they're asking for a CRB check they're not going to employ people with a criminal record, so that's limiting your options straight away.
>
> (Ben)

Individuals' perceptions of how potential employers will view their criminal histories is, to some extent, borne out in the research on employers' perceptions of employing ex-offenders (Metcalf *et al.*, 2001; Haslewood-Pocsik *et al.*, 2008; Mears, 2008; Rhodes, 2008). Various factors may influence employers' perceptions, including conviction offence and whether or not the company has previously recruited ex-offenders (Atkin and Armstrong, 2012), yet it is unclear whether or not many would-be desisters would consider the variety of factors that could influence potential employers' perceptions. Rather, it is more likely that would-be desisters will make a decision to declare criminal history information based on their own perceptions of the stigmatising effect of the criminal record and the approach that they take to manage the stigmatising identity.

Winnick and Bodkin (2008) argued that most of the respondents in their study of 450 male prisoners anticipated rejection and stigmatisation as a consequence of their criminal records, but they found that most of these men wanted to be honest and open about declaring their criminal histories, rather than take a 'withdrawal and secrecy' approach. Although the authors acknowledged that there could be some sample bias (insofar as the men who volunteered to participate in the study might be more willing to declare criminal history information), they also found that men who experienced relationships premised upon support and inclusion were more likely to take an honest and open approach. The importance of this is that if positive and supportive relationships can be fostered between the would-be desister and their supervising officer, and between the desister and their family and friends, then it is more likely that the desister will be able to successfully manage the stigmatising identity. This could encourage greater engagement with the formal labour market.

Thus, the men in the study had constructed their own desistance strategies, involving changes to relationships, place of residence and employment, and employment was regarded by all of the men as being a necessary aspect of their strategies. However, the interviews also suggested that various structural barriers existed which would inhibit the development of these strategies, and these related in particular to the obtainment of regular employment. Past experiences of education and employment, and present economic and socio-cultural factors, were identified as constraining individuals' attempts to obtain work. On the whole, individuals were less inclined to actively seek employment, and were more likely to look for work in informal labour markets, if they lacked previous experience of formal employment.

While these men may have begun to envisage future possibilities of action and they may have constructed alternative versions of their identities, the pressing demands and constraints of the present social context may have led them towards reverting to old habits. Individuals may resort to past actions in response to a perceived inability to overcome certain structural barriers, or as a reaction to the perceived irreconcilability between traditional masculine identities and alternative forms of contemporary masculine identity. Nayak (2006) has argued that some masculine identities can become displaced in contemporary society. These identities may relate to particular forms of employment or gendered domestic roles. As certain forms of traditional working class masculine identity may become marginalised, individuals who would have previously adopted these are prompted to seek alternative forms of accepted identity. Some individuals may find positive ways of adopting new forms of masculine identity, but for others the draw of traditional identities may be too strong. This is not to argue that some would-be desisters would automatically resort to deviant behaviour in response to the marginalisation of traditional masculine identities (although some almost certainly would), but that some might seek to fulfil their desistance strategies whilst maintaining their masculine identity. As Nixon (2009) has argued, service work, characterised by deference and emotional labour, contradicts the habitus of traditional working class masculine employment identities. Therefore, while would-be desisters may construct strategies for desistance which incorporate employment, the marginalisation of traditional forms of masculine employment may result in these individuals seeking to repeat past patterns of action in order to obtain employment.

8 Probation

Enabling or constraining desistance?

There exists a small but growing body of literature which examines the impact of criminal justice interventions on desistance from crime (Rex, 1999; Farrall, 2002; McCulloch, 2005; Robinson, 2005; Farrall and Calverley, 2006). As desistance is best viewed as a process which evolves over time, it is appropriate to consider how interventions could be influential at various stages of an individual's sentence. Some authors have highlighted the possible effects that imprisonment could have on desistance and resettlement (Maruna and Toch, 2005; Maguire and Raynor, 2006; Crewe et al., 2011), while others have emphasised the role of community sentences on these processes (Robinson, 2005; McCulloch, 2010; Faulkner and Burnett, 2011; Williams and Ariel, 2012). A small body of literature has also begun to emerge in recent years which seeks to examine the role that particular types of intervention may have upon the desistance process, such as arts therapy (McNeill et al., 2011; Nugent and Loucks, 2011; Tett et al., 2012) and therapeutic communities (Stevens, 2012).

Several authors have found that the quality of the 'officer-offender' relationship can have a meaningful impact upon the likelihood of successful desistance (Barry, 2000, 2007; Burnett and McNeill, 2005). This relationship has been found to enhance levels of engagement, and desisters have suggested that they appreciated someone being concerned about them and taking an interest in their lives and wellbeing. Talking and listening have been identified as crucial skills, and previous research has found that a willingness to resolve personal and social problems is also an important part of the relationship (Rex, 1999; Burnett, 2004; McCulloch, 2005; McNeill, 2006a, 2006b; Barry, 2007). McNeill et al. (2012) have also argued that it is essential for the practitioner to develop a relationship where the individual is valued and respected, but that the interventions delivered by the practitioner also have to be implemented in such a way that the individual's goals and objectives are integrated within the overall process. Farrall (2002), on the other hand, found little evidence that probation had a meaningful impact on desistance, and suggested that resolving personal and social problems was beyond the control of supervising officers. His research concluded that conversational aspects of the 'officer-offender' relationship were, therefore, questionable.

This chapter examines the perceptions of probation supervision held by the men in the study. They were asked about past and present experiences of probation, aspects of probation that they enjoyed or found useful, whether there was anything that they would change about probation, and whether or not they felt that probation would help them to stay away from crime. The men were also asked whether probation helped them to overcome particular problems or difficulties that they were facing, and whether or not they felt probation would be able to help them in the future. The first part of this chapter examines the enabling influence of probation in the early transitions towards desistance. The interview data revealed that probation is instrumental in enhancing individuals' agency and plays a pivotal role in equipping individuals with the necessary skills to desist from crime. The interviews also revealed that supervising officers often played a crucial role in initiating a projective orientation of agency among the men that they worked with. The importance of this is that a future outlook, strategy or plan has already been identified as an important aspect of successful desistance (Maruna, 2001), but this study highlights the role that probation plays in helping to construct these future strategies.

The second part of this chapter examines the constraining effects of probation on the initial transition towards desistance. Very little attention has been paid in the literature to date towards the effect of the organisational structure and delivery of probation on processes of desistance. The interview data highlighted particular organisational or bureaucratic factors which restrict the functional ability of practitioners and their connection with the men's experiences of the supervisory relationship. The data also showed that limited practical assistance was provided and that one-to-one discussions were often limited to fairly short durations of time. This was because of the constraints placed upon the time of probation staff, largely because of various additional bureaucratic and managerial pressures. The effect of this is that there exists a discrepancy between the planning of strategies, and discussions of how best to achieve them. Many individuals who are in the early stages of desistance are therefore left in a situation where they tend to rely upon past experiences and understandings of particular social contexts to inform their actions.

Many of the men remarked that probation had helped them to develop their decision-making skills, and several suggested that their self-confidence had improved during their time under probation supervision. A number of men also commented that they felt more capable to make changes in their own lives after their experiences of probation. At times the men spoke in general terms about the positive effects of probation, and at other times they spoke about particular aspects of the sentence which were of assistance. One-to-one supervision and accredited programmes were particular aspects which were often discussed, although the men in the study had experience of a number of sentence requirements. For the current sentence at the time of interview, four of the men also had an unpaid work requirement; two had a residence requirement; one had a prohibited activity requirement; four had an exclusion requirement; and three had a curfew requirement.

More than half (n = 12) of participants had to complete an accredited programme as a requirement of their sentence. Five of the men had been required to undertake the Integrated Domestic Abuse Programme (IDAP), one had to undertake the Drink Impaired Drivers (DID) Programme, one had undertaken the Sex Offender Treatment Programme (SOTP), one had to undertake a Control of Violence for Angry Impulsive Drinkers (COVAID) Programme, two had to undertake a Low Intensity Alcohol Programme (LIAP), and two had to undertake the Controlling Anger and Learning to Manage (CALM) Programme[1] as part of their sentence. Most participants spoke positively about accredited programmes and most described the experience as worthwhile, although two of the men (Martin and Chris) in particular described the programme that they were required to complete as 'pointless' and 'not for me'. These negative perceptions of programmes will be discussed later, but most individuals suggested that the programmes had been beneficial, particularly with respect to developing personal agency. Typical responses included: 'The programme has helped me to see what I was doing was wrong', 'The programme has given me better knowledge' and 'The programme has helped me want to change'.

All of the men had a supervision requirement, and all had been supervised as part of the current sentence for a period of at least one month. Most (n = 16) were meeting with their supervising officer on a weekly basis at the time of interview. Most of the men spoke positively about their experiences of probation supervision, although many indicated that their initial perceptions were negative. This change in perception is, arguably, to be expected, and may even be indicative of desistance taking place. Almost all (n = 19) suggested that their supervising officers were trying to help them, and this was often linked to the aim of reducing offending behaviour, echoing earlier work in this area (Rex, 1999; Burnett, 2004; McCulloch, 2005).

The men valued honesty, openness, and reliability – also in keeping with existing research – and it was suggested by some individuals that sustaining desistance was an important means of demonstrating to their supervising officer that they valued the relationship. However, the interview data suggest that supervising officers are not important simply because they are 'friendly' and 'approachable', but that they were regarded as fulfilling an important role in the transition towards desistance. Many of the men also stated that probation supervision served a control or surveillance function, often remarking that part of the probation officer's role was to 'keep an eye' on the individual under supervision. Two of the men described probation in somewhat punitive terms, describing the sentences that they had received as being too harsh in proportion to the crimes that they had been convicted of. That said, even these men described the relationship with their supervising officer as being helpful and supportive.

The positive statements identified in the interviews may, of course, be the result of the selection effect of the study. Individuals who volunteered to participate in the interviews may be more willing to engage and participate in activities more generally. Furthermore, the men were recruited to participate in the study through their supervising officers, and it is possible that the supervising officers selected participants who would be more likely to speak positively about the experiences of probation. However, given that the sample broadly reflected national data and that the interview data echoed existing desistance research, it is suggested here that any possible selection effect was minimal. Moreover, given the assured nature by which the men highlighted negative aspects of probation where relevant, if these findings do represent the views of the most positive and engaged individuals under probation supervision, then the reality for many others might be rather bleak.

Probation – getting desistance going

Various aspects of the probation experience were highlighted as facilitating the desistance process. Generally, these related to enhancing an individual's agency or improving their personal skills. Many of the men stated that while they had been under probation supervision they had developed and improved their decision-making skills. For others, the experience of probation had empowered them to make changes in their lives, and this had helped them to develop their self-confidence. Some of the men also suggested that their experiences of probation supervision had helped them to develop an alternative sense of moral agency, whereby they had begun to think more about the consequences of their actions and how alternative courses of action might be more appropriate. All of the men commented that probation had encouraged them to envisage an alternative future, and some of the men suggested that this had given them a renewed outlook on their lives.

'Better information helps you make better decisions'

Many of the men stated that their decision-making skills had developed while they were under probation supervision. Those who had undertaken an accredited programme as part of their sentence, in particular, commented on their improved decision-making, and these men all stated that they felt more confident and more positive about the future and their ability to desist. Several of the men who had undertaken a programme element in their sentence suggested that active engagement in the sessions was important in order to ensure that they received the benefits from the programme. Tom, for example, described how performing role-playing games in some of the sessions he attended had helped to improve his decision-making skills:

> House games, as it were. Roles. One be the husband, one be the wife. Both drive, say, but the wife takes the car to go to the mother, but the other kid needs picking up later on, can you pick him up. So you think about going to the pub about two o'clock, you have four or five pints, then you pick up your kid at four, so you've got your own kid, plus other kids on the road, and you're putting lives in danger. You've got to substantiate why you went to the pub, and you can't. And it plays on your mind, and everything they've said is right. You've got no argument against it and after a few weeks it sticks....It's all to do with decisions. What you see, what you hear, and

what action you're going to take. So if a barman says leave your car keys, but you refuse cos you need your van for work the next morning. Nothing might happen, but something might happen, or you might get stopped in the morning. So it's all about making decisions.

(Tom)

Some individuals referred to improved decision-making skills in terms of having greater information, which then helped them to make better decisions. These men were referring to information in terms of having a greater awareness of the impact of their offending on victims and their families, and a greater understanding of the consequences of offending. For some of these men, the programmes that they had undertaken had not, in their eyes, fundamentally altered their character, but rather they had had a more nuanced effect upon their attitudes and behaviour:

I'm still the same person I was before I got in trouble and when I got in trouble, I've just got more information. I could still kick off and attack anyone at any minute, but I know the consequences, I know I won't stand to gain anything, and better information helps you make better decisions. That's what it is, I've got better information. Like I say, doing the IDAP's opened my eyes up, and I've got better information from doing it. I've learnt from it.

(Robert)

Several of the men also explained that their experience of one-to-one supervision had enhanced their decision-making skills. They explained that discussions during supervision sessions frequently involved the supervising officer presenting a hypothetical situation and asking the individual to consider a course of action and to reflect on the potential consequences of that action. The officer would also offer suggestions for alternative courses of action, which the individual would then consider in a similar way. Interviewees suggested that this was a helpful process as it enabled them to draw their own conclusions, rather than having ideas imposed upon them:

She'll ask me what I think I should do, I'll say something and then we'll talk about what might happen if I do that. It makes you think.

(Leroy)

To realise it yourself it's probably better because you can say, 'alright, this is a problem. I'm not sure how to deal with it, but it gives you something to work with'. You can then talk it through with others, get their opinions, take that on board, and work it through.

(Ben)

It was common for individuals who had a programme requirement to describe how their supervising officer would reinforce messages from the programme within one-to-one supervision sessions. This was identified as a useful way of exploring some of the programme messages in further detail:

> The IDAP's great. It does all different sessions about calming down....They help me out, and then I can come here and talk to [PO]. So we'll talk about what I've learned, what did I think about it, how am I going to use that, that sort of thing. Sometimes she'll ask me if there's a situation that I could use it in, or she'll give me an example of something that might happen and I have to come up with a way that I can use what I've learned, that sort of thing. It's good, cos I'm not just taking bits from the IDAP and saying, 'well, I don't need this, I don't need that', but [PO] is making me look at each bit and how it relates to me.
>
> (Charlie)

Improving decision-making skills was regarded as an important aspect of desistance. For some, this was because they would be less likely to reoffend if they were in similar situations to those in which they had previously offended. For others, having improved decision-making skills increased feelings of self-confidence and motivation, which made desistance appear to be more achievable.

'*It's about learning about yourself*'

Often individuals recited messages that they had learned during programme sessions, and spoke about the goals of the programme and what it would achieve. Assuming that these individuals were not simply repeating what had been said to them, this suggests that individuals internalise the messages that come from the programmes. Furthermore, it shows that individuals adopt the stated aims and objectives of the programme as their own, and incorporate them into wider objectives and courses of action in relation to desistance:

> It's about learning about yourself, why you did the things you did, and how to put them right. It's about recognising the signs of your temper building up, and doing something about it. You use a time-out, have a fag, nip outside, whatever, until you've calmed down.
>
> (Charlie)

Some individuals explained that they had been able to use some of the techniques that had been taught in the programmes, and that this had helped them during situations where offending had occurred in the past. As a result of becoming empowered by the programmes, therefore, some individuals were able to act differently and make better decisions in certain circumstances:

> I've tried [the technique] a few times and it does work. I've even used it with my friends, they had an argument just before Christmas and I said to

them, you go into that room and you go into that room and just take ten minutes to calm down and think about what you want to say, then come back and talk it through, and it works, it does work. So I'm learning and I'm passing that on to other people as well....They say it will keep getting better and better, so I'm just keeping it all in my head, take a time-out when I need one, and think positive.

(Ken)

Undertaking the programme elements of their sentences had clearly given some of the men a sense of empowerment, whereby they felt a greater sense of control over their lives and felt more equipped to make better decisions. This had also improved individuals' levels of self-confidence. Self-confidence was identified by many individuals as significant to the likelihood of sustaining desistance, which resonates with the work of Burnett (1992), who argued that desistance was more likely if individuals were motivated and optimistic. This also echoes Farrall's typology of orientations towards future offending (2002: 101). As it is now commonplace to regard desistance as a process rather than an event, it is reasonable to assume that sustaining confidence is more important than merely being confident at the beginning of the desistance journey. However, it might also be true to say that it is particularly important to be self-confident during the transitional phase of desistance, characterised as it often is by deep uncertainty, ambivalence and the stark juxtaposition of criminality and conformity. The interview data suggested that programmes help to develop agency by improving individuals' self-confidence, particularly with respect to being confident about the likelihood of not offending in the future:

SK: Do you think you might offend again in the future?

BEN: Erm. When I came out of prison I was unsure, I didn't want to reoffend, but I was unsure about the reasons why I offended in the first place....But doing the SOTP course, Sex Offender Treatment Programme, it gives you chance to explore emotions and feelings around that time. That really helped with my self-confidence issues, like I say I was really low when I first came out and that was a real problem for me. But doing the course, I've had chance to look at why I did what I did, and to talk it through with people has been good. It's made me more confident about the future.

Improving self-confidence was also related to the work undertaken during one-to-one supervision sessions. Individuals suggested that their confidence had increased through discussions with their supervising officer, and this was explicitly related to the likelihood of future offending:

What we talk about mostly is how I deal with day-to-day situations, trying to increase my independence, improve my self-confidence, because I've highlighted that as a problem. Because if I fall into a low mood state again, the danger is that I allow myself open to the suggestion of the sort of feeling I had for [victim]. So it's all about keeping myself motivated, independent, and full of confidence.

(Ben)

Therefore, the interview data suggested that there is a reinforcing relationship between decision-making skills, empowerment and self-confidence. Moreover, the men in the study indicated that the synergy between programmes and one-to-one supervision may provide the most effective means of developing these agentic factors. Where these two aspects of probation operated in close harmony the men appeared to have internalised the key messages and utilised them in the formation of their own desistance strategies. The interview data also showed that a positive relationship between programmes and one-to-one supervision could enhance moral agency. Moral agency, here, refers to the capacity of individuals to effect change in their own lives through a greater understanding of socially and culturally accepted moral practices (Sugarman, 2005).

'It ain't the right way to be'

Earlier it was suggested that changes in moral agency had an effect upon an individual's decision to desist, insofar as individuals reinterpret their past actions as being incongruent with newly acquired values and beliefs. The interview data showed that experiences of programmes impacted upon attitudes and values such that individuals regarded past actions as wrong and were keen to show their repudiation of them. Ken, for example, explained how he had felt after he had been sentenced:

I just couldn't get my head round how unfair it seemed, I mean if you're married everything should be 50–50 down the middle. So that's what got me so angry cos I just couldn't see how she could do that to me.

(Ken)

He then went on to explain how his experience of undertaking the programme and supervision elements of his sentence had altered his understandings of 'right' and 'wrong'. It is interesting to note how Ken suggested that at the time of the offence he believed that he was acting in a moral way:

But now, since seeing the IDAP and coming here [probation supervision], I can see where she was scared and where the kids were scared. It makes me feel bad now, cos in my eyes I was trying to do the right thing to get my stuff, but since going to IDAP I can see that the way I was going about doing that was scaring her and the kids. So it's been a bad patch, but I can see a way out now, I'm easing up a bit, and times come when I don't even think about it [aggression] at all, which is good cos I don't want to be like that no more, I don't consider myself a violent person and I don't want to be a violent person. It ain't the right way to be.

(Ken)

For Ken, therefore, the combination of the programme element and the supervision element had altered his moral agency, but for others supervision alone had been enough to effect changes in this regard. Some individuals explicitly identified changes that had occurred in this respect over time as a result of discussions with their supervising officer:

I must admit, when I first started coming here I weren't too bothered about what I'd done, it didn't bother me. [PO] would be talking about what I'd done, but it didn't really bother me. But after a while I did start to listen and I did start to think about it, and now I don't really like what I done. I'm embarrassed by it to be honest.

(Leroy)

Discussions about the impact of offending upon victims were often cited as helping to develop moral agency in this respect, but more general conversations were also identified as impacting upon an individual's reinterpretation of past actions. These conversations had led the individual to determine that past behaviour was incongruent with their moral agency, and incompatible with the life they wanted to lead. Both offending and offending-related behaviour had been reinterpreted as a result of conversations with supervising officers, as Josh explained when he spoke about his alcohol intake, which had been instrumental in much of his offending:

When you first start probation, she sat down and talks to you, she explains things, what they call tasks. She makes you look at life how it should be, like when you go out and get drunk. And you do things, and you look back and you think, what a dickhead. You're above a cloud and you think you're untouchable....After that I thought, yeah, there is life out there without getting pissed up every week, and driving cars without licences. I don't live like that anymore, and I won't go back. And she sees the changes that I've tried to make and she says, 'yeah, you've done well, keep it up' sort of thing.

(Josh)

Josh's quote also illustrates how supervising officers certified positive changes by offering encouragement and praise. Encouragement and a supportive nature are valued as important traits in supervising officers, evidenced both by the interview data and existing research (for example, Rex, 1999). However, certification in this respect is of greater significance than more general encouragement, as it is directed at particular actions that the individual has undertaken. Praising specific successes in this manner was something that a number of practitioners consciously tried to incorporate into supervision sessions:

I think one thing that everyone needs to take on board is, okay these cases have all got something wrong in their lives, something they need to change, but they've also got a lot of positive things going for them and if you just keep droning on and on about them, then obviously it is going to pull them down, whereas I quite like to … identify the positive things and kind of just praise the things that are going well as well. I think it's nice for them to hear that, because quite a lot all they've heard in their lives is negative comments all the time, I know two of them who've never had any positive comments from either school or family et cetera, so to kind of give them that praise from time to time I think is nice for them to hear.

(PO2)

This practitioner also spoke about the importance of recognising success not only in dichotomous reoffending terms, but also in terms of gradual improvements over time:

One of my cases has regular drug testing and he produced a positive test the other day but out of the last six months that he's been released from prison he's only produced two positive tests, and compared to what it would've been a couple of years ago, I praised him and said yes you have produced a positive test but that's two out of a very long period of time, which compared to the past you would have been producing probably a positive test every week. Obviously we don't encourage them to have positive tests, but I think he needed reminding that he's doing well by not producing a positive for a very long time.

(PO2)

This approach to probation supervision clearly reflects much desistance research, with a focus on gradual reductions in offending and offending-related behaviours, positive messages about success, and certification of progress and change. Therefore, probation supervision can be seen to help individuals to effect changes in their own lives through developing greater understandings of what is good. This, then, enables individuals to develop a future orientation based around more meaningful life goals.

'She's helped me to see that I can have a future, a different future'

A future orientation can have a positive effect on the desistance process (Burnett, 2000; Farrall, 2002), and successful desistance may be more likely where individuals have a plan and feel able to enact it (Maruna, 2001). While a more general positive future outlook may help individuals arrive at a decision to desist, a more specific understanding of future plans and life goals may be required in order to sustain desistance. Indeed, confidence and motivation alone are likely to be inadequate to sustain desistance (Burnett, 2004), and it is likely that individuals will require a greater understanding of who they want to become and how to get there. The most prominent theme in the interview data with respect to probation experiences was the notion that supervising officers helped individuals to contemplate the future and consider strategies for sustaining desistance. Practitioners indicated that this was the approach they employed during the early stages of the supervision process:

> One of the first things I do with my cases is identify what they want to do, or where they want to be in five years time, which is normally always going to be a long-term goal, but then encourage them to set smaller short-term goals.
>
> (PO2)

This is indicative of the collaborative approach to probation supervision that appeared to exist for all of the men in the study. When discussing experiences of probation, all of the men, to a greater or lesser extent, suggested that one-to-one supervision included an element of developing future goals:

> SK: Could you tell me any plans you have for the future?
> JOHN: What I want to do in the new year, it might sound a bit cheesy, but one of the sessions in [probation supervision] was about me writing a plan for what I want to do for the year, like a planning lesson. Like get a job what I know can take me through the year, maybe into next year.

The men in the study explained that these discussions had helped them to envisage alternative future life goals, which did not involve offending or offending-related behaviours. They also suggested that self-confidence and self-efficacy had increased following such discussions with their supervising officer:

> She's helped me to see that I can have a future, a different future, not falling back on drink, not getting into trouble, offending and what-have-you. And, erm, I've got a different outlook on life now, cos of her helping me to see things differently really, and it's good, I'm making different decisions, I'm making things better for myself, and it's from talking with [PO] really what's done that.
>
> (Nath)

While some individuals were able to conceive of future objectives without prompting from their supervising officers, many were reliant upon their officer to suggest possible objectives that would help them to make changes in their lives. In some cases these objectives related to drinking or drug taking (notably for Tom, Dean, Alan, Kev, Charlie and Kurt). Most often, however, proposed objectives tended to be related to employment, relationships, or living arrangements. These objectives were discussed in the previous chapter, where it was shown that individuals clearly associated the achievement of these goals with the increased likelihood of desistance. However, in discussions about probation supervision, it became clear that, for some individuals, objectives were directly suggested by the supervising officer:

> Right, in one of the sessions we done she said to me, 'where do you want to be in a year's time?' And I said, 'I dunno, really. Not here!' And she said to me, 'well, you could be in a job, earning some money on a regular basis, and you could be living in a flat of your own'. I thought, yeah that sounds good. So, that's what we'll look at.

(Kurt)

This is not to argue that practitioners should not suggest objectives, or help to construct future plans, for their cases. Indeed, these factors have been shown to increase the likelihood of desistance, so the fact that practitioners are under taking this kind of work with Probationers is a positive message for those who would argue that probation should retain a rehabilitative dimension. However, discussions about how these objectives might be realised appeared to be largely absent from supervision sessions, which meant that individuals were more likely to have to formulate projects to achieve their goals on their own, which the following section explores in further detail.

Probation – stopped in their tracks

While the interviews revealed that probation supervision and programme requirements had helped individuals to develop a range of personal skills and agentic factors, they also highlighted a number of factors relevant to the experience of probation that would likely constrain the transition towards desistance. Echoing previous research (Farrall, 2002), many of the men in the study indicated that they felt that probation was of little assistance in helping them to overcome practical difficulties that they were experiencing. However, while previous work has indicated that Probation Officers may feel reluctant to become involved in assisting with the resolution of practical difficulties, the interviews here revealed that supervising officers were more likely to refer individuals to external agencies for this type of assistance. The men in this study suggested that this raised more difficulties, rather than resolving existing ones. In part, supervising officers may be more likely to refer individuals to external agencies because of time constraints, and this was recognised by some men in the study as being a constraining factor in relation to achieving desistance. For these men it appeared that they felt a more intensive probation experience could increase the likelihood of desistance taking place. Others, by contrast, felt that their sentence was too onerous and that parts of their sentence were perceived to be irrelevant. In a similar vein, some men believed that within their experience of probation there was too much emphasis upon public protection and the negative criminogenic aspects of their lives.

'Talking, great, but getting stuff done, nothing'

The men in the study generally commented favourably upon the probation experience, and most of the men had commented that probation had helped them to develop various personal skills, such as decision-making and self-confidence. However, several individuals commented that supervision was less helpful in terms of helping them to overcome practical difficulties that they were experiencing. All of the men self-reported experiencing at least one problem. Most reported problems in relation to employment (n=14), or issues relating to finance/debt (n=12). Almost two-thirds (65 per cent) of the men self-reported experiencing three or more problems at the time of interview. Most of the men, however, indicated that probation was of little assistance in helping them to overcome these problems. While most individuals suggested that their supervising officer was 'friendly' or 'good to talk to', there was also a suggestion that they did not provide much practical assistance:

> She's good to talk to, I just wish she'd do a lot more for me. Like help out a bit more. Cos I've asked her a few times if she'd be able to help me, sort something out that'll help me get moved and that, help me get some ID and that. But she just says she can't do that. All she wants to do is talk about how I'm feeling, what I've been up to and that, but I say, 'look, I need help with this' and I get nothing. So, talking, great, but getting stuff done, nothing.
>
> (Brian)

This echoes Farrall's (2002) study on probation and desistance from crime. Farrall (2002) found that probation offered little assistance in the resolution of obstacles to desistance.[2] However, in my study some individuals did remark positively on assistance that they had received from their supervising officer. Where individuals did make reference to practical support from supervising officers, this tended to involve relatively menial tasks such as form-filling, telephone calls, letter writing, and so forth. However, this is not to devalue the importance of such support, as individuals clearly stated that these tasks were significant and that, without assistance, they would have been a burden on time and finances. Further, they could act as a barrier to desistance, particularly in the early stages of transition when it is less likely for individuals to be fully committed:

> They've been a big help. With all the phone calls they've made for me, it would've cost me a bomb if I tried to do it myself! So they've been very supportive to me getting these things sorted. If I had any hair I'd've pulled it out by now!
>
> (Dean)

Therefore, while some of the men in the study remarked that probation was of little assistance in helping them to overcome problems, others indicated that probation could provide some practical support to help individuals to help themselves. However, many of the men stated that they had been referred to external agencies for help in resolving problems, and this was verified in the interviews with supervising officers.

'You're getting pushed from one side to another'

The men had described their strategies for desistance, and this had entailed various objectives primarily in relation to relationships, living arrangements and employment. It became clear in the interviews that often these strategies were collaboratively produced within the probation supervision experience, if not suggested directly by the supervising officer. The men in the study were able to identify various obstacles to the achievement of these objectives, and it appeared that little practical assistance was forthcoming within the supervision experience. Rather, it was more common for individuals to be directed to external agencies for assistance:

> SK: So you've mentioned to [PO] that you want to get a job, right?
> JOHN: Yeah.
> SK: And have you discussed it any further with her?
> JOHN: No, basically she just said, 'I can set up a meeting with APEX', who are there to help you find work, so we ain't really spoken about looking for work or how I'm going to do it or whatever, that's what APEX is there for.

It was clear from exchanges such as this that some of the men were clearly under the impression that the responsibility for providing assistance to overcome problems rested with external agencies. Individuals were most often referred to external agencies to provide assistance in relation to employment and accommodation, although there were some examples in the data of referrals to external assistance with regard to alcohol or drug misuse problems. Most individuals who had experience of external agencies suggested that they were unimpressed by the service that was offered. Some individuals complained that there was a lack of clarity, understanding or knowledge regarding rights and responsibilities, particularly in relation to the disclosure of criminal history information. These individuals had suggested that some employment agencies provided unclear or inconsistent messages about what information the men had to provide about their criminal records when applying for jobs. One of the men (Ben) stated that he had been disappointed by the professionalism of the external agency he was referred to for employment assistance. Ben had described the first time that he had visited the employment agency and the nature by which he had been required to disclose information about his criminal history:

> It was the first time I'd disclosed my offence anyway, so I'm nervous anyway. As soon as I disclosed to him he said, 'could you just wait here?'

He left the room, went upstairs, and came back with three other people, but as he left he got someone else to come and sit with me … and one woman was the spokesperson and she said, 'because of the nature of your offence it won't be feasible', and so on, and I thought, 'it would've only took one of you, you know? This ain't no circus freak show, you know?' It only took one of them to say, 'look we know you're looking for work, looking to train, but it's not practical that you get your training here', and that would have been sufficient and fine. We could've all shook hands and walked away. There's no need to treat it like a circus. And being the first time I disclosed, it did really knock my confidence.

(Ben)

Other individuals stated that they had become frustrated and weary over the amount of time it had taken staff in external agencies to perform tasks, and that there was little attempt made to meet individual needs. The men and their supervising officers also suggested that there was a lack of communication between probation and external agencies. Collectively, these issues resulted in individuals feeling undervalued or neglected when they had been referred to external agencies, and some suggested that the experience of visiting various agencies had become somewhat burdensome:

You're getting pushed from one side to another. I mean, I know they [agencies] are professionals, but your PO knows your offence. I don't know whether they [other agencies] know what problems arise from having a criminal record or not, but I'm pretty certain they could work a bit closer. Rather than just saying, 'okay we've got these people to help you to find a job and that's that, you're dealing with them for that bit'. And going from place to place requires quite a bit of effort. And, like I say, I haven't had much joy with them, so I've tended to say, 'alright, I'll do this on my own'.

(Ben)

Practitioners, too, commented upon the lack of communication between agencies and the Probation Service, suggesting that it constrained their ability to work constructively as well as having a negative impact upon the person they were supervising:

It's very hard to get any information out of them [APEX]. They're quite difficult to get in touch with or make an appointment with for your case, so you end up having to send them along blind really. And then they'll arrange whatever they can with them, and it can come back on you, because you don't know what they're doing and they end up missing an appointment with you because they've got one with APEX or whoever, and really that's a warning for your case.

(PO5)

Some of the men had also experienced difficulties in trying to make contact with particular agencies, which had clearly left them feeling demotivated. Naz, for example, explained that he had tried to contact an agency he had been referred to for assistance with his accommodation:

> I went to see them last week and I was there from twenty past ten until the end of the day, and nobody came to see me. Then I was there again from about half nine until twelve-thirty and again, I saw nobody. We have no sofa, no nothing. If you want to talk to them, you can call from six in the morning until six in the evening and you will maybe, maybe, get to talk to someone. It's very difficult.
>
> (Naz)

Naz later explained that, as a result of his experience, he had decided not to try to improve his accommodation circumstances. For some, the assistance offered by external agencies did not appear to be responsive to their needs, and did not help the individual to overcome perceived barriers, in Charlie's case with respect to employment:

> SK: Have you had any help from probation in trying to find work?
> CHARLIE: Not directly from probation, but I went to a meeting with APEX, you know? Erm, they weren't really helpful to be honest; they were very friendly, but I don't think they really knew why I was there, it just seemed like they was trying to tell me about having a criminal record, not really talking about how to get a job or helping me find a job or whatever. I came out of it thinking, 'that was a waste of time', so I never went back, I just thought, 'I'll sort this out on my own'.

Further, the data suggested that some individuals had relatively low expectations prior to visiting external agencies for assistance, anticipating that they would receive minimal support. Ryan, for example, had a forthcoming appointment with an employment agency:

> I don't really know what it'll be like, I don't know what it's all about. But I'll give it a go. I'll go along and see what it's all about. But I won't hang around if it's shit. If it's shit I'll do something else.
>
> (Ryan)

Initially, this may suggest that individuals believe external agencies to be of little assistance because they approach situations with a negative mentality, a form of self-fulfilling prophecy. This may suggest that poor outcomes, with respect to assistance from external agencies, is influenced by personal agency, insofar as it is individual choice that determines whether to engage with, and when to disengage from, the agency. However, the interview data suggested that past experience of agencies had been unhelpful, and this had influenced their definition of the situational context, as Ryan suggested in relation to his interview:

I've been waiting for the Job Centre to set this [interview later that day] up. I was meant to have one before, but when I got there no-one had heard anything of me, so that was a waste of time. If they mess me around like that again I won't bother with them no more. It's daft really. A waste of my time, especially if I'm walking all the way from [AREA].

(Ryan)

Therefore, Probationers are frequently referred to external agencies for practical assistance to overcome or manage problems, and to remove barriers to desistance. Largely this is a corollary of the time constraints and bureaucratic pressures faced by practitioners, and the emerging inclination towards utilising external agencies to assist Probationers. However, the interview data reveal a number of factors which limit the extent to which agencies help individuals to overcome certain difficulties. This is likely to have a negative effect upon transitions towards desistance, not least because particular structural barriers to desistance remain in place. The data suggested that individuals' experiences of agencies are detrimental to self-confidence and motivation, and that individuals are more likely to resort to past experience and pre-existing understandings of social contexts in order to achieve particular objectives.

'*Okay then, same time next week okay?*'

The proclivity towards referring individuals to external agencies may be the result of the expansion in partnership-working within the criminal justice system over the past two decades (Glendinning *et al.*, 2002; Gough, 2010; Pycroft, 2010), and the gradual shift towards greater emphasis upon private and Third Sector involvement in the delivery of criminal justice interventions (Tarry, 2006; Corcoran, 2009, 2011; Hill, 2010; Ledger, 2010; Cabinet Office, 2011; Collins, 2011a, 2011b; Fox and Albertson, 2011; Hogg and Baines, 2011; Nicholson, 2011). The tendency towards using external agencies may also be a collateral result of the limited amount of time spent in one-to-one supervision with each individual. Discussions of experiences of probation during the interviews led towards an exploration of the content and scope of conversations during one-to-one sessions. Many men indicated that these conversations were often brief and restricted to a limited range of topics. Often the focus was upon activities between supervision sessions, as opposed to any meaningful discussions about future objectives and strategies to achieve them. Naz, for example, explained that he wanted to go to college in order to train to be a car mechanic, but that he was not sure how he would achieve this. He was asked whether he had discussed this with his supervising officer:

SK: Is that something you've spoken with [PO] about?
NAZ: Er, no.
SK: How come?

NAZ: Actually because there are so many things to talk about that we don't have time. She asks me about everything. She asks me about my friends, my girlfriend. Every little thing. What I've been doing, where I've been, every little detail. I have to tell her everything about what I'm doing every day. She's asking me if I'm getting into any trouble. There's no time to talk about anything else.

The quote from Naz suggests that discussions about future objectives and how they could be achieved were adversely affected by the length of one-to-one supervision, and the priority afforded to the content of each discussion. Of course, it is important that supervision sessions explore individuals' activities inbetween each meeting, as this would serve a vital function both in terms of monitoring each individual's progress throughout their sentence and also in terms of aiming to ensure public protection. Discussions of future objectives, particularly where these may be of a more long-term nature, should not preclude discussions of more day-to-day activities in the present or more immediate future. Indeed, during the early transitional stage of desistance it may be highly important to attend to day-to-day issues, as individuals are likely to experience substantial uncertainty and conflict between their emotions and personal and social contexts during this phase of the desistance process. The transitional phase is, for many individuals, likely to be chaotic and confusing, so long-term objectives and future strategies will be irrelevant in this context if individuals cannot navigate the trials of day-to-day living. Regular one-to-one supervision sessions within probation are highly important for this reason.

The interviews revealed, however, that the duration and scope of supervision sessions varied considerably, both between individuals and also for each individual on a week-by-week basis. Individuals suggested that supervision sessions could vary from five minutes to over an hour:

It does vary. Sometimes it's just, 'hello', 'hello', 'is everything okay?', 'yeah, fine', 'work going well?', 'yeah, great', 'okay then, same time next week okay?', 'yeah, see you then'. Literally, five minutes. But other times, like I say, you might have more to talk about, or [PO] might have a task she wants us to work through, or we might have to talk about the IDAP, and then you might be here for half an hour or so.

(Chris)

This may indicate that the duration of supervision is driven by the demands which arise week by week, or where there is an appropriate link to other sentence requirements, such as the timing of accredited programmes. Practitioners suggested that the time they could spend with their cases was more dependent upon the amount of paperwork that they had to complete. Also, it was apparent that supervision sessions were explicitly linked to targets, and that meeting these targets was given greater credence than the work that was actually undertaken within the session:

[AREA] is really high-performing and the focus of work in [AREA] is actually about meeting your targets and completing all your paperwork, and if you only spend ten minutes with your clients then you do....I mean there's targets across the board because they're national targets, but in [AREA] they up the ante so national standards say that you only have to see a high-risk case once a week, in [AREA] we have to see them twice a week. It's about visibility of the Service, doing something to protect the public virtually. If you see someone twice a week for maybe ten minutes one session, what benefit is there from seeing them in that second appointment? When actually I could've spent longer with them in the first appointment and done some really good quality work, rather than trying to squeeze in more appointments in the week. I don't really see any benefit to doing that, other than it looks good on paper.

(PO1)

In this respect, the supervising officers who participated in the study believed that the limited time spent in one-to-one supervision was the consequence of bureaucratic pressures at the organisational level. The necessity to meet targets clearly curtailed the amount of time available to spend with individuals, and while none of the practitioners stated that they referred to external agencies in response to this, it is possible that some practitioners would be more likely to utilise external agencies if they felt that the individual needed more support. The rationale behind such bureaucracy and targets, from the practitioners' perspective, was to provide a signal that the Probation Service was acting to protect the public. Clearly there is a public protection dimension to the work undertaken in probation, and this may be manifested in so-called tougher community penalties and a focus upon negative criminogenic factors in the individual's life.

'She ain't got any right to judge me like that'

Some of the men clearly felt that the focus upon negative factors had a detrimental effect upon their experiences of probation, and supervision sessions in particular. Some individuals suggested that they had felt at times as though they were being judged, or that their supervising officer was sceptical of the responses that they provided. This had the effect of discouraging the individual from talking openly with their supervising officer, and also damaged the relationship between them. Although it is impossible to tell from this research, it is also reasonable to assume that for some individuals this could lead to a self-fulfilling prophecy, or what has been referred to as the 'looking-glass self-concept' (Maruna *et al.*, 2004), which could lead individuals back to offending:

I thought she was just mental, she used to say: 'You're negative, you're this, you're that, you've got a bad attitude.' And I used to think, she ain't got any right to judge me like that. And that's what it felt like, like I was being judged. She might be my PO, she might be here to help me, but she's not helping me, she's making me worse.

(Raj)

A certain degree of conflict between the need to balance public protection and a desire to facilitate desistance is, perhaps, to be expected, and individuals will need to challenge previous attitudes and behaviours as part of both the probation and desistance processes. However, it is possible that individuals may find this to be particularly difficult during the early transition towards desistance, where individuals may respond more defensively to challenging approaches. Practitioners frequently raised the issue of balancing the demands of public protection and law enforcement against objectives of facilitating desistance. The need to balance public protection with attempts to effect change can lead to conflicting messages for the Probationer, and uncertainty about the nature of the officer-offender relationship. Public protection is a fundamental aspect of the wider risk management agenda that has emerged in probation, and elsewhere, in recent decades, and the potential for risk management and rehabilitation ideologies to coexist within the Probation Service has been discussed elsewhere (Robinson, 1999). This is not to argue that risk and rehabilitation are incompatible, but rather to draw attention to a site of conflict specifically in relation to desistance, one which practitioners are charged with the responsibility of reconciling:

I think boundaries are really important, enforcing the boundaries definitely. And obviously it's part of our role, law enforcement, so we do have to do that. But at the same time the relationship's really about trying to facilitate change, so there are certain boundaries and enforcement procedures that have to take place, but essentially I'm trying to work with that person so that they can make changes in their life ... but sometimes you're the only person that they have ever opened up to or that's been consistent in their lives, so it is a sort of funny relationship really because you have such a big part in someone's life for quite a period, you talk about really personal things, and sometimes it's really hard for them....It's really hard, because we do really dig deep and ... I don't think it's often clear, and it's obviously not clear to me, but I don't think it's clear to them what our relationship is supposed to be.

(PO1)

The emphasis upon risk management and public protection also impacted upon other aspects of practitioners' work, in addition to the relationship between officer and offender. There was a definite sense that practitioners felt constrained by the prominence of risk management in their role, in terms of both bureaucratic pressures and public and media attitudes towards risk:

It is at the back of our minds. We're all just so worried about ending up in the papers, you just do everything you can to cover your back, and it's only after you've done that, that you can start to think about anything else.

(PO4)

When we do the reassessments, more often than not you won't lower the risk of harm, cos you don't want to be in a position where you've said, 'he's less of a risk now', if he goes out and commits a serious crime.

(PO5)

'It's good for the people that need it, but not for me'

The emphasis upon public protection may also be manifested in the sentence requirements that individuals had to complete. Some of the men felt that the demands placed upon them as part of their sentence were irrelevant or unduly restrictive. Two of the men – Martin and Chris – suggested that their programme requirements were of little value. Chris explained that he did not actively participate in the group sessions on his programme as he did not believe that it was relevant to him. He was also keen to distance himself from others on the programme:

I don't really have much input, cos I don't really think I should be there. I'm not like the other people in there, with me it was a mistake, I know what I did was wrong, it won't happen again, it's not for me. It's good for the people that need it, but not for me.

(Chris)

Thus, Chris did not identify any meaningful outputs from the programme, as he perceived it to be irrelevant and he defined the programme as being intended for more serious offenders. In Martin's case, he did not regard the programme he was about to undertake as worthwhile due to his past experience of other interventions that had been intended to challenge his behaviour:

I don't want to do it, I don't think I need it. I've done courses like this before and it don't do nothing, there's no point to it. She says I need help with my anger and that, but I've changed, I'm not like that no more....But if I don't do it I go back to jail, I'll breach, so I have to do it! I've done courses like this before and it doesn't do nothing, I still think the same and do the same, but obviously I'm going to have to do what she suggests or it's back to jail.

(Martin)

One supervising officer offered an explanation for the apparent lack of engagement among some individuals on one programme in particular, the Integrated Domestic Abuse Programme (IDAP):

> [The course] is intensive, it challenges the individual in their own domestic environment. A lot of the time they don't see themselves as an offender or a criminal because that's what they've done for years, some of them, and it's normal behaviour. So then when someone comes along and says, 'what you're doing is wrong, you need to change this, this and this', they tend to be a bit stand-offish.
>
> (PO5)

For these individuals, then, programmes were not defined as being integral to their desistance strategies, and this was reflected in their unwillingness to engage with the programme. Passive involvement in probation is unlikely to be enough to achieve a reduction in reoffending, and offenders are more likely to succeed if they are committed to the objectives of their probation supervision and are motivated to benefit from the various elements of their Probation Order (see Mason and Prior, 2008, on engaging young offenders). Only one individual, Nath, had experience of one-to-one preparation work with his supervising officer prior to the programme beginning. For Nath, this preparatory stage was valuable, both in terms of increasing his engagement with the programme and with respect to offering him some knowledge of what the course entailed prior to its beginning:

> Erm, you know I'd got a good understanding of what the course was about before I went there, whereas some chaps went there completely blind. They didn't know what it were about and it was a bit of a shock when they realised what they were trying to teach us, basically. Whereas I'd done all this preparation with [PO] which was quite good. When I first got told I'd have to do this [IDAP] course I thought, 'you're kidding me? No thanks' sort of thing, you know? But doing the preparation work really helped me understand what it'd be like before I got there. It was a bit intense, but I'm glad she did all that preparation work with me.
>
> (Nath)

The importance of pre-programme work was also acknowledged by supervising officers. One practitioner suggested that it was possible to distinguish between individuals who had experienced pre-programme work, and those who had not:

> It's about getting them ready….I think it's really important work, I don't think they'd be ready, sometimes the programmes start early and you don't have chance to do the pre-programme stuff and you can tell the difference.
>
> (PO3)

However, such preparatory work occurs sporadically, which is largely a corollary of programmes running to fixed timetables, which means that the possibility of conducting pre-programme work is by virtue of there being enough time between the individual beginning their sentence and the next available date for a programme commencing for the preparatory work to take place. Further, this is driven by the target-oriented nature of contemporary probation practice, as one practitioner suggested:

> We're under a lot of pressure to get people started on [the programmes] as soon as possible. We do try to make sure people get the pre-programme work, but they're not always ready for it, and there often isn't enough time between them being sentenced and the start date.
>
> (PO4)

Programme targets also impact upon whether or not an individual would receive a programme requirement as part of their sentence, which was recognised as problematic by one practitioner:

> Where I used to work if we were recommending supervision we had to recommend a programme requirement as well unless the Assistant Chief Officer agreed it wasn't required, and that's two rungs above me. Here, they're looking into programmes at the moment, but it's better because they weren't picking holes if you weren't proposing a requirement, or if you were only proposing supervision, so it's better. But it looks like they are picking holes in that here now. Maybe that's something we're going to have to do here, I don't know.
>
> (PO1)

Practitioners discussed particular cases where the emphasis upon meeting targets for programme completions had had a detrimental effect upon the Probationer, although these did not relate to any individual in this sample. Some targets are competing, and a consequence of this is that some individuals receive, perhaps, unnecessarily burdensome sentences with numerous requirements. As a result, some individuals may be unable to complete all aspects of their sentence, because of the sheer volume of requirements:

> The problem is that when the cases are running they're quite intensive and fitting the programme dates and times around your case's other commitments can be quite difficult sometimes, and I've had to take some cases back to court for that reason, because they simply can't fit it all in.
>
> (PO2)

> I've got one guy, I've had to ask the court to take off his programme cos otherwise he'd be here or somewhere to do with probation every day of the week. I mean, it's ridiculous.
>
> (PO4)

As discussed earlier in this book, a plethora of targets has emerged in the criminal justice system more generally, and the Probation Service in particular, in recent years. In 2007–2008 the target for accredited programme completions was

17,319, which was surpassed by the National Probation Service (NPS, 2008: 10). Such targets can be of an arbitrary nature, that there is a clear distinction between objectives, priorities and objectives, and that the target-oriented culture of contemporary probation may create an unhelpful working environment for staff and Probationers (see also: Whitehead, 2007: 40–6). The interview data reflect this aspect of probation, suggesting that some individuals receive a programme requirement when it may not be entirely suitable and that it is principally the completion of the programme that is of interest, as opposed to the positive impact upon the individual subjected to it. This is not to argue that programmes are not worthwhile, or that they do not contribute towards the facilitation of desistance. The interview data clearly showed that for most individuals programmes are a positive experience. The data do suggest, however, that developing the Probationer's engagement is a crucial aspect of probation practice.

It is not intended that this chapter be read as an evaluation of probation or any particular aspects of probation, including supervision, accredited programmes, or the work carried out by external agencies. The emphasis here has been specifically upon the relationship between probation practice and desistance from crime, rather than exploring the more general role of probation or individual attitudes towards it. The focus is, instead, upon individuals' experiences of various aspects of probation in relation to their attempts to desist from crime. The interviews revealed that probation facilitated the transitional phase of desistance by enhancing individuals' agency, but that there was little assistance in terms of resolving problems. Where practical assistance was offered this tended to be of a more menial nature, or in the form of a referral to an external agency. Individuals were generally critical of the assistance they received from external agencies, often identifying particular causes of their dissatisfaction. This frequently resulted in the individual stating that they would attempt to overcome particular difficulties on their own.

Certain changes to the organisation and structure of probation in recent years have restricted the functional ability of practitioners to provide practical support, and limited the amount of time that could be spent with each case. This leaves a number of structural barriers to desistance largely unaffected, and it also leads to a situation whereby individuals adopt certain objectives but are left with little guidance with respect to how to achieve them. The consequence of this is that individuals tend to shift towards an iterational orientation of agency, such that past repertoires of thought and action inform the projects that individuals would dedicate themselves to. In other words, individuals become more likely to rely upon past experiences of action as a blueprint for future activity, at least partly because of the inability of practitioners to deliver a more individualised service.

9   Active agents and social contexts

The interview data provided an insight into the prospective viewpoints of individuals seeking to move away from crime. They allowed for an exploration of intended strategies for sustaining desistance, and the identification of perceived challenges that individuals may face along the way. Moreover, the interviews offered an insight into how individuals anticipated reacting to such challenges if and when they should arise. In doing so, the interview data have shown that individuals in the transitional phase of desistance are 'active agents' in considering the possibility of change, in considering objectives to achieve change, and in planning how to achieve those objectives (see also Simmonds, 1989). Various structural factors condition would-be desisters to consider a particular type of conformity to which they aspire, and this stems, in part, from the role of probation in proposing future objectives. However, past structures furnish individuals' present situational contexts with constraining factors that they perceive will inhibit their commitment to these objectives. This chapter examines how individuals consider desistance and how they aim to achieve it in light of the social context within which they find themselves. In doing so, this chapter offers an account of the role of human agency in the transitional phase of desistance.

Agency is frequently juxtaposed to structure and is, therefore, often considered to involve free will. It is something that is unique to human beings who, through an interplay of knowledge, intention and adjustment, are able to choose between various courses of action: 'By nature, humans are flexible and adjusting. Human action is driven by reason; animal behaviour by causes. Humans have free wills; they can always do otherwise or nothing' (Fuchs, 2002: 26). Even in doing nothing, individuals may make a conscious decision to do so. However, agency is more complex than choosing a particular course of action (Elster, 1989). Individuals may choose one course of action even though an alternative was available, but this does not account for why or how they came to settle on that particular course of action. Likewise, individuals may make adjustments, alter plans, or change courses of action altogether, but again this does not offer any insight into the underpinning processes which led the individual to this. In order to more fully understand the nature of human agency in the transitional phase of desistance, a more comprehensive understanding of agency is required.

The interview data from this study indicate how individuals in the transitional phase reflexively consider their social contexts in light of determining particular objectives that they believe would enable them to sustain desistance. There are various structural turning points to which individuals demonstrated some attachment, and various life-course events which appeared to be relevant to the men in the study. This is important because in the absence of such relevance it is unlikely that the event or turning point would be as effective in helping to secure the move away from crime (Farrall, 2002; Haigh, 2009; Serin and Lloyd, 2009). In this respect, the men in the study were seeking to transform particular aspects of their lives. Emirbayer and Mische (1998) argued that there are different temporal orientations of agency, and that, depending on the particular orientation of an individual at a given time, the socio-structural context within which the individual operates may either be reproduced or transformed. They defined agency as:

> the temporally constructed engagement by actors of different structural environments – the temporal-relational contexts of action – which, through the interplay of habit, imagination, and judgement, both reproduces and transforms those structures in interactive response to the problems posed by changing historical situations.
>
> (1998: 970)

Agency is, therefore, the capacity of individuals to respond to problematic situations and, in relation to this, the ability of individuals to alter their temporal orientations and thus reproduce or transform their social contexts (Biesta and Tedder, 2006a: 11). Further, Emirbayer and Mische (1998) argued that there should be greater exploration of transformative agency. This is clearly relevant to the study of early desistance as individuals who are encountering this transitional stage are likely to face problematic situations. It is also relevant as it can enable an exploration of how individuals prospectively approach the task of sustaining desistance in the long-term. The existing literature clearly shows that individuals will need to overcome challenging circumstances if they are to successfully desist, and an exploration of desistance which incorporates this conceptualisation of agency can provide an insight into how individuals approach such tasks.

The perspective outlined here contends that agency involves the capacity to exert influence over an individual's social context, and possibly alter the trajectory of their life-course. Emirbayer and Mische (1998) argued, however, that agency should be understood as being three-dimensional: that is, that agency refers to the past, orients towards the future, and engages with the present. They call this distinction the 'chordal triad of agency' (1998: 970), and argued that the importance of recognising these agentic dimensions is 'that agentic processes can only be understood if they are linked intrinsically to the changing temporal orientations of situated actors' (1998: 967). Crucially, these orientations are only analytical distinctions and each is present within all action, although not in equal measure, and to understand agentic processes necessitates an understanding of the interplay between these dimensions, and how the interplay varies according to the structural context of action (Biesta and Tedder, 2006b: 3). The orientations of agency that Emirbayer and Mische (1998) referred to are the iterational, the projective, and the practical-evaluative. It is argued here that individuals may alter their temporal orientation to agency in relation to the future objectives and the circumstances of their social contexts at particular moments in time. A positive sense of self, whereby the individual believes that they are making progress towards achieving their goals, and a social context that includes enabling structural properties, may be more likely to lead to a projective dimension of agency, leading to innovation on the part of the individual.

Projective agency – making the transition towards desistance

There is some evidence to suggest that individuals can 'desist by default', by seeking out life-course changes, without ever intending to desist or committing to it (Laub and Sampson, 1993). This explanation of the desistance process contends that such life-course changes will gradually steer the individual away from criminal activity, either by reducing time spent with delinquent peers, limiting criminal opportunities, or increasing the individual's stake in society. However, there is also much evidence which indicates that individuals are more active in the process of deciding to desist and formulating intended future actions on the basis of such a decision (Burnett, 2000; Maruna, 2001; Serin and Lloyd, 2009). Such an approach contends that desistance is constructed, at least in part, by the would-be desister themselves. The individual plays an active role in reproducing or transforming certain aspects of their personal and social contexts, with the intention of changing their life in order to sustain desistance.

The findings from this study support the latter of these perspectives on desistance from crime. The interviews revealed several agentic themes within discussions of the decision to cease offending and strategies designed to sustain desistance. This was somewhat in contradistinction to existing findings in relation to individuals' experiences of the early stages of desistance. Healy and O'Donnell (2008), for example, found that primary desisters in their sample, while highly motivated to change, were ambivalent about the process of desistance and that the '"language of agency" appeared to be lacking' (2008: 34). Rather, the men in the present study generally demonstrated high levels of self-confidence, an inclination towards developing alternative identities, and increased levels of moral agency and self-control. However, the men clearly did not maintain a consistent desistance narrative throughout the interviews, and they would, to a greater or lesser extent, interject with comments or statements which seemed to be more relevant to the maintenance of past patterns of behaviour.

The early stages of desistance mark a transitional phase between offending and desisting; it is a time when the individual is neither an offender nor an 'ex-offender' or 'reformed character'. The transitional phase of desistance is one where the individual is replacing a concern for the factors which sustain offending with a concern for factors which will sustain desistance. Given that past experiences, including historical structures, would condition individual action, including routine activities, replacing offending-related factors with those which entail desistance is a considerable under taking for an individual to embark on. As such, it is reasonable to assume that early desisters would display only a tentative commitment towards the process of desistance, and this may account for any contradictions or ambivalence in the interviews.

The present study employed a wider range of subjective-level factors than has been used in previous studies of desistance (Maruna, 2001; Healy and O'Donnell, 2008; Healy, 2010), and this offered an alternative insight into the phenomenon of the transitional phase of desistance. The men in this study were keen to articulate that they felt in control of their decisions to desist and the initial transitions away from offending. This was, perhaps, most clearly evidenced by participants' expressions of self-confidence and self-efficacy, insofar as individuals expressed both the willingness and the perceived ability to achieve their desired outcomes. The present study also highlighted that several participants envisaged an alternative future identity. Often these were identified by early desisters as being, as Giordano *et al.* (2002: 1001) wrote, 'fundamentally incompatible with continued deviation'. The assumption of a new non-offender identity is central to the concept of secondary desistance (Maruna and Farrall, 2004), yet the interview data collected in this study suggested that individuals in the early stages of desistance may regard such an identity as a future objective which can facilitate the transition towards longer-term desistance. Clearly, there is an argument to be made that many offenders may envisage alternative future identities, but that this does not entail that they will be able to assume them. However, LeBel *et al.* (2008) argued that envisaging identities such as these future objectives, can help to avert problems that may occur during the desistance process. Indeed, they argued more generally that a strong sense of agency can work both positively and negatively: a sense of agency that is motivated and committed to desistance will help the individual to overcome difficulties and gain from life-course events, 'while a negative frame of mind leads to drift and defeatism in response to the same events' (2008: 155).

Therefore, it can be seen that the men in the study, to a greater or lesser extent, were open to the possibility of change and had considered the possibility of an alternative future. This is consistent with the projective orientation within the chordal triad of agency (Emirbayer and Mische, 1998). The projective dimension of agency 'is linked to the intention to bring about a future that is different from the present or the past' (Biesta and Tedder, 2006b: 3). Agency, therefore, involves more than merely repeating past actions, but instead entails that individuals are active in producing new possibilities of action. The projective dimension of agency is defined as the 'imaginative generation by actors of possible future trajectories of action, in which received structures of thought and action may be creatively reconfigured in relation to actors' hopes, fears, and desires for the future' (Emirbayer and Mische, 1998: 971). This aspect of agency has been neglected in many contemporary theories, although a number of authors have argued that individuals are capable of 'active agency' in effecting change. May and Cooper (1995: 77), for example, suggest that humans possess the capacity to 'resituate' themselves and transform various aspects of social activity. For Giddens (1998: 37), under conditions of late-modernity individuals must live in a more reflective manner, which can generate new possibilities of thought and action. However, these frameworks do not allow for the analysis of agency as leading to change (Emirbayer and Mische, 1998: 983 fn).

Drawing upon Mead's notion of 'distance experience', the projective dimension of agency explains how individuals are able to distance themselves from past repertoires of action, including the habits and traditions of social structures that constrain their identities and activities. It is this capacity for distanciation that allows for individuals to undertake new schemas of action and alter life-course trajectories, through the 'narrative construction' of future possibilities and their 'hypothetical resolution' prior to the actual execution of appropriate courses of action (Biesta and Tedder, 2006a: 14). These future possibilities encompass both 'strongly purposive ... goals, plans, and objectives' (Emirbayer and Mische, 1998: 984), and potentially more transient aspirations and desires.

The projective dimension of agency is, therefore, future-oriented as individuals 'construct changing images of where they think they are going, where they want to go, and how they can get there from where they are at present' (ibid.). Thus, the projective dimension of agency can be regarded as, 'an essential element in understanding processes of social reproduction and change' (ibid.: 991), and any adequate understanding of these processes needs to acknowledge 'the relevance and influence of future expectations' (Biesta and Tedder, 2006a: 15). There are five key components to projective agency. First, anticipation of future trajectories. Individuals will identify future possibilities, but these are informed by past knowledge, such as awareness of 'morally and practically appropriate courses of action' (Emirbayer and Mische, 1998: 989). Second, the construction of a future-oriented narrative, providing a roadmap, albeit mutable and incomplete, to follow. Third, the reconstruction of possible courses of action, allowing for creative and imaginative constellations of possible future trajectories. Fourth, the hypothetical resolution of future objectives with knowledge of past actions and behaviours, and understandings of what is morally and practically acceptable. Finally, the initial enactment of future projects. This may involve experimentation with particular courses of action, or a flirtation with possible future identities and social roles, without having to commit to them.

Laub and Sampson (2001: 51) argued that the desisters in their sample 'made a commitment to go straight without even realising it' and that certain roles altered 'short-term situational inducements to crime', while allowing for the development of 'long-term commitments to conformity'. The authors suggested that the men they studied were active in the desistance process, thus acknowledging the role of agency, yet they also argued that new identities emerge following investment in, and the realisation of a commitment to, particular social roles. The data analysed in the present study, however, shows that individuals envisage a new identity as a non-offender during the early stages of desistance *prior to* investing in a social role and, further, display a willingness to assume such an identity. This is illustrative of the projective orientation because individuals are generating possible future trajectories of action through a reflexive consideration of received structures. The received structures may be the possibility of a new social role, such as 'good father' or 'good partner', or a more general pro-social role.

It should be noted that Laub and Sampson's (2001) research reported findings from the narratives of long-term desisters who had assumed a non-offender identity and, moreover, that it is unknown how many of the men in the present study would make the transition to longer-term desistance. It should also be noted, however, that their research was conducted retrospectively, whereas the analysis presented in this study explored desistance prospectively. Therefore, it is possible that the men in Laub and Sampson's (2001) study envisaged a future non-offender identity, and then changed their identities over time as they gradually committed to particular social roles. Indeed, several of the would-be desisters in the present sample envisaged specific future identities that they wanted to assume. It is reasonable to assume that some of these men may, over time, develop long-term commitments to marriage or parenthood and assume the envisaged identities they referred to during the interviews.

Other men in the study did not appear to envisage alternative identities, but they did suggest that they wanted to make changes to their personal and social contexts. Often this involved distancing themselves from delinquent peers. While this type of transition towards desistance might not involve the envisaging of an alternative future identity, it is possible that a new identity could emerge over time as a result of a change to the structure of the individual's social relationships. As Baumeister (1994: 283) argued: 'When all of one's social relationships remain constant, personality change is considerably more difficult, because people tend to assume that others' personalities will remain stable and consistent.' Therefore, it is reasonable to assume that (accounting for other desistance-related factors, such as sustained motivation and social bonds to work or family) the individual might gradually assume the new identity of non-offender. This proposition may appear to be aligned with Laub and Sampson's (2001) argument that desisters gradually adopt an identity of non-offender following a series of 'side-bets'. However, the findings from the present study also show that early stage desisters create the structures that allow for the development of longer-term desistance as a result of their own agency. Projective agency is evident here in the individual's determination to distance themselves from past repertoires of thought and action. Although the individual might not yet have a purposive future to commit to, they do demonstrate some commitment to wanting to move away from crime and a desire to leave behind past habits and activities. This agency is evident in Ryan's decision to cut ties with his previous peer group. He did not have a clear future pathway in mind, but he did show some determination to leave behind his past. This indicates that he made a choice from a set of possible courses of action which is 'the central point that is implied in all definitions of agency' (Hays, 1994: 64). The argument that Ryan chose from a range of possibilities is reinforced by John's assertion that he would not cut ties with his peer group, despite his awareness that they were, at least partly, culpable in his offending.

While projective agency is future-oriented, and entails a substantial degree of creativity and imagination, the received structures that individuals operate within may also have a constraining effect upon their deliberations. The choices that are available to individuals are limited by the range of structurally provided opportunities, and it can be argued that structure creates the agency that appeared to be evident in the interviews with early desisters. Both Ryan and John had served custodial sentences, they were of a similar age, and neither wanted to reoffend as they expected that they would be returned to prison. Thus, the structural deterrence of prison prompted a re-evaluation of their involvement with offending and this, in turn, encouraged each to consider how they would make the transition towards desistance. John appeared to be more confident about the possibility of gaining employment; he suggested that he was willing and able to move away from his locality, and stated that he wanted to start a family. Ryan, by contrast, had few job prospects and, instead, seemed to be almost resigned to claiming benefits, in the short-term at least. He also stated that he was unable to move away from his area, and was unwilling to start a family. For Ryan, therefore, the future did not seem to include as many opportunities or possibilities as some of the men in the study, and this was reflected in his rather more limited discussions about his future intentions.

Thus, the situational context of two different individuals had furnished each with a different range of possible courses of action, yet each was able to display agency in making the initial transition towards desistance and, therefore, trying to effect change in their lives. Moreover, while each was presented with a range of structurally provided opportunities (however limited they may have been), the origin of their decision to desist could be found in the structural effect of incapacitation. Indeed, this was the case for several participants (notably: Ryan, John, Leroy and Josh), yet other structural factors could also be identified in the interview data which triggered particular displays of agency.

Echoing existing literature (Shover, 1983; Burnett, 1992), it was found that for some men the threat (perceived or real) of longer custodial sentences also prompted a decision to desist, and increases in the risk of harm from offending had a similar effect. Changes to the nature of relationships also triggered particular displays of agency among early desisters, particularly where family members provided a supportive environment. This also resonates with McNeill's (2009) suggestion that desistance-focused interventions should encourage engagement with families of origin, and with the evidence from the wider desistance literature which suggests that family formation can facilitate longer-term desistance (Horney *et al.*, 1995; Laub and Sampson, 2003). However, it is argued here that relationship changes can act as a structural trigger for particular aspects of agency that facilitate the initial transition towards desistance. As family members show support and encouragement, individuals may respond in an agentive manner by making particular decisions that initiate the transition towards desistance. Finally, some participants suggested that structural changes to the nature of their accommodation experiences had acted as a trigger for them to move away from crime, eliciting displays of self-confidence, motivation and a desire to desist. It is these changes to the immediate environment that the men lived in which altered the way in which they regarded their futures. The changes enabled them to consider alternative trajectories and possibilities of future action, social roles and identities.

Thus, the data presented here indicate that structural changes both prompt individuals to make decisions to desist, and provide the impetus for projective agency to emerge, which enables individuals to make the initial transition towards desistance. These structural factors, therefore, 'offer the very possibility of human choice' (Hays, 1994: 65). The forms of agency displayed by the participants in the present study did not emerge from nothing, but rather they are responses to particular situational contexts. Desistance transitions, therefore, are enabled by particular formations of social structure which prompt individuals to make a decision to desist and formulate strategies to sustain desistance. In doing so, early desisters also seek to change their situational context. For some this involves the envisaging of an alternative future identity to which they aspire, while others attempt to distance themselves from past habits of thought and action. This is the essence of projective agency.

Therefore, it is argued here that agency is highly relevant to the transitional phase of desistance, yet that such agency is only possible as a result of the enabling and constraining properties of particular social structures. In particular, the transition towards desistance can be facilitated by improvements to relationships, which resonates with McNeill's (2009) recommendation that desistance-focused interventions should involve the family of origin, and through interventions that target individuals' moral agency. Finally, the data presented here has shown that the transition towards desistance can be fostered by empowering individuals to undertake the transition themselves, and this can also emanate from one-to-one contact with supervising officers. The following section will explore how individuals make strategies to sustain their moves towards desistance.

From projective to practical-evaluative agency – strategies for sustaining desistance

Within the existing desistance literature there is much evidence to suggest that particular social factors can have a positive effect upon the desistance process (LeBel *et al.*, 2008). Indeed, the prototypical desistance journey may be one which involves the acquisition of sustainable legitimate employment, marriage, parenthood, and regular association in pro-social networks. It has also been suggested that desistance becomes more likely where individuals are able to overcome particular obstacles in their social contexts (Farrall and Calverley, 2006; McNeill *et al.*, 2011). Finally, the desistance literature has also provided evidence to suggest that desistance becomes more likely if individuals formulate plans and feel confident that they are able to achieve them (Burnett, 2000; Maruna, 2001). Following this, various authors have argued that desistance occurs as a result of a process, which begins with individuals being at least willing to consider the possibility of change, followed by a consideration of possible vehicles for change, the envisaging of and commitment to an alternative future, and finally the condemnation of past behaviours (Giordano *et al.*, 2002; Rumgay, 2004; Vaughan, 2007; Shapland and Bottoms, 2011). Research to date, however, has not meaningfully explored whether individuals construct strategies during the early stages of desistance which they would seek to enact and, if they do so, what the nature and content of such strategies might be.

The men in the present study were asked about their future plans, both in general terms and more specifically in relation to sustaining desistance. The aim was to explore how individuals explore desistance prospectively, reflecting the assertion within the 'chordal triad of agency' that agency involves an orientation towards the past, present and future (Emirbayer Mische, 1998). This was also to examine how individuals construct desistance strategies prospectively, rather than exploring retrospective accounts of how individuals were able to sustain desistance. Within existing studies of early desistance, it has been found that individuals are more likely to commit to intermediate social bonds which may lead indirectly towards longer-term desistance (Healy and O'Donnell, 2008). However, it was found in the present study that individuals were more agentic in considering how they might sustain their moves away from offending and offending-related behaviours.

The men were able to identify a number of barriers that they would need to overcome in order to sustain desistance, and were also able to highlight several positive changes that they wanted to make in their lives which would also support their attempts to desist. Several references were made to overcoming barriers in the areas of individuals' lives which have been highlighted in the recent literature (Farrall and Calverley, 2006; Raynor, 2007b; Byrne and Trew, 2008), including: employment; alcohol and drugs; accommodation; area of residence; family and relationships; and attitudes. In this regard, the men in the study demonstrated a certain degree of projective agency by considering what they would need to achieve in order to sustain desistance. This shows that the men had reflexively considered how they might begin to make the transition from a life which had led them to offending in the past, to a life which would preclude offending in the future.

Responses showed that the men perceived relationships (both positive and negative), living arrangements and employment to be the most significant factors in helping them to sustain desistance. Moreover, for many individuals, employment was perceived to be necessary to overcome other barriers, or achieve other objectives, in relation to sustaining desistance. Perhaps somewhat surprisingly, alcohol and drugs were not frequently cited as important factors that needed to be overcome, but this can be explained by the small proportion of the sample that were experiencing problems in this regard. Both Tom and Nath referred to themselves as alcoholics, and both regarded overcoming their drinking problems as a necessary and significant factor in sustaining desistance, yet there were few others who identified alcohol or drugs as obstacles. Thus, a range of structural factors were identified as being particularly important in relation to sustaining desistance.

Most participants related the structural barriers that they would need to overcome to previous social contexts that had led to involvement in offending, to future objectives, or to both. For example, many individuals spoke about social structural factors that had influenced their offending in the past, notably in relation to the neighbourhood they grew up in (as also suggested by Webster *et al.*, 2006) or family conflict (see also Loeber and Stouthhamer-Loeber, 1986; Graham and Utting, 1996). In turn, they stated that changes would need to occur in these areas of their lives if they were to sustain desistance. Many participants were also able to discuss why these social factors influenced their involvement in offending, most often related to environmental factors (high crime, drug use, unemployment), peer pressure, routines involving delinquent or antisocial behaviour, and a lack of stability in their lives. Similarly, many participants also spoke about why changes to certain structural factors in their social context would entail positive outcomes and help to sustain desistance. Often, particular changes were related to greater responsibility, increased independence and a stable lifestyle.

Thus, there appeared to be a range of subsidiary factors influencing the structural aspects that participants identified as needing to change in order to sustain desistance. The men, therefore, wanted to submit to certain structural changes in order to reduce their own risk of reoffending. Indeed, they variously stated that they wanted to settle down, move out of their neighbourhood, get a secure place to live, and find a 'proper' job. Moreover, responses suggested that these desired objectives are not simply 'hard-wired', normative goals, but rather that early desisters explicitly stated these objectives in relation to reducing their own risk of reoffending and increasing the likelihood of sustaining desistance. This desire to alter their situational context is a clear expression of understanding that their present circumstances are similar to those which previously led to offending, and that they wanted to commit to an alternative social structural environment in order to sustain desistance. Further, there is a clear consideration among early desisters of the implications of maintaining their present situational contexts in relation to their sustaining desistance.

The men were also future-oriented in considering the changes that would need to be made to their present situational contexts in relation to the alternative future identities that they envisaged. As mentioned earlier, several of the men wanted to assume the identity of 'good father', 'good partner', or, more generally, 'non-offender'. In envisaging such identities, many individuals spoke about the structural changes that would be necessary if they were to achieve them. For a number of individuals, assessments of relationships, locality and accommodation interacted in relation to the future identity they wanted to adopt. John, for example, described how he wanted to move out of the area he lived in, find a nice place to live, and start a family. These future orientations incorporate a range of life-course events or changes and, when combined with the envisioning of an alternative identity, this creates a version of conformity to which individuals intend to strive for.

Bottoms *et al.* (2004) wrote that conformity is both a lifestyle and a self-identity, and that one such conformity (which they refer to as the 'English Dream') involves a secure job in a stable company, 'enough money', ownership of consumer goods, attachment to an intimate relationship, and possibly children. They ask whether this is attainable, particularly for those with a criminal history, and whether alternative conformities exist for desisters in contemporary society (2004: 384). Among the men in the present study, most held aspirations for a similar conformity involving: strong family-based relationships, stable accommodation in a nice area, and a secure, reasonably well-paid, job. Precisely where the commitment to this particular conformity emerges is unknown, but it seems reasonable to assume that an understanding of how past social contexts led to involvement in offending influences individuals towards seeking alternative lifestyles to conform to. The self-confidence, empowerment and envisaging of future identities that were shown to be prominent in the interview data allow for early desisters to develop an initial desire and commitment to move away from crime. In reflecting on this aspiration, certain structural factors within each individual's social context condition future actions which formulate the strategy to sustain desistance.

In the strategies for sustaining desistance that many individuals articulated, therefore, there was evidence of the past, present and future orientations of agency (Emirbayer and Mische, 1998), with a particular emphasis upon projective agency. Moreover, there was evidence of a consideration of how past structures had influenced the present situational contexts individuals found themselves in and, in turn, how the present (unchecked) could affect their futures in relation to certain objectives. There is dissonance here between the accounts of early desisters in this study and the narrative accounts of desistance provided by Sampson and Laub (2001; Laub and Sampson, 2003). Sampson and Laub (2001) highlight the need to 'examine desistance as a process consisting of interactions between human agency, salient life events, and historical context' (2001: 4). The central proposition in their thesis is that desisters take on family and work responsibilities, which 'knife-off' the criminogenic environment, reordering 'short-term situational inducements to crime' (2001: 51). Over time, desisters occupy these roles which coerce the individual into acting in a particular manner, eventuating in long-term conformity (Laub and Sampson, 2003: 149). Their account of desistance is, therefore, essentially structuralist. The analysis presented here, however, demonstrates that individuals in the early stages of desistance may formulate strategies to sustain desistance that do involve the structural inducements to which Sampson and Laub (2001) refer, and, moreover, that they establish an initial commitment to these structural 'turning points' in direct relation to conformity. Indeed, the evidence here suggests that early desisters envisage a particular form of conformity in order to achieve 'self-progression'

(Farrall, 2002: 225) in terms of sustained desistance. This suggests a more complex form of 'active agency' to that which Sampson and Laub (2001) suggested, but one which both remains structurally induced and structurally conditioned.

There were clearly some participants who did not share the same strategies for sustaining desistance based on the conformity described above, or others for whom strategies for desistance included a commitment to conformity that also contained some internal contradictions (such as Alan, whose offending was drink-related, but he wanted to retain ties with people he drank with). While some early desisters demonstrated commitment to some of the structural turning points referred to above, there were other aspects of their social context that they were unwilling to change. This marks the shift from projective agency to a practical-evaluative orientation of agency. An underlying component of projective agency is the presence of knowledge about morally and practically acceptable courses of action. As individuals construct alternative futures they will inevitably consider the moral and practical aspects of their lives. For some men this will lead to a reconsideration of future trajectories and possible identities, as they seek to balance this with knowledge received from past repertoires of action. This balancing act is the essence of practical-evaluative agency.

The practical-evaluative dimension of agency relates to the actions of individuals in response to the contextual demands of the present. There are four key elements to practical-evaluative agency (Emirbayer and Mische, 1998: 998–1000). First, the problematisation of the present situation as somehow inconsistent with, or resistant to, the realisation of projects. Second, the characterisation of present circumstances in relation to past experience. Third, the deliberation between potential courses of action as a response to situational contexts in relation to broader objectives. Fourth, the decision of how to act 'in the here and now' following deliberation among various possibilities, and the execution of the decision in the correct manner at the right time. As such, the practical-evaluative dimension involves a consideration of both the means and the ends of action; that is, what individuals want to achieve and how they intend to achieve it (Biesta and Tedder, 2006a: 15).

This aspect is defined by Emirbayer and Mische (1998: 971) as the 'capacity of actors to make practical and normative judgments among alternative possible trajectories of action, in response to the emerging demands, dilemmas, and ambiguities of presently evolving situations'. In this respect, the practical-evaluative dimension of agency can be understood as the manner by which individuals incorporate knowledge of past actions, and their orientations towards the future, into the circumstances of the present (Biesta and Tedder, 2006a: 15). For the men in the transitional phase of desistance this orientation of agency emerges as they attempt to balance a desire to distance themselves from past habits and actions and move towards an alternative future, within the constraints of the present day. As Emirbayer and Mische (1998: 994) argue, 'relatively unreflective routine dispositions must be adjusted to the exigencies of changing situations; and newly imagined projects must be brought down to earth within real-world circumstances'. For some of the men, they may not have been ready to distance themselves completely from past habits and relationships, and this may explain why they appeared to alter their desistance strategies to accommodate some perpetuation of old routines. As they are faced with the dilemmas and demands of the present situation, an entirely new routine may be too overwhelming. Thus, crucially, the practical-evaluative dimension is not merely an adaptation to certain problematic situations, but also encompasses the judgement and deliberation that individuals exercise in their decision-making strategies. Practical-evaluative agency, therefore, becomes more prominent as individuals consider their strategies for sustaining desistance.

Practical-evaluative agency, in the form of difficulties in balancing the dilemmas of the present with knowledge of the past and concerns for the future, was also present in discussions of possible future offending. Some of the men remarked that future offending could be justified under certain circumstances, or that particular 'small crimes' were defensible due to a perceived lack of severity. John, for example, gave a clear account of the changes that were required for him to sustain desistance, yet although he stated that his peer group influenced his involvement in offending he was unwilling to sever ties with them. Largely, this was because he referred to them as his family, and they provided a social network within which he felt comfortable. This suggests that, while early desisters are willing to commit to certain structures in relation to conformity, there are other structural factors that serve to constrain attempts to sustain desistance. As such, certain structures may lead to a transition from projective to practical-evaluative agency, reflecting the 'continual reconstruction of ... orientations towards past and future in response to emergent events' (Emirbayer and Mische, 1998: 971).

The transition between agentic orientations may also, in part, explain some drift between criminality and conformity. Bottoms *et al.* (2004) argued that, 'there may not be one end-point of criminality' and desistance may involve 'a complicated oscillation' between several end-points (for example, reduced severity, reduced frequency), 'whilst moving in the main towards conformity' (2004: 383). The evidence from the men in this study may suggest that this continuum of conformity, gradually resulting in desistance, may result from a complex amalgam of structural turning points to which individuals want to commit, and existing structural conditions which they either want to retain or are constrained by. This, however, is not the same as the 'side-bets' to which Sampson and Laub (2001) referred, as early desisters consciously choose what they want to commit to within the boundaries of structural possibility. The findings in the present study also resonate with those from the Sheffield Desistance Study. Shapland and Bottoms (2011) found that desistance was a process which involved new ways of living in the community, and that while the individuals in their study may have held conventional goals and aspirations, there were certain contexts or scenarios where deviant behaviour was seen to be more acceptable. The data from the present study suggest that it is likely that individuals in the transitional phase of desistance will hold fairly conventional aspirations and that they will construct strategies to achieve them, but that there are particular situational contexts where those individuals will determine that a deviant course of action or behaviour is appropriate.

Overwhelmingly, the men in the present study identified a strategy for sustaining desistance that was based upon a commitment to a small number of structural turning points. This was similar to the 'English Dream' referred to by Bottoms *et al.* (2004: 384), but it has been shown that many early desisters also hold employment as an overarching objective, necessary to achieve other aims. Often individuals spoke about the need to provide an income, taking greater responsibility, providing stability, and proving that they had changed in order to achieve various objectives, and that employment could fulfil all of these needs. This was in addition to employment being held as an objective in its own right by many of the sample. Thus, employment was regarded by many participants as a necessary, if not sufficient, condition for their desistance strategies. For some of the men this was because employment was seen in instrumental terms, as capable of resolving various practical difficulties. For other men, employment was regarded as being a means of demonstrating that they were a person who could be trusted and relied upon. This was part of fulfilling the new social role and identity that they wanted to adopt. However, when discussing individuals' future strategies for employment, the majority of participants suggested that they would obtain work informally. This is an example of individuals recognising that their present situations are inconsistent with the realisation of their objectives, which is a fundamental aspect of practical-evaluative agency.

Most of the sample was unemployed at the time of interview, and several had never had formal employment. Participants who did have experience of formal employment were more confident that they would be able to secure formal employment again in the future. Furthermore, those with formal experience appeared to be more active in trying to obtain work, while many of those with informal experience suggested that they would wait until a friend or family member offered them some work. For some this was compounded by a lack of education or poor skills and qualificiations. It was, perhaps, somewhat surprising that some participants did not perceive their criminal record to be a barrier to gaining formal employment, especially given the wealth of evidence that suggests many employers discriminate on the basis of criminal record information (Metcalf *et al.*, 2001; TUC, 2001; Boyle, 2007; Maley *et al.*, 2007). However, among those, such as Ben, who had recently disclosed criminal record information, their experiences of doing so had led them to believe that their criminal record would prohibit them from gaining formal employment. As such, it could be argued that it is not the criminal record itself that is problematic (although later in the desistance process the symbolic removal of the 'criminal record' label may be more pertinent to the individual's desistance journey), but rather it is the experience of negative attitudes towards the record that has implications during the transitional phase. Finally, several participants stated that they believed that current economic conditions limited their opportunities to gain formal employment, reflecting the structural constraints of rising unemployment at the time of interview (Autumn/Winter 2008–2009), which had reached between 6 and 7 per cent (Hughes, 2009: Chapter 4).

The effect of these structural factors led many to determine that they would need to seek work in informal labour markets. This suggests that participants' strategies for gaining employment involve agency factors in terms of a consideration of the past (previous experiences of employment), the present (qualifications, criminal record, employment opportunities) and the future (the most likely routes to employment), yet these considerations are significantly constrained by structure. There exists, therefore, a paradox between early desisters demonstrating a desire and commitment to gain employment in order to satisfy other objectives which they are also committed to, while being excluded from these structural turning points by the very nature of these structures.

Thus, to sustain desistance, agency is relevant insofar as early desisters actively construct their own strategies giving consideration to the past, present and future. These strategies are purposefully devised in order to sustain desistance, and the structural turning points that are identified as future objectives are personally relevant to each individual. Collectively, these structural turning points create a particular conformity to which many individuals in the transitional phase of desistance aspire; that is primarily based upon an alternative future identity and social context, and which generally requires employment to achieve. However, structure provides the possibility for such a conformity, and it is structure that enables desisters to consider such a future orientation. Moreover, it is structure that constrains and limits the range of possible courses of action, and which guides individuals towards courses of action that, although they may be more familiar with, may not lead to the types of change initially envisaged. For early desisters formulating strategies to sustain desistance, agency is relevant because many are projective in the way in which they imagine their futures, and they are also evaluative in their consideration of available possible courses of action. The possible courses of action are conditioned by structure, and it is to these structures that desisters wish to conform. However, it is also the structural context that constrains desisters and excludes them from a range of opportunities. This illustrates the power of structure as individuals attempt to sustain desistance – structure both conditions the turning points to which individuals determine that they want to conform to, and it constrains the range of possible courses of action to achieve them.

Iterational agency – the impact of probation

In recent years a small body of literature has emerged which has explored the interface between experiences of probation and processes of desistance from crime (Rex, 1999; Farrall, 2002; McCulloch, 2005; Farrall and Calverley, 2006; Weaver and McNeill, 2010). There are various factors which have been shown to facilitate the process of desistance, and others which may act as more of a hindrance. There is some evidence to suggest that a strong relationship between the would-be desister and the supervising officer can assist the process, and it has also been shown that where practical assistance in overcoming difficulties can be offered that this can also facilitate a move away from crime. Evidence has also shown that the likelihood of desistance occurring can be improved when the supervising officer has strong interpersonal skills, such as talking, listening and having an empathetic attitude (Rex, 1999; McCulloch, 2005).

While this body of literature continues to grow, there has been relatively little attention paid towards the impact of probation specifically on the transition from criminality to conformity and on the formulation of strategies to sustain desistance. The men in the study were asked about their experiences of probation in general, and also about the impact of probation on perceived structural barriers to desistance. The men, generally, spoke positively about their experiences of probation, and the interview data reinforced messages which have emerged from the existing literature. The men indicated that they valued having someone who believed in them and various personal characteristics which helped to develop a strong relationship between the supervising officer and the would-be desister. In addition to this, however, the men also suggested that probation had helped them to develop various agentic characteristics, including enhanced decision-making skills, increased self-confidence and an altered sense of moral agency. Some individuals also stated that they felt more in control of their lives and empowered to make changes in their lifestyles.

These agentic factors correspond with those found in the existing literature (McAdams, 1992; Maruna, 2001; LeBel *et al.*, 2008), but the interview data here indicate that probation enhances individual agency during the early stages of desistance. One-to-one supervision and accredited programmes were shown to be of most benefit in this regard, and this was enhanced further when these two elements of probation worked in synergy. This appeared to help to concretise the overall probation experience, such that the men would be more likely to move away from crime and reflect upon their strategies for sustaining this move. This appeared to occur in two distinct ways. First, when supervision and programme requirements were sequenced appropriately, the supervising officer was able to provide some preparatory work prior to the programme beginning. This appeared to offer crucial groundwork, so that the men were better equipped to benefit from the programme requirement. Second, a greater synergy could be achieved between supervision and programme requirements where the supervising officer reinforced messages which were delivered during the programme element. This would allow for knowledge and understanding to be confirmed, whilst also emphasising key points from the programme. McNeill (2006b) argued that the hegemonic focus upon programmes may have 'supplanted and marginalized' the traditional role of individual relationships (2006b: 245), and it may be the case that some developmental work that might have previously been undertaken during one-to-one supervision sessions has been transferred to the group-based environment of accredited programmes. The interview data from the present study, however, indicate that a potentially fruitful form of probation may be one which involves supervision and programmes working in unison. Indeed, this illustrates how probation can initiate projective agency among individuals contemplating desistance.

Through this combination of supervision and programme elements, many of the men had developed various agentic skills and this was prompted, in several cases, by supervising officers encouraging individuals to contribute to discussions both during supervision and programme sessions. At times this involved exploring Probationers' thoughts in relation to the impact of their offending on victims, possible responses to scenarios in their current everyday lives, and aspirations for the future. This suggests that probation can provide a structural context that triggers certain aspects of agency that can facilitate the transition towards desistance. The evidence indicates that this was most successfully achieved with those individuals who appeared to be most engaged with the supervision and programme sessions. This was achieved through the development of a strong officer-offender' relationship, and through preparatory work undertaken before programme commencement.

The most prominent, and arguably most important, theme, to emerge from the interview data with regard to probation experiences was in relation to discussions about future objectives and the strategies for achieving them. A minority of the men appeared to have engaged in a collaborative approach with their supervising officers towards identifying future objectives. For most of the men, however, objectives were predominantly developed by the supervising officer alone. These were often in relation to employment, living arrangements and relationships. This can be seen as a positive dimension of work with early desisters, as a future outlook can facilitate longer-term desistance (Maruna, 2001). Indeed, the Liverpool Desistance Study (LDS) showed that one of the key distinctions between desisters and persisters was the lack of a future-orientation among active offenders (Maruna *et al.*, 2004). However, the data showed an absence of discussions about how to achieve certain objectives, which renders many would-be desisters with the responsibility of formulating projects to achieve these objectives. There are a number of possible explanations for this, which are discussed below, which leaves individuals with little support for the practical-evaluative dimension of agency (Emirbayer and Mische, 1998). The risk inherent here is in the problematisation component of practical-evaluation (Emirbayer and Mische, 1998: 998). Future objectives are inconsistent with present situations, and individuals must rectify this. A judgement must be made which renders the situation unproblematic, and it is assistance with this judgement which probation neglects. Consequently, the iterational orientation of agency may become more prominent.

The iterational element of agency involves reflecting on past actions and the individual's understandings of them. There are five key components to iterational agency. First, individuals will selectively draw upon particular habitual actions as they are regarded as appropriate to sustain particular objectives. Second, individuals recognise emerging interactions or events as being similar to particular past experiences, and respond accordingly with habitual actions. The emerging events will never completely replicate previous ones, but individuals are able to assimilate emerging events with habitual actions. Third, as well as assimilating similar emerging and past events, individuals will also identify emerging events with other people or contexts. Fourth, individuals will man-oeuvre between past repertoires of habitual action. Under certain circumstances such manoeuvring may be semi-conscious, but at other times individuals may have to be more instrumental in manoeuvring between various patterns of habit-ual action. Finally, iterational agency provides expectation maintenance, as indi-viduals are able to predict the outcomes from particular actions, or how others will react to certain interactions. Iterational agency is defined by the authors (Emirbayer and Mische, 1998: 971) as the 'reactivation by actors of past patterns of thought and action, as routinely incorporated in practical activity, thereby giving stability and order to social universes and helping to sustain identities, interactions, and institutions over time'. Thus, the iterational dimension of agency is the individual's ability to recall and select schemas of thought and action that they have developed through historical interactions. However, 'the agentic dimension [of iteration] lies in *how actors selectively recognise, locate and implement* such schemas' (ibid.: 975, emphasis in original), rather than simply referring to the possession of these schemas. This builds upon Giddens's notions of 'practical consciousness' and 'routine practices'. Routine practices constitute the foundation of individuals' habitual activities (1984: 282), while practical consciousness refers to the ability of individuals to be able to accom-plish these everyday tasks, without necessarily being able to describe them (Farrall and Bowling, 1999: 255). This practice of recursively activating struc-tures to enable the routinisation of action (Giddens, 1979) can be explained by reference to the notion of 'ontological security'.

According to Giddens (1991) individuals have to constantly locate their own sense of ontological security, a point which is shared by Beck and Beck-Gernsheim (2002) when they write that 'modern guidelines actually compel the self-organization and self-thematization of people's biographies' (2002: 31). Individuals will routinely try to maintain a sense of ontological security, or else they would be paralysed by anxiety, and this is most effectively achieved by establishing circumstances of familiarity and routine (Liddle, 2001: 56). Thus, for Giddens, it is the need to achieve ontological security that coerces individu-als to routinise their activities, in order to obtain a sense of stability.

It is argued here that probation encourages projective agency through sug-gesting particular objectives for the future. However, probation is largely absent while individuals exercise practical-evaluative agency. As such, when would-be desisters encounter the *problematisation* component of practical-evaluative agency they have limited support in being able to rectify the situation. When individuals seek a resolution they will *characterise* the problem at hand and are likely to draw upon past schemas of thought and action for assistance. Would-be desisters may seek familiar habits or routines in an attempt to achieve future objectives (such as informal labour markets to obtain employment), or they may reconsider future objectives altogether. Given the perceived array of possible courses of action – which, for many would-be desisters is likely to be somewhat limited given their personal and social contexts – individuals will then *deliberate* over the best course of action to take. Crucially, this is not merely a reactivation of habitual routines, but individuals will actively try to identify the most effective action to achieve broader objectives. Individuals will then make a *decision*, but these are not necessarily unambiguous or fixed, but rather tenuous. The final component of practical-evaluative agency is *execution*, whereby individuals will enact the decisions that they have arrived at. The capacity to execute is differentially distributed among individuals, and not all individuals will be able to execute their decisions effectively (Emirbayer and Mische, 1998: 998–1000).

Would-be desisters may revert to iterational agency in response to problematic situations that they encounter due to the lack of support within probation. The social contexts that individuals find themselves in may limit the range of possibilities available, particularly in the pursuit of employment. This may lead individuals towards past repertoires of thought and action. Others may attempt alternative courses of action, but may lack the capacity to execute them, and this may then lead individuals to alter objectives or their strategies for achieving them. It is argued here that the experiences of probation for the men in the study were such that they lacked support with regard to practical-evaluative agency and were, therefore, more likely to revert to iterational agency.

The interviews identified various constraints within contemporary probation practice that hinder the transition to desistance. Of particular prominence in the interview data were references to a lack of guidance in relation to achieving objectives, and a lack of practical assistance to overcome problems. These constraints not only left participants with the responsibility of formulating projects on their own, but also had deleterious effects in terms of self-confidence and motivation. Sustaining motivation and confidence, particularly during challenging times, is vitally important to the desistance process (Maguire and Raynor, 2006b: 25), and the early desistance stage is likely to be especially characterised by ambivalence. There were other instances where practitioners demonstrated the belief in the individual that can contribute to desistance (McNeill, 2006b: 245), such as the supervising officer who praised the Probationer who had not had a positive drug test for a long period of time. However, if supervising officers are not helping them to overcome problems, or providing specific guidance for how to achieve certain objectives, this may implicitly send a message that they do not 'believe in' the would-be desister.

There are a number of aspects of contemporary probation practice that conspire to constrain desistance. The interview data suggested a focus upon particular sentence requirements, notably accredited programmes. Programmes have become a cornerstone of probation practice since the rise of 'What Works?' from the early- to mid-1990s. Chief among these have been programmes which are based upon cognitive behavioural approaches, designed to challenge attitudes and thinking. While several participants spoke positively about their experiences of programmes, some stated that they did not feel that the programmes were personally relevant. There are a number of possible explanations for this. First, a lack of time to undertake pre-programme work results in a lack of engagement. Second, the content of the programme challenges the individual in environments in which they are unaccustomed to being challenged. Third, the individual is sentenced to complete a requirement for which they are an unsuitable candidate, as a result of the 'bums on seats' demands placed on probation areas (Robinson and Crow, 2009: 116).

The latter of these explanations resonates with the emergence of a 'target culture' within contemporary probation. As mentioned earlier, in 2007–2008 the target for accredited programme completions was 17,319, which was surpassed by the National Probation Service (NPS, 2008: 10). However, 'the initial targets for completion of programmes were based on negotiations with the Treasury in 1999 rather than on any measurement of the need for them or the numbers of offenders likely to benefit' (Raynor, 2007b: 136). Clearly, there is a danger that emphasising completions instead of who is likely to benefit will lead to many individuals having a programme as a requirement of their sentence which is largely irrelevant. This is likely to result in a lack of engagement, a decline in motivation, and an unwillingness to participate in other activities that may support desistance. Some practitioners also described the pressure to complete a certain number of sentence requirements, and the impact that this had on the people with whom they work. In some cases, the demands of sentence requirements placed extreme pressure on the individual. On the one hand, this can be regarded as a positive use of sentencing powers as there is a clear argument that a variety of requirements could provide the structure and routine necessary to develop conformity and a range of positive personal attributes. On the other hand, however, if sentence requirements are administered with little consideration for the individual receiving them then this is likely to be detrimental to the desistance process.

Desistance is also constrained by the demands of public protection and risk management, which produce considerable bureaucratic obligations. For example, it has been estimated that the average time taken to complete an OASys assessment is two-and-a-half hours (Raynor, 2007b: 136). In many cases, the practitioners who took part in the present study stated that bureaucratic demands place a considerable demand on their own resources, as they are under immense pressure to meet targets and complete necessary paperwork. Targets take prominence because they are linked to budgets, and participants stated that there could be few excuses for not reaching targets. This has significant implications for the amount of time available for one-to-one supervision sessions, with some participants reporting that supervision can last for as little as five minutes. One consequence of this is that practitioners are unable to develop agency among others to its fullest potential. A corollary of this is that it remains unclear how the objectives that are internalised by individuals, but which are often proposed by practitioners, can be completed. Farrall and Calverley (2006) argued that probation can plant the seed of desistance that can gradually influence Probationers towards long-term crime cessation. They argued that, 'the "seeds" will probably only be sown in one-to-one supervision' (2006: 66). It is argued here that there is evidence of the 'seeds' being 'sown' as probation can both trigger the initial transition towards desistance and encourage a projective orientation of agency. However, to continue their analogy, for desistance to flourish, regular care, attention and nurturing would be required. This could come from a variety of sources and relationships, including family, partners and friends. The individual would also need to regularly work on their own desistance journey, to ensure that they remain on the right pathway. However, criminal justice practitioners can play a crucial role in providing this level of nurturing, particularly during the early transitions when individuals may be most tentatively poised between criminality and desistance. That is, interventions to sustain desistance need to provide more one-to-one support with the individuals who are attempting to make the transition from criminality to desistance. The evidence presented in the present study has suggested that this is not currently the case, as early desisters who undertake a practical-evaluative orientation resort to the familiarity of past experience (past structures), by repositioning themselves to an iterational form of agency.

The lack of one-to-one time between officer and offender is also 'the result of recent governmental pressure to contract out services' (Vennard and Hedderman, 2009: 225). Responses from the men in the present study indicated that efforts to overcome problems (particularly in relation to accommodation and employment) tended to involve referral to external agencies. Most participants who had experience of external agencies spoke negatively about them, stating that they were unresponsive, time-consuming and poorly managed. Some individuals were apprehensive about being referred to external agencies due to negative experiences in the past. These experiences of external agencies were also damaging to self-confidence and motivation but, moreover, had the effect of directing would-be desisters to resort to past experiences to determine how they would achieve certain objectives. This is exemplified in Ben's case; his experiences of external agencies were particularly negative, and this had led to him seeking work in informal labour markets.

Thus, it can be argued that probation enables the initial transition towards desistance by triggering certain aspects of agency to prompt individuals to consider the possibility of change, and in motivating individuals to attempt longer-term crime cessation. This is achieved through the highly important role of one-to-one supervision, and the positive characteristics of supervising officers, described by participants in this study and elsewhere (Rex, 1999; McCulloch, 2005). Accredited programmes can also play an important role in the enhancement of agency, but it is argued here that this is more likely if engagement is secured and if individuals feel as though the programme is personally relevant. Further, programmes are likely to be more beneficial if they are integrated with supervision sessions so that messages are reinforced and Probationers are afforded the opportunity to discuss particular aspects of programmes in greater detail away from a group environment. Probation also plays an important enabling role in the transition towards desistance by encouraging a projective orientation of agency, which allows for individuals to envisage an alternative future. Often, however, this future outlook is proposed by the supervising officer and accepted by the Probationer.

While this can be regarded as an important dimension of supporting desistance, the contemporary structure of probation, with its attendant emphasis upon targets and bureaucracy, reduces the time spent with individual Probationers to the extent that ways of achieving objectives remain unaddressed. Rather, recent government policy has aggressively encouraged the use of external agencies to provide services which, it is argued here, creates a fissure within the officer-offender relationship. Negative experiences of external agencies are likely to lead would-be desisters towards past experience to guide their thoughts and actions and, for many, this may lead to a resumption of offending behaviour.

Enhanced agency versus the power of structure

The discussion presented thus far has shown that probation can play an instrumental role, both in prompting desistance and in suggesting objectives which could help to sustain desistance. In exploring the initial transitions towards desistance and the subsequent formulation of strategies to desist in the aftermath of this transition, a range of subjective factors were identified which correspond with those identified in the existing literature (LeBel *et al.*, 2008; Maruna, 2001; McAdams, 1992). The broader conception of agency employed in this exploratory study of early desistance, and the wider range of subjective factors identified in the analysis, identify a stronger sense of agency among early desisters than that found by Healy and O'Donnell (2008). This sense of agency also suggests that would-be desisters are more active in their transitions to desistance and plans for the future than suggested by Sampson and Laub (2001; Laub and Sampson, 2003). Whereas these authors suggest that desistance is achieved through a succession of 'side-bets' that gradually secure conformity, the evidence presented here suggests that individuals are more active in envisaging an alternative non-offending future.

This argument, therefore, follows the work of LeBel *et al.* (2008), who argued that subjective factors emerge prior to structural changes in the social context in the process of desistance. During the transition towards desistance individuals possess a strong sense of agency which involves the envisaging of alternative future identities, motivation, and a sense of self-confidence in their ability to make changes in their lives. The work of Emirbayer and Mische (1998) suggested that different structural contexts can trigger particular aspects of agency, and alter orientations of agency. The discussion presented here indicates that the structure of probation generates a sense of agency through encouraging a reflection on past offending (to develop moral agency) and through discussions of the future (to develop motivation and an alternative future outlook). This is not to argue that structures in the wider context of desisters' lives do not influence agency in similar respects. Indeed, the analysis in the present study has shown that structural changes to individuals' lives, particularly in relation to their relationships, accommodation, and experiences of risk, also activate certain aspects of agency.

The work of Emirbayer and Mische (1998) has also been shown to be relevant to the discussion of the transition towards desistance in contemporary probation by drawing upon their notion of a 'chordal triad' of agency. It is argued here that would-be desisters exercise a projective dimension of agency, and this has been shown in the strategies to sustain desistance that participants articulated during the interviews. Most often, these strategies are based upon the envisaging of alternative identities such as 'good father' or 'good partner', and the adoption of future objectives in relation to having somewhere nice to live, starting a family, and securing employment. These objectives are similar to those outlined by Bottoms *et al.* (2004), and may be considered to be normative 'hard-wired' aspirations, but it should be noted that objectives were discussed explicitly in relation to sustaining desistance. Moreover, for a group of individuals who experience marginalisation and inequality in a range of areas of their lives, it is likely that the envisaging of such objectives will only be triggered within a particular social context.

The projective dimension of agency can be seen first within individuals' descriptions of their initial decisions to desist, as many begin to consider how they would like to act in the future and who they would like to become. The projective dimension continues in individuals' strategies for desistance, yet here there is also evidence of what Emirbayer and Mische (1998) referred to as the practical-evaluative dimension of agency. Within this orientation of agency, would-be desisters are able to consider their future objectives in relation to their present structural circumstances. It is at this point that the influence of probation upon the transition towards desistance begins to unravel. For many, the combination of a projective and practical-evaluative orientation generates the envisaging of a particular conformity to which they initially desire and commit to. However, upon deliberating about how it is possible to achieve this, many perceive various structural constraints, which allows for the emergence of an iterational orientation to agency, whereby they reflect on past experiences to reactivate past thoughts and actions.

As a result of various bureaucratic pressures, the emphasis on public protection, and increased government pressure towards contracting-out, the policy context of contemporary probation practice limits the amount of time supervising officers can spend with Probationers. It is argued here that it is this dimension of probation that would allow for the generation of a projective orientation among would-be desisters, and that the continuation of regular one-to-one supervision is likely to facilitate efforts to sustain desistance. Collectively, the various changes which have characterised the modernisation of the Probation Service have reduced the potential for interactions between the would-be desister and the supervising officer. The effect of this is that the while the would-be desister may exercise projective agency through considering the possibility of change, and envisaging alternative future objectives, they are likely to revert to habitual action because there is limited assistance from the supervising officer both in overcoming practical difficulties and in considering strategies for achieving objectives.

This was identified in the data as individuals suggested employment was the most important objective, yet a lack of support to overcome structural barriers led many to determine that informal labour markets would be their most likely pathway to gaining work. It is possible that this is partly a corollary of the need to satisfy ontological security (Giddens, 1990, 1991), as individuals revert to 'what they know' in order to retain stability, sustain identities and engage in familiar interactions. However, the data suggested that would-be desisters demonstrate transformative agency (Hays, 1994); that is, that they want to make changes in their lives, they desire new interactions, and they aspire to new social contexts. As individuals seek to make such transformations they encounter the constraining effects of past structures that furnish their present situational contexts with properties which serve to marginalise and exclude them from mainstream activities. Individuals are, therefore, constrained by a lack of resources and, thus, the courses of action that they determine may be unlikely to enable them to achieve the overall objective of sustaining desistance. This does not discount from the agential activities of individuals in the early stages of desistance, because, it is argued here, individuals selectively enact past patterns of action and behaviour. This, however, should not be conflated with Bourdieu's habitus or Giddens's routine practices.

Such approaches would suggest that individual agency is habitual and repetitive, rather than purposive and transformative. Nor is this a concession to voluntarism, as action does not automatically follow intention. Individuals cannot know the precise interactions that they will encounter as they seek to achieve certain objectives (Fuchs, 2002). A would-be desister may wish to cut ties with delinquent peers but cannot predict if or when they may encounter such an individual, nor what the nature of any ensuing interactions may be. Likewise, a would-be desister may hold the objective of obtaining legitimate employment, but they cannot know when employment opportunities may arise, or whether they will encounter an understanding or a prejudicial employer. Accommodation may be part of the would-be desister's plans, but they cannot control what neighbours they would have, or what impact that could have upon their attempts to desist. Such encounters may have an impact upon the future objectives held by the would-be desister, or the manner by which they seek to achieve them.

Individuals formulate future objectives and construct plans to achieve them based upon reflexive deliberations concerning the social context that they find themselves in. At times, individuals may selectively re-enact past patterns of action and behaviour if such reflexive deliberations lead towards the individual determining that to be the most appropriate course of action in those circumstances. Therefore, it is the dynamic interplay between purpose, judgement and habit which encapsulates the nature of agency for men in the transitional phase of desistance. In addition, men in the transitional phase may find that selectively reverting to habit is part of the process of learning to live in a more conventional manner. Shapland and Bottoms (2011) found that desisters have to learn how to live in the pro-social community, but this will inevitably take time. It is possible that individuals in the early stages of desistance demonstrate some degree of iterational, or habitual, agency as part of this process.

The impact of probation in the transitional phase of desistance appeared to be most prominent with regard to projective agency. The experience of probation, for many men, had helped them to be more positive about the possibility of change and had enabled them to envisage an alternative future which did not include offending or offending-related behaviours. Probation had also provided many of the men with objectives which would help them to sustain desistance. These are positive aspects of probation, and they demonstrate a degree of desistance-focused practice. Probation enhances projective agency because it helps men to see the destination that they could aim for. However, due to constraints on time and resources, probation appeared to be less able to provide the men with the 'roadmaps' required to 'get there'. Instead, the men were either referred to external agencies, or had to determine courses of action for themselves. Consequently, practical-evaluative agency became more prominent, as the men had to reflexively deliberate on their personal and social contexts and consider what would be possible given the structural constraints that surrounded them. Under particular conditions, iterational agency then became more prominent for many of the men. After reflecting on their social contexts they selectively re-enacted certain past actions and behaviours in order to try to achieve their goals.

This builds upon the arguments presented by Farrall (2002) and McNeill (2006, 2009), who suggested that probation helps to develop human capital in the form of motivation and personal capacities, but does not generate the social capital necessary for individuals to exercise new capabilities. The men in the study had visions for the future; they had constructed 'change narratives'. They identified aspects of their lives that they wanted to change in order to improve the lives of themselves and others (for example, partners or children), but it was clear that some were frustrated at the lack of opportunities to be able to achieve this (for example, through accommodation and employment). It is argued here, therefore, that probation allows for the emergence of particular forms of agency in the form of motivation, self-confidence, moral agency and the envisaging of alternative identities. However, a lack of support at critical moments in the transitional stage of desistance then leads to a form of agency whereby individuals revert to past experience and familiarity, which is likely to hinder individuals' efforts to make the transition towards longer-term sustained desistance.

This, it is argued here, is primarily because probation policy and practice under New Labour was underpinned by a focus on responsibilisation and individualisation. As such, the role of practitioners became constrained by an overly prescribed policy framework, and a focus upon bureaucracy and managerialism. This entails that individuals have less support in trying to navigate difficult and challenging social environments, which can in turn lead to them experiencing turbulence in their transitions between crime and desistance. Long-term goals and strategies are meaningless if the individual is struggling with the task of attending numerous appointments at multiple locations, or with concerns about CRB checks and criminal history disclosure (not to mention even more day-to-day tasks such as paying bills, or providing for one's self and family). Such turbulence could affect decision-making, attitudes and behaviour. Consequently, the decisions that individuals initially made – in terms of choosing to desist, becoming a 'good father/partner', and so on – may not have been lived up to.

But this is not to argue that individuals choose to desist, and then subsequently choose not to anymore. Rather, it is to suggest that the social environment that individuals face when they make the initial transition towards desistance is one which includes particular structures which prevent certain choices from being realised. In other words, individuals are structured into making certain choices, and these may be to revert to past repertoires of action and behaviour.

Wikstrom and Treiber (2007), in their situational action theory, similarly argued that individuals' actions occur in an environmental setting, and that this setting can provide individuals with opportunities to act in pro-social ways, or that it can provoke individuals to act in an immoral fashion if they experience obstacles or challenges (what they refer to as 'frictions'). It is argued here that as individuals make the transition towards desistance they are likely to encounter such 'frictions', and this can lead the individual towards an iterational form of agency as this is deemed to be an appropriate response to the perception that the particular challenge or obstacle encountered is likely to be too difficult to surmount. In part this may be because the men in this study reflexively considered their future goals in line with 'traditional' perceptions of appropriate life-courses. These may be incongruent with the structure of modern society (for example, changes to family formation, changes to labour market formation, and so on) and so individuals' goals may be unrealistic. However, it is also likely that this is the result of a lack of support (both perceived and real) during the transition towards desistance, and that in the absence of such support individuals will be more likely to revert to past repertoires of action. Differences between individuals in this respect can therefore be explained either as (1) differential experiences of obstacles; (2) differential levels of support, or; (3) differences in perceptions of the social environment. Unless community supervision can help individuals to overcome obstacles and help individuals to perceive their social environments in a positive and desistance-focused way then individuals are more likely to regard past actions and behaviours as an appropriate response to their social circumstances.

10 Concluding thoughts

The argument that has been presented in this book has suggested that probation policy under New Labour emerged as an attempt to produce responsibilised citizens. Alongside this, the aim of probation became an attempt to control and manage risky populations, with the tasks of the individual practitioner, underpinned by a 'surveillant managerial' discourse (Nellis, 2005), delineated as: assessing risk; enforcing breach sanctions; and, challenging criminogenic deficits, all in adherence to a centrally prescribed policy framework with explicit guidance and tools. These changes marked a shift away from welfare concerns towards a risk-based penology, as well as the emergence of rehabilitation *through* responsibilisation. As suggested above, this builds upon the arguments of Farrall (2002) and McNeill (2009) who have argued that probation helps to develop human capital, in the form of motivation or individual capacities, but neglects social capital, in the form of opportunities to exercise these capacities (McNeill *et al.*, 2005: 32).

It has also been argued here that agency is multi-contextual – that is, that different contexts influence how individuals exercise agency by providing conditions which enable and constrain agency which, in turn, influences the possibilities of action for particular individuals at a given time. This has been achieved by arguing that the various contexts that would-be desisters encounter solicit alternative temporal orientations of agency which can enable, constrain or suppress these possibilities of action. Different contexts can encourage individuals to exercise agency in a transformative manner, but this can only be sustained if individuals have the necessary resources to be able to overcome particular difficulties, and the guidance required to acquire new habits of thought and action. Where this is absent, individuals may be more likely to revert to past habits of thought and action.

The probation context developed by New Labour facilitates desistance by developing agency in the form of confidence, motivation, decision-making, and a future orientation. However, it is argued here that this is, somewhat, effaced by the lack of support in relation to individuals' broader contexts. In other words, probation develops human capital but neglects the social capital required to make the transition towards desistance (Farrall, 2002; McNeill, 2009). The argument here is that this social capital is neglected *because* probation policy is designed to produce responsibilised, remoralised, prudent citizens, *and* because it is designed to manage offenders through centrally prescribed processes. The dilemma here lies within the proposition that agency is personalised, active and dynamic (Archer, 2007), and is, therefore, unsuited to the dogmatic actuarial and managerial nature of modernised probation.

Would-be desisters, social contexts and human agency

Personal identities, comprised of individual goals and objectives, are what make us heterogeneous. Although individuals' objective positions may be similar, their subjectively determined ends may be radically different. Furthermore, the personalised nature of agency means that even where objective positions and ends are the same, the subjectively determined pathways to achieve them may also be different. It is reasonable to assume that a significant number of individuals under probation supervision may not hold any aspirations to desist (at least at that moment in time). Indeed, some may have the objective of completing their sentence and then returning immediately to the life of crime they had before. Recent work which explores the nature of compliance and community penalties illustrates this point – that some individuals may only comply with the formal requirements of the sentence, without ever 'buying in' to the possibility of change, while others may substantively comply, taking on board the ideology and principles of desistance (Robinson and McNeill, 2008, 2012; see also Ugwudike, 2010). Thus, although objective positions may be similar, individuals' end goals may be radically different. However, among the sample interviewed for this research, all stated that they wanted to desist from crime, yet the goals which were identified as necessary to achieve this varied between interviewees. The point to be made here is that even where objective positions and subjectively determined ends may be similar, the pathways that individuals design for the achievement of these may also be radically different. There is, therefore, substantial heterogeneity among would-be desisters, and this is, at least in part, a consequence of individuals' capacity to exercise agency.

Agency is active in the sense that individuals can adjust their goals and pathways in light of incoming information and may change their preferences accordingly. Individuals continuously assess their social contexts in relation to their goals, and this may lead to a re-evaluation of these, such that a reordering of preferences takes place. It is, perhaps, unlikely that would-be desisters would retain the same set of goals over a long duration. They may hold some long-term objectives, or 'pipe dreams' perhaps, but in the short- to medium-term at least, their goals, and, more importantly, their priorities, are likely to change. For individuals who are making the early transition towards desistance this is particularly likely to be the case as they encounter new and unknown, as well as old and familiar, contexts. Each context is furnished with certain roles and resources (Bhaskar, 1979), and these actively produce different forms of agency from individuals, which leads to different forms of action.

Finally, agency is dynamic in that it is constantly exercised by active individuals, but also because it can radically alter as a response to particular contexts. In this regard, agency is context-dependent, and action that results from agency depends upon its contextual feasibility (Archer, 2007: 81–3). As a consequence, individuals may exercise agency in different ways as they encounter different contexts. A would-be desister, for example, might exercise a projective form of agency during conversations with their supervising officer, perhaps because this is a context within which they feel empowered to think about the future. While they are in their local community, however, they may revert to an iterational orientation, because their surroundings offer a 'dire prognosis' (Maruna, 2001) for the future, or perhaps because they want to avoid being an 'outsider' in their own neighbourhood.

There is also the possibility that different contexts could produce unexpected events and unrehearsed responses to them. An individual, for example, may hold employment to be the most important objective to achieve desistance. They may have also given proper consideration to how they can gain legitimate employment; visited recruitment agencies, and received information about the types of job they may be suitable for, and what skills they can offer. As such, they have contextual knowledge of gaining employment and draw upon this in formulating their plans. This contextual knowledge might help them to gain an offer of work, but later they are told by their supervising officer that they cannot accept the offer as it involves working away from home for a certain period of time. The individual was previously unaware of this, and how they react upon receiving this information is likely to alter their future pathways, and possibly the success or otherwise of their desistance transitions. They might not, for example, follow the formal channels to employment again, if they consequently perceive their previous attempts to have resulted in failure.

Importantly, the multiple contexts within which agency is exercised are interconnected, and the actions that result as a consequence of the interaction between context, agency and the individual, are interdependent. Would-be desisters need to navigate multiple contexts: employment, accommodation, community, and probation, to name a few. It has been argued here that conditions within some of these contexts produce different forms of agency, which leads to different intentions among similarly placed individuals. For desistance to be sustained, individuals will need to navigate these multiple contexts and ensure that the conditions within them are oriented away from those which are likely to lead to offending, and towards those which will sustain non-offending. Probation policy and practice in recent years has added further contexts to individuals' lives through the use of external agencies, which adds a further dimension that would-be desisters are required to navigate. Further use of external agencies, for example through contestability or Payment-By-Results, reinforces the need for further research to examine the contextual nature of agency in the desistance process. This navigation of multiple contexts is at the root of the complexity of desistance transitions, and explains why desistance is plagued by ambivalence and uncertainty. Future desistance research needs to explore the interactive effect between these multiple contexts, and the effect on agency and attempts to sustain non-offending. The task for practitioners is highly complex because they operate in an environment which promotes technocratic, managerial solutions to the highly uncertain, multi-contextual difficulties of individuals' lives.

Practitioners, human agency and probation policy and practice under New Labour

The modernisation of probation under New Labour was driven, in part, by fears about the effectiveness of community sentences. Policymaking will continue to be heavily influenced by media and public anxieties about the problem of reoffending and the need for crime control which, in turn, is likely to necessitate increased risk assessment and offender management. The danger that this presents is that interventions will continue to be matched to offenders based on their criminogenic 'deficits', with a relative lack of consideration for individual needs, contexts or aspirations. This contributes to the delimiting of agency to the iterational dimension, and to would-be desisters reverting to past repertoires of thought and action which is likely to inhibit longer-term desistance. For frontline workers to deliver desistance-focused interventions, in the short-term at least, will require the individual practitioner to navigate any potential disjunctures, connections or possibilities that lie between centrally prescribed rules and guidance, and the conditions and contexts of individual cases. In other words, desistance will depend on the agency of the practitioner as well as the agency of the offender.

This may involve the practitioner making decisions about the rationing of time and resources which may, in turn, involve a contradictory decision between, for example, meeting key performance indicators or surrendering these to the achievement of one-to-one work with individual offenders (a point of tension that was alluded to in the fieldwork for this book). The choices that individual practitioners make will depend on how they exercise agency in determining the outcomes they want and the way in which they set out to achieve them. As has been argued throughout this book, agency is enabled and constrained by an individual's personal and social contexts, potentially limiting or expanding what they perceive to be possible in the future. The environment within which practitioners have to work will, therefore, influence the capability of individuals to act in a desistance-focused manner.

Of course, this is in many ways drawing upon the notion of street-level bureaucracy developed by Lipsky (1980), but it is worth highlighting the possibility of alternative interpretations of the probation context among frontline workers. This is an area which has attracted a small amount of recent attention (Deering, 2010; Gregory, 2010), where it has been suggested that practitioners do resist some of the punitive managerial discourses and instead retain some more traditional ethics of probation work through their reflective practice. Robinson and McNeill (2008, 2012) have also explored the notion that practitioners might be able to combine the logics of compliance and desistance in their day-to-day work. A potential obstacle here is that practitioners may be constrained by fears of accountability if they deviate from centrally administered policy and guidelines, and there is an argument to be made that such policy and guidelines intend to produce particular types of practitioner. These 'types' relate to the intentions of policymakers and managers to produce individuals who act according to certain dispositions. For example, policies designed to initiate certain breach practices may be intended to produce practitioners who are 'enforcers'; that is, individuals whose disposition to act is more attuned to securing formal compliance. However, it is argued here that agency can determine how individuals in similar positions act differently, and practitioners may interpret policy guidance in various ways, or may subvert certain policies to achieve alternative aims. Future desistance research should explore the contextual contingencies that allow for the flexible interpretation of policy, guidelines, and the role of 'supervising officer', such that probation interventions become more desistance-focused.

The importance of probation supervision becoming more desistance-focused is highlighted by the body of literature which has shown that sustained desistance is more likely where a relationship between officer and offender is developed that addresses individual needs in a collaborative and participative manner. This finding may suggest that longer-term desistance is more likely where practitioners exercise agency to subvert the existing policy framework, which is designed to delimit practice of this nature. This is supported by the findings presented in this book. However, this has been, and continues to be, limited by the modernisation of probation. There exists a paradox where offenders embarking on desistance transitions wish to submit to the structures of mainstream society, but find themselves excluded by those same structures. There is also a paradox where, to support desistance, practitioners are required to adopt a flexible individualised approach to working with offenders, but operate within a policy framework that is rigid, technocratic and managerial. Such flexibility is required if the type of relationship described above is to be developed to facilitate desistance. In its absence, would-be desisters are considerably less likely to be able to navigate the multiple contexts that constitute their lives. Policy should allow for a more flexible, personalised relationship between officer and offender, but this is unlikely, in the foreseeable future at least, given the media and public anxieties about crime and the hegemonic managerial ethos developed under New Labour.

Desistance under the Conservative-led Coalition government

The fieldwork for this book took place between 2009–2010, during the final months of the New Labour government. Therefore, much of the policy and practice relevant to the community supervision of offenders discussed in this book so far is, in part, a critical reflection on the development of probation policy under New Labour. When the Conservative-led Coalition formed a government in May 2010 this signalled the beginning of a series of changes to criminal justice policy in particular, and probation policy and practice more specifically. Although the exact nature and extent of these changes remains unclear at the time of writing, it is timely to reflect on those changes that have already taken place, and those that are proposed, in the context of the findings from this study.

The Cameron-Clegg Coalition government quickly signalled its intentions regarding criminal justice with the publication of the Green Paper, *Breaking the Cycle: Effective Punishment, Rehabilitation and Sentencing of Offenders* (Ministry of Justice, 2010). The document condemned the sharp increase in the prison population, and the use of short-term prison sentences with little opportunity for rehabilitation or reform. These progressive messages have also been made elsewhere by the Coalition government. In July 2010 Crispin Blunt (then Prisons and Probation Minister) paraphrased Winston Churchill in a speech, stating that responses to crime and the treatment of offenders are a test of a nation's civilisation, and that rehabilitation should be a central part of the overall response to crime (National Archives, 2011). Later in the same year, the Justice Secretary, Ken Clarke, gave a speech arguing for more community sentences (BBC, 2010). The Coalition's early plans also indicated a move away from the 'bureaucratic positivism' that had been a central aspect of probation work over the past decade:

> A top-down approach has concentrated on process instead of results. Prisons and probation services were assessed on the basis of hitting multiple targets and whether they had complied with detailed central requirements. There was insufficient focus on whether they were delivering the right result for the public and communities.
>
> (Ministry of Justice, 2010: 6)

Such rhetoric may indicate a progressive stance on rehabilitation. However, the approach outlined to achieve this has led to cause for concern among some commentators (for example: Ledger, 2010). There are two key strands to the Coalition government's approach. First, the government has advocated a Payment-By-Results scheme which would offer a financial incentive to providers on the basis of their success in reducing reoffending (Fox and Albertson, 2011). While this may prompt greater innovation and a focus on rehabilitation, there are also concerns that such competition may lead to fractured partnerships between agencies (Hough, 2011: 224). Second, offenders themselves may be incentivised to engage in programmes designed to rehabilitate, in return for shorter sentences or less social control. However, this is underpinned by an assumption that compliance is based on rational decision-making and appears to neglect the fact that the transition from crime to conformity is a long and complex one, characterised by lapse and uncertainty (Bottoms *et al.*, 2004; Burnett, 2004; Maguire and Raynor, 2006).

The *Breaking the Cycle* Green Paper also encourages greater contestability within probation, and it envisages probation trusts, private- and third-sector organisations, competing to provide services. In some respects this points towards an uncertain future for probation (Silvestri, 2012), particularly with regard to the manner in which probation services will be delivered in a climate of public spending cuts and staff reductions (NAPO, 2011). Such uncertainty has also been voiced in relation to the nature of commissioning that is expected to take place:

Probation services have been uncertain about their future since the idea of wider competition was first mooted almost ten years ago. The Government must clarify its intentions for the future of probation. We would welcome a clear statement from NOMS about which elements of probation work are considered appropriate for commissioning from other providers (and which are not).

(House of Commons Justice Committee, 2011: Para. 227)

In response, the government has stated that a diverse range of providers will be able to compete for various services, including: Community Payback; Electronic Monitoring; Bail Accommodation and Support Services; Approved Premises; Attendance Centres; Victim Liaison; Accredited Programmes; Activity Requirements; Supervision; and some aspects of Offender Management[1] (Ministry of Justice, 2012b: 14). The government has also indicated that Probation Trusts will commission these services, but will retain overall responsibility for offender management. Probation Trusts will be responsible for initial risk assessments, advice to courts and the Parole Board, supervision and decision-making in MAPPA cases, recalls and breaches, and early revocation of sentences. Probation Trusts will be responsible for public protection and reducing reoffending, and budgets will be devolved to the local level so that Trusts can target resources more effectively by commissioning the most appropriate services in their area:

Under our proposals, therefore, a Probation Trust would conduct the initial assessment of all offenders and determine the level of management they need at this stage based on their risk. Where the management of offenders presenting a lower risk had been completed in that area, the contracted provider would then be responsible for them. The Probation Trust would continue to manage and supervise all higher risk offenders.

(Ministry of Justice, 2012b: 17)

Under the current Coalition government the exact constitution of probation's culture is still emerging, but it would appear that disaggregation of service delivery is a key aspect of the contemporary approach to probation. Payment-by-results will clearly feature as an organising principle for the delivery of probation services, and while there may be some benefits in terms of the transference of risk, increased efficiency, and public expenditure savings (Cabinet Office, 2011; Collins, 2011a, 2011b; Corcoran, 2009, 2011; Fox and Albertson, 2011; Nicholson, 2011), there are also question marks around the possible effects upon the 'officer-offender' relationship, and upon the additional barriers that this could present to the would-be desister. It remains to be seen whether organisations from the private or Third Sectors will be able to offer the degree of support that has traditionally been associated with probation, or whether they will be able to develop engaging relationships with offenders. A lack of support and engagement is likely to lead to a continuation of the responsibilisation of offenders that emerged under the New Labour government. It is also unclear whether or not providers from the private or voluntary sectors will be equipped with the skills and expertise to deliver desistance-focused services. Furthermore, many existing services are currently delivered at a localised level and are highly responsive to individualised needs as a result. This is in keeping with knowledge about effective desistance practice, but the emergence of a Payment-By-Results scheme could jeopardise this, particularly if smaller organisations are marginalised from the tendering process.

At the time of writing, the Coalition has also announced plans to develop peer mentoring as a strand within the delivery of community supervision, in particular as a through-the-gate initiative to provide support for individuals released from prison as they attempt to reintegrate into the community. Clearly this raises a number of questions, not least in relation to how appropriate mentors would be recruited and trained, what services they would offer, and what level of monitoring would be available. However, peer mentoring could also offer an additional service which would fill the gap left by Probation Officers having to devote so much of their time to bureaucratic exercises and managerialist demands. Mentoring could also offer existing desisters with the opportunity to 'give something back', and to pass on the benefit of their experience. Clearly more research is required which would examine the benefits of peer mentors from a desistance perspective, and how such services could be effectively administered.

Desistance-focused practice in the future

The New Labour government undoubtedly made substantial changes to probation policy and practice between 1997–2010. Not least was the creation of the National Probation Service, the implementation of the National Offender Management Service, and the enhancement of various bureaucratic practices. The New Labour government also drove forward the use of one-to-one and group work programmes, largely based on a cognitive-behavioural model[2] to help to reduce reoffending. However, despite the emergence of literature around 'What Works' in relation to desistance (for example Rex, 1999; Burnett, 2000; Farrall, 2002), the New Labour government never fully embraced desistance theory or the idea of desistance-focused practice. The argument presented in this book and, arguably, in much of the desistance literature is that desistance-focused practice is crucial if community supervision is to enable individuals to change. Change is a crucial aspect of reducing reoffending, so any attempt to reduce it which neglects to consider desistance theory or practice is necessarily going to be limited.

The Conservative-led Coalition government appears to have been more receptive to the key ideas which underpin desistance-focused practice. There has also been a growing interest in desistance from those within probation, and community supervision practices appear to be changing vis-à-vis desistance theory and knowledge about 'What Works'.[3] However, there are some contradictions here too. Concerns have been raised about the potential fragmentation that could be caused by the Payment-By-Results project, and the findings from this study indicate that having more providers involved in community supervision could adversely impact upon attempts to desist (see Chapter 8). More research needs to be conducted which examines the way in which individuals experience supervision from a variety of providers, and how this impacts upon attempts to desist. There is no question that providers from the Third Sector[4] could provide some highly individualised supervision experiences that would be beneficial to the overall desistance process, but more work needs to be done to identify what particular aspects are useful and how these can be harnessed effectively. There is also more work that needs to be done to identify how different groups of individuals can be effectively supervised in the community (for example, young people, BME groups, and women offenders[5]).

This book has highlighted some of the difficulties and challenges faced by individuals in the early stages of desistance. Some of these challenges relate to the individual, in terms of, for example, moral agency, motivation or substance use. Other challenges relate to the wider social context, such as employment opportunities, availability of housing, or peer associations. The study has shown that many individuals display the human agency required to envisage alternative future goals, but that when faced with challenges such as those indicated here they may be more likely to revert to past habits and behaviours. This is, partly at least, because probation practitioners are constrained in their endeavours to initiate and support change by an overly prescriptive and bureaucratic policy framework. Much of this is based upon an understanding that successful community supervision can be measured in terms of simplistic reoffending rates. The aim of community supervision should not be based upon simple 'yes/no' measures of reoffending, but instead should be about helping individuals to develop more effective and productive approaches to self-management.

The findings from this study show that many individuals have some reserves of human agency, which is necessary for desistance to occur. Community supervision should be directed towards capitalising these reserves, and supporting them further, so that individuals become more empowered to manage their own behaviours effectively. The approach towards community supervision should also not be directed towards enforcing compliance, as this is more likely to be of a formal and short-term nature. Instead, community supervision should be directed towards enabling individuals to secure longer-term compliance themselves. It is argued here that this may not be achievable within policy frameworks which constrain the actions of individual practitioners and dilute discretion and autonomy. It is hoped that this book will be of interest to practitioners, particularly in terms of identifying approaches towards working with individuals in the community which may be considered to be desistance-focused. It is also hoped that this book will be of interest to policymakers, such that conditions can be developed which allow practitioners to operate more freely from the constraints of bureaucracy and managerialism, and instead remain desistance-focused.

Notes

2 Reoffending and the response from probation

1 A first offence is defined as an offence which results in a first reprimand, warning, caution or conviction. A further offence is where an individual who already has a criminal history recorded on the PNC receives another reprimand, warning, caution or conviction (Ministry of Justice, 2012).

2 In 2002 the government, based on the finding that a disproportionate amount of crime was committed by a small percentage of offenders, introduced a strategy to ensure that all agencies within the criminal justice system had a focus upon those defined as 'persistent offenders.' This led to the introduction of the Persistent Offender Scheme in 2003, and was closely followed by the Prolific and other Priority Offender (PPO) programme in 2004. The approach has been at the forefront of criminal justice policy for the last decade. The Labour government stated that efforts to target the 'most prolific' offenders had been 'the major shift over the last five years [2004–2009]' (HM Government, 2009). The focus on persistent and prolific offenders has, in turn, fed into the development of Integrated Offender Management (IOM) which would provide a strategic umbrella framework within which PPO schemes could continue to operate. IOM has a key focus on reducing reoffending, and provides 'the opportunity to target those offenders of most concern' (Home Office/Ministry of Justice, 2010: 1).

3 Some recent Ministry of Justice figures do incorporate frequency and severity, and the recent Payment-By-Results pilot at HMP Peterborough measured the success of interventions by examining reductions in the frequency of reconviction as opposed to the binary measure of whether or not an individual was reconvicted (Disley *et al.*, 2011).

4 Various excellent accounts of the history of probation exist elsewhere. The series of articles published in *The Howard Journal of Criminal Justice* by Bill McWilliams (1983, 1985, 1986, 1987) are often cited as offering an excellent insight into the changing ethos of probation in England and Wales. Maurice Vanstone's (2004) text offers a comprehensive historical account of probation, while Oldfield's (2002) monograph provides discussion of the gradual transition from a welfare-focused to a risk-focused service. Whitehead (2007, 2011) has provided an analysis of the theoretical, cultural and organisational changes to the Probation Service since its inception. See also: Canton's (2011) *Probation: Working With Offenders*, and Mair and Burke's (2011) *Redemption, Rehabilitation and Risk Management*.

5 Between 2002–2006 the number of qualified Probation Officers fell by 4 per cent, while the number of trainee Probation Officers fell by 30 per cent (see Oldfield and Grimshaw, 2007).

6 The number of Senior Probation Officers increased by 63 per cent between 2002–2006, while the number of Deputy Chief Officers/Directors increased by almost 200 per cent. Over the same time period there was a 26 per cent increase in the number of court

orders passed to the Probation Service, and a 17 per cent increase in the amount of pre-post release work undertaken (see Oldfield and Grimshaw, 2007).

3   Persistence, desistance and the transitional phase

1 Cusson and Pinsonneault make reference to a man who shot dead a police officer in the commission of a crime and who subsequently spent several years on Death Row. This, he exclaimed, changed his outlook on life, and prompted a reconsideration of who he wanted to be.
2 Clearly, one argument against this position is that many crimes occur in the workplace (Croall, 2001; Friedrichs, 2002), and that certain opportunities to offend or engage in antisocial behaviour may result from associations with co-workers (Robinson and O'Leary-Kelly, 1998).
3 A subsequent follow-up study was reported by Farrall and Calverley (2006), and another is being conducted at the time of writing (see Farrall *et al.*, 2011, 2012).
4 The Oxford Dynamics of Recidivism study has also been the subject of follow-up projects (see Burnett, 2004; LeBel *et al.*, 2008).
5 The Sheffield Desistance Study is formerly known as the Sheffield Pathways Out Of Crime Study (SPOOCS) and formed part of the broader Social Contexts of Pathways in Crime (SCOPIC) research consortium. Other studies in this consortium included the Environmental Risk Longitudinal Twin Study (E-Risk), and the Peterborough Adolescent Development Study (PADS). The SPOOCS researchers offered a model of desistance which begins with a triggering event, which leads to a decision to desist. In turn, this prompts a re-evaluation of identity. This is followed by action and maintenance in order to achieve desistance.

4   Agency, narratives and social context

1 It is worth noting that desistance was neither the explicit nor a main focus of Clarke and Cornish's work. Their work was also entirely theoretical, in the sense that they did not provide any data to support their argument. Instead, they constructed a hypothetical 'decision tree' to illustrate how an offender might make the decision to stop offending.

6   First steps – the transition to desistance

1 For a comprehensive account of the internal conversation see Margaret Archer (2003) *Structure, Agency and the Internal Conversation*. This is preceded by her book *Being Human: The Problem of Agency*, published in 2000 and which provides an excellent grounding in the key concepts. *Making our Way through the World: Human Reflexivity and Social Mobility* (2007) offers an account of the internal conversation and illustrates its application.

7   Strategies for desistance

1 Steven Roberts (2012) has reported on findings from a qualitative study of 24 young men employed in the service sector. He found that these men were able to resist the hegemonic masculinity reported in earlier studies, and commit to a 'softened' version of masculinity involving work in the service sector and a rejection of 'traditional gendered domestic responsibilities'. Arguably, the men in Roberts's study would be more attuned to the notion of an emergent masculine identity congruent with the changing nature of contemporary society, given their position in the labour market.

8 Probation – enabling or constraining desistance?

1 IDAP – Integrated Domestic Abuse Programme. This programme is designed to challenge the patterns of thinking which underpin male domestic abuse. It is based on the belief that men who domestically abuse are trying to control their victim. Participants learn about the abuse that they carry out and develop alternative skills and behaviours so that they can have healthy relationships in the future.

DID – Drink Impaired Drivers Programme. This programme is aimed at challenging attitudes and behaviour surrounding drinking alcohol, specifically in relation to driving. Participants self-monitor their drinking, and learn about the effects of alcohol. The aim is to change attitudes and behaviour surrounding drinking, and to promote safer driving. Participants also learn about the effects of drink driving on victims and their families.

SOTP – Sex Offender Treatment Programme. There are various versions of treatment programmes for men who have committed a sexual offence. These can take place in custody and in the community. Men can complete various modules, and courses can last up to 250 hours. The variations of the programme can enable better targeting of the programme (e.g. towards individuals with social or learning difficulties), but the core aims are to help individuals to understand why they have offended and to promote meaningful life goals and to encourage individuals to develop new patterns of thinking and behaviour.

COVAID – Control of Violence for Angry Impulsive Drinkers Programme. This programme is targeted towards young men who have a history of violent behaviour while intoxicated (not necessarily resulting in crime). It is directed more towards individuals who engage in binge drinking, rather than individuals defined as alcoholics. It can be delivered in custody or in the community, and it can be delivered either in groups or on a one-to-one basis.

LIAP – Low Intensity Alcohol Programme. This programme aims to motivate individuals to change patterns of thinking and behaviour in relation to drinking alcohol. It raises awareness of alcohol misuse and aims to prevent relapse.

CALM – Controlling Anger and Learning to Manage Programme. This programme is aimed at male offenders who have a history of offending which involves emotional arousal. Individuals learn about the triggers to their offending, and learn skills and techniques to control and manage their emotions.

For further information on accredited programmes see: www.justice.gov.uk/offenders/before-after-release/obp.

2 Although in the follow-up to the original study, Farrall and Calverley (2006) found that probation had 'planted a seed' from which the process of desistance could grow.

10 Concluding thoughts

1 In July 2012, it was announced that Serco (a private sector organisation) would begin to provide Community Payback from October of the same year, with London Probation Trust as the sub-contractor.

2 Perhaps the two most commonly used programmes under New Labour were Reasoning and Rehabilitation (R&R) and Enhanced Thinking Skills (ETS). See Raynor and Vanstone (1996) for an evaluation of the R&R based Straight Thinking on Probation (STOP) programme, and see Friendship *et al.* (2003c) for a review of cognitive skills programmes in UK prisons.

3 The 'Journal of a Desistance Development Officer' (Available at: http://desistanceaspt.blogspot.co.uk/) provides a highly interesting and engaging example of the growing interest in desistance from practitioners.

4 By 'Third Sector' I am referring here broadly to voluntary, charity and other community-based organisations.

5 But see Sharpe (2011) and Calverley (2013) for existing research in this area.

References

Ajzen, I. (1991) 'The theory of planned behaviour' in *Organizational Behavior and Human Decision Processes*. 50: 179–211.

Anderson, S., Kinsey, R., Loader, I. and Smith, C. (1994) *Cautionary Tales: Young People, Crime and Policing in Edinburgh*. Avebury: Ashgate.

Antonowicz, D.H. and Ross, R.R. (1994) 'Essential components of successful rehabilitation programs for offenders' in *International Journal of Offender Therapy and Comparative Criminology*, 38: 97–104.

Archer, M.S. (1995) *Realist Social Theory: The Morphogenetic Approach*. Cambridge: Cambridge University Press.

Archer, M.S. (2000) *Being Human: The Problem of Agency*. Cambridge: Cambridge University Press.

Archer, M.S. (2003) *Structure, Agency and the Internal Conversation*. Cambridge: Cambridge University Press.

Archer, M.S. (2007) *Making our Way through the World: Human Reflexivity and Social Mobility*. Cambridge: Cambridge University Press.

Arnett J.J. (2000) 'Emerging Adulthood: A Theory of Development from the Late Teens through the Twenties' in *American Psychologist*, 55: 469–80.

Arnett J.J. (2003) 'Conceptions of the Transition to Adulthood among Emerging Adults in American Ethnic Groups' in Arnett, J.J. and Galambos, N.L. (eds) *Exploring Cultural Conceptions of the Transition to Adulthood*. San Francisco: Wiley.

Arnett J.J. (2007) 'Emerging Adulthood: What Is It, and What Is It Good For?' in *Child Development Perspectives*, 1: 68–73.

Ashworth, P. (2009) 'What Happened To Probation? Managerialism, Performance & The Decline Of Autonomy' in *British Journal of Community Justice*, 7(3): 61–76.

Atkin, C.A. and Armstrong, G.S. (2012) 'Does The Concentration of Parolees in a Community Impact Employer Attitudes Toward the Hiring of Ex-Offenders?' in *Criminal Justice Policy Review*, 24 (1): 71–93.

Attride-Sterling, J. (2001) 'Thematic networks: an analytical tool for qualitative research' in *Qualitative Research*, 1 (3): 385–405.

Bandura, A. (2001) 'Social Cognitive Theory: An Agentic Perspective' in *Annual Review of Psychology*, 52: 1–26.

Barry, M. (2000) 'The mentor/monitor debate in criminal justice: "what works" for offenders' in *British Journal of Social Work*, 30 (5): 575–95.

Barry, M. (2007) 'Listening and learning: The reciprocal relationship between worker and client' in *Probation*, 54 (4): 407–22.

Barry, M. (2009) 'Youth Justice Policy and its Influence on Desistance from Crime' in Barry, M. and McNeill, F. (eds) *Youth Offending and Youth Justice*. London: Jessica Kinsgley.

Barry, M. (2010a) 'Promoting Desistance Among Young People' in Taylor, W., Earle, R. and Hester, R. (eds) *Youth Justice Handbook: Theory, Policy and Practice*, Cullompton: Willan.

Barry, M. (2010b) 'Youth transitions: from offending to desistance' in *Journal of Youth Studies*, 13 (1): 121–36.

Barry, M. (2012) 'Young women in transition: From offending to desistance' in Losel, F., Bottoms, A. and Farrington, D. (eds) *Young Adult Offenders: Lost in Transition?* Oxon: Routledge.

Bateman, T. (2005) 'Reducing Child Imprisonment: A Systemic Challenge' in *Youth Justice*, 5 (2): 91–105.

Bauman, Z. (1992) *Intimations of Postmodernity*. London: Routledge.

Bauman, Z. (2002) 'Foreword' in Beck, U. and Beck-Gernsheim, E. *Individualisation: Institutionalised Individualism and its Social and Political Consequences*. London: Sage.

Baumeister, R.F. (1994) 'The crystallization of discontent in the process of major life change' in Heatherton, T.F. and Weinberger, J.L. (eds) *Can Personality Change?*. Washington, DC: American Psychological Association.

Beck, U. (1992a) *Risk Society: Towards a New Modernity*. London: Sage.

Beck, U. (1992b) 'How Modern is Modern Society?' in *Theory, Culture and Society*, 9 (2): 163–9.

Beck, U. and Beck-Gernsheim, E. (2002) *Individualisation: Institutionalised Individualism and its Social and Political Consequences*. London: Sage.

Beck, U., Giddens, A. and Lash, S. (1994) *Reflexive Modernization: Politics, Tradition and Aesthetics in the Modern Social Order*. Cambridge: Polity Press.

Becker, H.S. (1963) *Outsiders: Studies in the Sociology of Deviance*. New York: The Free Press.

Benda, B., Harm, J. and Toombs, J. (2005) 'Survival analysis of recidivism of male and female boot camp graduates using life-course theory' in *Journal of Offender Rehabilitation*, 40 (3/4): 87–113.

Bennett, J. (2008) 'They hug hoodies, don't they? Responsibility, irresponsibility and responsibilisation in Conservative crime policy' in *Howard Journal*, 47(5): 451–69.

Bersani, B.E., Laub, J.H. and Nieuwbeerta, P. (2009) 'Marriage and Desistance from Crime in the Netherlands: Do Gender and Socio-Historical Context Matter?' in *Journal of Quantitative Criminology*, 25 (1): 3–24.

Bhui, H.S. (2004) 'Assessing Carter' in *Probation Journal*, 51 (2): 99–100.

Biesta, G. and Tedder, M. (2006a) 'How is agency possible? Towards an ecological understanding of agency-as-achievement'. Working Paper 5. Online. Available at: www.tlrp.org/project%20sites/LearningLives/papers/working_papers/Working_paper_5_Exeter_Feb_06.pdf [Accessed: 14/02/2008].

Biesta, G. and Tedder, M. (2006b) 'Agency and learning in the lifecourse'. Paper for the ESRC/TLRP Thematic Seminar Series 'Transitions through the lifecourse: The effects of identity, agency and structure'. London, 16/05/2006. Online. Available at: www.learninglives.org/papers/LL_TLRPSeminar_Series_May_2006.pdf [Accessed: 14/02/2008].

Blair, T. (1993) 'Why crime is a socialist issue' in *New Statesman and Society*, 6 (29/01): 27–8.

Blokland, A.A.J. and Nieuwbeerta, P. (2005) 'The Effects of Life Circumstances on Longitudinal Trajectories of Offending' in *Criminology*, 43 (4): 1203–40.

Blumstein, A., Cohen, J. and Farrington, D.P. (1988) 'Criminal career research: Its value for criminology' in *Criminology*, 26: 1–35.

Blumstein, A., Cohen, J., Roth, J.A. and Visher, C.A. (1986) *Criminal Careers and 'Career Criminals'*, Vol. I. Washington, DC: National Academy Press.

Bottoms, A. (1977) 'Reflections on the Renaissance of Dangerousness' in *The Howard Journal of Criminal Justice*, 16 (2): 70–96.

Bottoms, A. (1995) 'The Philosophy and Politics of Punishment and Sentencing' in Clarkson, C. and Morgan, R. (eds) *The Politics of Sentencing Reform*. Oxford: Clarendon Press.

Bottoms, A., Shapland, J., Costello, A., Holmes, D. and Muir, G. (2004) 'Towards Desistance: Theoretical Underpinnings for an Empirical Study' in *The Howard Journal of Criminal Justice*, 43 (4): 368–89.

Bottoms, A. and Shapland, J. (2010) 'Steps toward desistance among male young adult recidivists' in Farrall, S., Sparks, R., Maruna, S. and Hough, M. (eds) *Escape Routes: Contemporary Perspectives on Life After Punishment*. London: Routledge.

Boyle, M. (2007) *Unemployment and Re-offending: An International Literature Review*. Edinburgh: APEX Scotland.

Braithwaite, J. (1989) *Crime, Shame and Reintegration*. Cambridge: Cambridge University Press.

Brame, R., Bushway, S.D. and Paternoster, R. (2003) 'Examining the prevalence of criminal desistance' in *Criminology*, 41: 423–48.

Braun, V. and Clarke, V. (2006) 'Using thematic analysis in psychology' in *Qualitative Research in Psychology*, 3: 77–101.

Brody, S.R. (1976) *The Effectiveness of Sentencing*, London: HMSO.

Brown, M. and Bloom, B. (2009) 'Reentry and Renegotiating Motherhood: Maternal Identity and Success on Parole' in *Crime and Delinquency*, 55 (2): 313–36.

Budd, T., Sharp, C. and Mayhew, P. (2005a) *Offending in England and Wales: First Results from the 2003 Crime and Justice Survey*. Home Office Research Study 275. Online. Available at: www.homeoffice.gov.uk/rds/pdfs05/hors275.pdf [Accessed: 14/12/2009].

Budd, T., Sharp, C., Wier, G., Wilson, D. and Owen, N. (2005b) *Young people and crime: findings from the 2004 Offending, Crime and Justice Survey*. Home Office Statistical Bulletin No. 20/55. Online. Available at: www.homeoffice.gov.uk/rds/pdfs05/hosb2005.pdf [Accessed: 14/12/2009].

Burke, L. (2011) 'Revolution or evolution?' in *Probation Journal*, 58 (1): 3–8.

Burke, L. and Collett, S. (2010) 'People are not things: What New Labour has done to Probation' in *Probation Journal*, 57(3): 232–49.

Burnett, R. (1992) *The Dynamics of Recidivism*. Oxford: Centre for Criminological Research, University of Oxford.

Burnett, R. (2000) 'Understanding criminal careers through a series of in-depth interviews' in *Offender Programs Report*, 4 (1): 1–16.

Burnett, R. (2004) 'One-to-one ways of promoting desistance: in search of an evidence base' in Burnett, R. and Roberts, C. (eds) *What Works in Probation and Youth Justice: Developing evidence-based practice*. Cullompton: Willan.

Burnett, R. (2007) 'The Personal Touch in Ex-Offender Reintegration'. Paper presented to the Deakin University Third Annual Conference on 'The Reintegration Puzzle: Fitting the Pieces Together', held at the Waterview Convention Centre, Sydney,

07–08/05/2007. Online. Available at: www.deakin.edu.au/hmnbs/psychology/research/ease/2007%20Conference/files/burnett-paper.pdf [Accessed: 11/11/2009].

Burnett, R. (2010) 'Post-corrections reintegration: prisoner resettlement and desistance from crime' in Adler, J.R. and Gray, J.M. (eds) *Forensic Psychology 2nd edition*. Cullompton: Willan.

Burnett, R. and Maruna, S. (2004) 'So "Prison Works" – Does It? The Criminal Careers of 130 Men Released from Prison under Home Secretary Michael Howard' in *The Howard Journal of Criminal Justice*, 43 (4): 390–404.

Burnett, R. and McNeill, F. (2005) 'The place of the officer-offender relationship in assisting offenders to desist from crime' in *Probation Journal*, 52 (3): 247–68.

Burnett, R. and Roberts, C. (eds) (2004) *What Works in Probation and Youth Justice*. Cullompton: Willan.

Burns, G. (1998) 'A Perspective on Policy and Practice in the Re-Integration of Offenders' in *European Journal on Criminal Policy and Research*, 6 (2): 171–83.

Burrowes, N. and Needs, A. (2009) 'Time to Contemplate Change? A framework for assessing readiness to change with offenders' in *Aggression and Violent Behaviour*, 14 (1): 39–49.

Bushway, S.D., Piquero, A.R., Broidy, L.M., Cauffman, E. and Mazerolle, P. (2001) 'An Empirical Framework for Studying Desistance as a Process' in *Criminology*, 39 (2): 491–516.

Bushway, S.D., Thornberry, T.P. and Krohn, M.D. (2003) 'Desistance as a developmental process: A comparison of static and dynamic approaches' in *Journal of Quantitative Criminology*, 19 (2): 129–53.

Byrne, C.F. and Trew, K.F. (2008) 'Pathways Through Crime: The Development of Crime and Desistance in the Accounts of Men and Women Offenders' in *The Howard Journal of Criminal Justice*, 47 (3): 238–58.

Cabinet Office (2011) *Modernising Commissioning: Increasing the Role of Charities, Social Enterprises, Mutuals and Cooperatives in Public Service Delivery*. London: Cabinet Office.

Calverley, A. (2013) *Cultures of Desistance: Rehabilitation, Reintegration and Ethnic Minorities*. Abingdon: Routledge.

Canton, R. and Hancock, D. (2007) *Dictionary of Probation and Offender Management*. Cullompton: Willan.

Carter, P. (2003) *Managing Offenders, Reducing Crime: A New Approach*. London: Home Office Strategy Unit.

Catalano, R.F., Park, J., Harachi, T., Haggerty, K.P., Abbott, R.D. and Hawkins, J.D. (2005) 'Mediating the effects of poverty, gender, individual characteristics, and external constraints on antisocial behavior: A test of the social development model and implications for developmental life-course theory' in Farrington, D.P. (ed.) *Integrated Developmental and Life-Course Theories of Offending*. New Brunswick, NJ: Transaction.

Cauffman, E. and Steinberg, L. (2000) '(Im)maturity of judgment in adolescence: why adolescents may be less culpable than adults' in *Behavioral Sciences and the Law*, 18 (6): 741–60.

Cavadino, P. (2000) 'Improved housing will cut crime' in *The Guardian* 14/11/2000. Online. Available at: www.guardian.co.uk/society/2000/nov/14/societyhousing.comment [Accessed: 12/08/2006].

Chapman, T. and Hough, M. (1998) *Evidence-Based Practice*. London: Home Office.

Chartered Institute of Personnel and Development (CIPD) (2001) *Employing People with Conviction*. London: CIPD.

Chartered Institute of Personnel and Development (CIPD) (2004a) *Employing Ex-Offenders: A Practical Guide*. London: CIPD.

Chartered Institute of Personnel and Development (CIPD) (2004b) *Employers and Offenders: Reducing Crime through Work and Rehabilitation*. London: CIPD.

Clarke, R.V. and Cornish, D.B. (1985) 'Modeling Offender's Decisions: A Framework for Research and Policy' in Tonry, M. and Morris, N. (eds) *Crime and Justice: An Annual Review of Research*. Chicago: University of Chicago Press.

Coffey, A. and Atkinson, P. (1996) *Making Sense of Qualitative Data: Complementary Research Strategies*. London: Sage.

Collins, J. (2011a) 'Payment by results in the criminal justice system' in *Criminal Justice Matters*, 85 (1): 8–9.

Collins, J. (2011b) 'Payment by results in the criminal justice system: can it deliver?' in *Safer Communities*, 10 (2): 18–25.

Corcoran, M. (2009) 'Bringing the penal voluntary sector to market' in *Criminal Justice Matters*, 77 (1): 32–3.

Corcoran, M. (2011) 'Dilemmas of institutionalization in the penal voluntary sector' in *Critical Social Policy*, 31 (1): 30–52.

Cornish, D.B. and Clarke, R.V. (eds) (1986) *The Reasoning Criminal*. New York: Springer-Verlag.

Crewe, B., Liebling, A. and Hulley, S. (2011) 'Staff culture, use of authority and prisoner quality of life in public and private sector prisons' in *Australian and New Zealand Journal of Criminology*, 44 (1): 94–115.

Croall, H. (2001) *Understanding White Collar Crime*. Buckingham: Open University Press.

Cromwell, P., Olson, J. and Avary, D. (1991) *Breaking and Entering*. London: Sage.

Crow, I. (2006) *Resettling Prisoners: A Review*. York: York Publishing Services.

Cusson, M. and Pinsonneault, P. (1986) 'The decision to give up crime' in Cornish, D.B. and Clarke, R.V.G. (eds) *The Reasoning Criminal: Rational Choice Perspectives in Offending*. New York: Springer-Verlag.

Dean, H. (2003) 'Re-conceptualising Welfare-to-Work for People with Multiple Problems and Needs' in *Journal of Social Policy*, 32 (3): 441–59.

Deering, J. (2010) 'Attitudes and beliefs of trainee probation officers: A "new breed?"' in *Probation*, 57 (1): 9–26.

Denney, D. (2005) *Risk and Society*. London: Sage.

Denno, D.W. (1990) *Biology and Violence: From Birth to Adulthood*. Cambridge: Cambridge University Press.

DiClemente, C.C. and Prochaska, J.O. (1982) 'Self-change and therapy change of smoking behavior: A comparison of processes of change in cessation and maintenance' in *Addictive Behaviors*, 7: 133–42.

DiIulio, J. (1988) 'What's wrong with private prison' in *Public Interest*, Vol. 29: 66–83.

Disley, E., Rubin, J., Scraggs, E., Burrowes, N., Culley, D. (2011) *Lessons learned from the planning and early implementation of the Social Impact Bond at HMP Peterborough*. Research Series 5/11. London: Ministry of Justice.

Ditton, P.P (1999) *Mental Health and Treatment of Inmates and Probationers*. Washington, DC: US Department of Justice, Bureau of Justice Statistics.

Dominey, J. (2012) 'A mixed market for probation services: Can lessons from the recent past help shape the near future?' in *Probation Journal*, 59 (4): 339–54.

Dowden, C. and Andrews, D. (2004) 'The importance of staff practice in delivering effective correctional treatment: A meta-analytical review of core correctional practice' in *International Journal of Offender Therapy and Comparative Criminology*, 48 (2): 203–14.

Doyle, J. (2008) '"Murder a week" by criminals on probation'. *The Independent* 30/10/2008. Online. Available at: www.independent.co.uk/news/uk/crime/murder-a-week-by-criminals-on-probation-979724.html [Accessed: 12/02/2010].

Duff, A. (2001) *Punishment, Communication and Community*. Oxford: Oxford University Press.

D'Unger, A.V., Land, K.C. and McCall, P.L. (2002) 'Sex Differences in Age Patterns of Delinquent/Criminal Careers: Results from Poisson Latent Class Analyses of the Philadelphia Cohort Study' in *Journal of Quantitative Criminology*, 18 (4): 349–75.

Eden, K., Nelson, T.J. and Paranal, R. (2004) 'Fatherhood and Incarceration as Potential Turning Points in the Criminal Careers of Unskilled Men' in Pattillo, M., Weiman, D. and Western, B. (eds) *Imprisoning America: The social effects of mass incarceration*. New York: Russell Sage Foundation.

Elder G.H., Johnson M.K. and Crosnoe R. (2003) 'The Emergence and Development of Life Course Theory' in Mortimer, J.T. and Shanahan, M.J. (eds) *Handbook of the Life Course*, New York: Plenum Publishing: 3–19.

Elliott, D.S. (1994) Serious violent offenders: Onset, developmental course, and termination – The American Society of Criminology 1993 Presidential Address' in *Criminology* 32 (1): 1–21.

Elliot, D.S., Huizinga, D. and Menard, S. (1989) *Multiple Problem Youth: Delinquency, Substance Use, and Mental Health Problems*. New York: Springer.

Emirbayer, M. and Mische, A. (1998) 'What is Agency?' in *American Journal of Sociology*, 103 (4): 962–1023.

Ezell, M.E. and Cohen, L.E. (2004) *Desisting from Crime*. Oxford: Oxford University Press.

Farrall, S. (2002) *Rethinking What Works with Offenders: Probation, social context and desistance from crime*. Cullompton: Willan.

Farrall, S. (ed.) (2009) 'Explorations in Theories of Desistance: Societal-Level Approaches' in *Theoretical Criminology*, 13 (1): 1–146.

Farrall, S. (2013) *Investigating the Long term Impact of Probation Supervision: Offender Engagement Research Bulletin, Issue 15*. National Offender Management Service. Online. Available at: http://blogs.iriss.org.uk/discoveringdesistance/files/2011/09/NOMS-Bulletin_Issue-15FINAL1.pdf [Accessed: 24/03/2013].

Farrall, S., Bottoms, A. and Shapland, J. (2010) 'Social structures and desistance from crime' in *European Journal of Criminology*, 7 (6): 546–70.

Farrall, S. and Bowling, B. (1999) 'Structuration, Human Development and Desistance from Crime' in *British Journal of Criminology*, 39 (2): 253–68.

Farrall, S. and Calverley, A. (2006) *Understanding Desistance from Crime: Theoretical directions in resettlement and rehabilitation*. Maidenhead: Open University Press.

Farrall, S. and Maruna, S. (eds) (2004) 'Desistance-Focused Criminal Justice Policy Research: Introduction to a Special Issue on Desistance from Crime and Public Policy' in *The Howard Journal of Criminal Justice*, 43 (4): 358–67.

Farrall, S., Jackson, J. and Gray, E. (2009) *Social Order and the Fear of Crime in Contemporary Times*. Oxford: Oxford University Press.

Farrall, S., Sharpe, G., Hunter, B. and Calverley, A. (2011) 'Theorizing structural and individual-level processes in desistance and persistence: Outlining an integrated perspective' in *Australian & New Zealand Journal of Criminology* 44 (2): 218–34.

Farrall, S., Sharpe, G., Hunter, B. and Calverley, A. (2012) 'The Long-Term Impacts of Probation Supervision: Is Impact Detectable After 15 Years? Presentation for the Discovering Desistance Project. Online. Available at: http://blogs.iriss.org.uk/discoveringdesistance/files/2012/03/Presentation3.pdf [Accessed: 27/07/2012].

Farrington, D.P. (1986) 'Age and Crime' in Morris, N. and Tonry, M. (eds) *Crime and Justice: An Annual Review of Research*. Chicago: University of Chicago Press.

Farrington, D.P. (1989) *The Origins of Crime: The Cambridge Study in Delinquent Development*. Home Office Research Bulletin 27. London: Home Office.

Farrington, D.P. (1995) 'The development of offending and antisocial behaviour from childhood: Key findings from the Cambridge Study in Delinquent Development' in *Journal of Child Psychology and Psychiatry*, 36: 929–64.

Farrington, D.P. (1997a) 'Human Development and Criminal Careers' in Maguire, M., Morgan, R. and Reiner, R. (eds) *The Oxford Handbook of Criminology*, 2nd edn. Oxford: Oxford University Press.

Farrington, D.P. (1997b) 'Early prediction of violent and non-violent youthful offending' in *European Journal on Criminal Policy and Research*, 5 (2): 51–66.

Farrington, D.P. (2000) 'Explaining and preventing crime: The globalization of knowledge – The American Society of Criminology 1999 Presidential address' in *Criminology*, 38(1): 1–24.

Farrington, D.P. (2003) 'Developmental and Life Course Criminology: Key Theoretical and Empirical Issues' in *Criminology*, 41: 201–35.

Farrington, D.P. (2005) 'The integrated cognitive antisocial potential (ICAP) theory' in Farrington, D.P. (ed.) *Integrated Developmental and Life-Course Theories of Offending*. New Brunswick, NJ: Transaction.

Farrington, D.P. (2007) 'Advancing knowledge about desistance' in *Journal of Contemporary Criminal Justice*, 23: 125–34.

Farrington, D., Coid, J., Harnett, L., Jolliffe, D., Soteriou, N., Turner, R. and West, D. (2006a) *Criminal Careers and Life Successes: New Findings from the Cambridge Study in Delinquent Development*. Home Office Research Findings 281. London: Home Office.

Farrington, D., Coid, J., Harnett, L., Jolliffe, D., Soteriou, N., Turner, R. and West, D. (2006b) *Criminal Careers up to Age 50 and Life Success up to Age 48: New Findings from the Cambridge Study in Delinquent Development*, 2nd edn. Home Office Research Findings 299. London: Home Office.

Farrington, D.P. and Hawkins, D.J. (1991) 'Predicting participation, early onset, and later persistence in officially recorded delinquency' in *Criminal Behaviour and Mental Health*, 1: 1–33.

Farrington, D.P. and West, D.J. (1995) 'Effects of marriage, separation and children on offending by adult males' in Blau, Z.S. and Hagan, J. (eds) *Current Perspectives on Aging and the Life Cycle: Vol. 4. Delinquency and disrepute in the life course*. Greenwich, CT: JAI Press.

Faulkner, D. and Burnett, R. (2011) *Where Next For Criminal Justice?* Bristol: Policy Press.

Ferguson, D.M., Lynskey, M.T. and Horwood, L.J. (2006) 'Alcohol misuse and juvenile offending in adolescence' in *Addiction*, 91 (4): 483–94.

Fernee, U. and Burke, I. (2010) 'Cultural Diversity and the Probation Service' in *Irish Probation Journal*, 7: 140–51.

Fielding, N. (2004) 'Grounded theory, analytic induction, coding and computer-assisted analysis' in Becker, S. and Bryman, A. (eds) *Understanding Research for Social Policy and Practice: Themes, methods and approaches*. Bristol: The Policy Press.

Fleisher, M.S. and Krienert, J.L. (2004) 'Life-course events, social networks, and the emergence of violence among female gang members' in *Journal of Community Psychology*, 32 (5): 607–22.

Fletcher, D.R. (2001) 'Ex-offenders, the labour market and the new public administration' in *Public Administration*, 79 (4): 871–91.

Fletcher, D.R. (2007) 'Offenders in the post-industrial labour market: lubricating the revolving door?' in *People, Place and Policy*, 1 (2): 80–9.

Fletcher, D.R. (2008) 'Offenders in the post-industrial labour market: from the underclass to the undercaste?' in *Policy and Politics*, 36 (2): 283–97.

Fletcher, D.R., Taylor, A. and Hughes, S. (2001) *Recruiting and Employing Offenders*. York: Joseph Rowntree Foundation.

Fletcher, D.R., Woodhill, D. and Herrington, A. (1998) *Building Bridges into Employment and Training for Ex-Offenders*. York: Joseph Rowntree Foundation.

Flood-Page, C., Campbell, S., Harrington, V. and Miller, J. (2000) *Youth Crime: Findings from the 1998/99 Youth Lifestyles Survey*. Home Office Research Study 209. Online. Available at: www.homeoffice.gov.uk/rds/pdfs/hors209.pdf [Accessed: 14/12/2009].

Flynn, J. (2008) 'Thinking Beyond Prison Borders: Rehabilitation as an educational "project"'. Online proceedings of the Canadian Association for the Study of Adult Education (CASAE) 27th National Conference at the University of British Columbia, Vancouver, BC. Online. Available at: www.oise.utoronto.ca/CASAE/cnf2008/Online-Proceedings-2008/CAS2008-Flynn.pdf [Accessed: 27/02/2009].

Folkard, M.S., Fowles, A.J., McWilliams, B.C., McWilliams, W., Smith, D.D. and Walmsley, G.R. (1974) *IMPACT. Intensive Matched Probation and Aftercare Treatment: Volume I. The Design of the Experiment and an Interim Evaluation*. Home Office Research Study 24. London: HMSO.

Folkard, M.S., Smith, D.E. and Smith, D.D. (1976) *IMPACT Volume II: The Results of the Experiment*. Home Office Research Study 36. London: HMSO.

Ford, R. (2009) 'Crime figures row as 48 on probation are charged with serious offences' in *The Times*, 26/10/2009. Online. Available at: www.timesonline.co.uk/tol/news/uk/crime/article6890656.ece [Accessed: 12/02/2010].

Forrest, W. and Hay, C. (2011) 'Life-course transitions, self-control and desistance from crime' in *Criminology and Criminal Justice*, 11 (5): 487–513.

Forste, R., Clarke, L. and Bahr, S. (2010) 'Staying Out of Trouble: Intentions of Young Male Offenders' in *International Journal of Offender Therapy and Comparative Criminology*. Online. Available at: http://ijo.sagepub.com/cgi/rapidpdf/0306624X09359649v1 [Accessed: 29/01/2010].

Fox, C. and Albertson, K. (2011) 'Payment by results and social impact bonds in the criminal justice sector: New challenges for the concept of evidence-based policy' in *Criminology and Criminal Justice*, 11(5): 395–413.

Francis, B., Soothill, K. and Fligelstone, R. (2004) 'Identifying patterns and pathways of offending behaviour: a new approach to typologies of crime' in *European Journal of Criminology*, 1: 48–87.

Friedrichs, D.O. (2002) 'Occupational crime, occupational deviance, and workplace crime' in *Criminology and Criminal Justice*, 2 (3): 243–56.

Friendship, C., Bates, A., Patel, V., Corbett, C. and Friendship, C. (2003a) 'Assessing reconviction, reoffending and recidivism in a sample of UK sexual offenders' in *Legal and Criminological Psychology*, 8 (2): 207–15.

Friendship, C., Beech, A.R. and Browne, K.D. (2002) 'Reconviction as an Outcome Measure in Research' in *British Journal of Criminology*, 42 (2): 442–4.

Friendship, C., Blud, L., Erikson, M., Travers, R. and Thornton, D. (2003c) 'Cognitive-behavioural treatment for imprisoned offenders: An evaluation of HM Prison Service's cognitive skills programmes' in *Legal and Criminal Psychology*, 8 (1): 103–14.

Friendship, C., Falshaw, L. and Beech, A.R. (2003b) 'Measuring the real impact of accredited offending behaviour programmes' in *Legal and Criminological Psychology*, 8 (1): 115–27.

Fudge, S. and Williams, S. (2006) 'Beyond Left and Right: Can the Third Way Deliver a Reinvigorated Social Democracy' in *Critical Sociology*, 32 (4): 583–602.

Furstenberg, F., Kennedy, S., McCloyd, V.G., Rumbaut, R.G. and Settersten, R.A. (2004) 'Becoming an Adult: The Changing Nature of Early Adulthood' in *Contexts*, 3: 33–41.

Gardner, M. and Steinberg, L. (2005) 'Peer Influence on Risk Taking, Risk Preference and Risky Decision Making in Adolescence and Adulthood: An Experimental Study' in *Developmental Psychology*, 41 (4): 625–35.

Garland, D. (1985) *Punishment and Welfare: A History of Penal Strategies*. Aldershot: Gower.

Garland, D. (1996) 'The Limits of the Sovereign State: Strategies of Crime Control in Contemporary Society' in *British Journal of Criminology*, 36 (4): 445–71.

Garland, D. (2001) *The Culture of Control: Crime and Social Order in Contemporary Society*. Oxford: Oxford University Press.

Garside, R. (2004) *Crime, Persistent Offenders and the Justice Gap*. London: Centre for Crime and Justice Studies.

Giddens, A. (1979) *Central Problems in Social Theory*. Los Angeles: University of California Press.

Giddens, A. (1983) 'Comments on the Theory of Structuration' in *Journal of the Theory of Social Behaviour*, 13: 75–80.

Giddens, A. (1984) *The Constitution of Society*. Cambridge: Polity Press.

Giddens, A. (1986) *The Constitution of Society: Outline of the Theory of Structuration*. Cambridge: Polity Press.

Giddens, A. (1990) *The Consequences of Modernity*. Cambridge: Polity Press.

Giddens, A. (1991) *Modernity and Self-Identity: Self and Society in the Late Modern Age*. Cambridge: Polity Press.

Giddens, A. (1998) *The Third Way: The Renewal of Social Deomcracy*. Cambridge: Polity Press.

Giordano, P.C., Cernkovich, S.A. and Rudolph, J.L. (2002) 'Gender, crime and desistance: Toward a theory of cognitive transformation' in *American Journal of Sociology*, 107: 990–1064.

Giordano, P.C., Schroeder, R.D. and Cernkovich, S.A. (2007) 'Emotions and crime over the life course: A Neo-Meadian perspective on criminal continuity and change' in *American Journal of Sociology*, 112 (6): 1603–61.

Glaser, D. (1969) *The Effectiveness of a Prison and Parole System, abridged edition*. Indianapolis, IN: Bobbs-Merrill.

Glendinning, C., Powell, M. and Rummery, K. (eds) (2002) *Partnerships, New Labour and the Governance of Welfare*. Bristol: The Policy Press.

Glueck, S. and Glueck, E. (1940) *Juvenile Delinquents Grown Up*. New York: Commonwealth Fund.

Glueck, S. and Glueck, E. (1945) *After-Conduct of Discharged Offenders*. London: Macmillan.

Glueck, S. and Glueck, E. (1968) *Delinquents and Nondelinquents in Perspective*. Cambridge, Mass.: Harvard University Press.

Glueck, S. and Glueck, E. (1974) *Of Delinquency and Crime: A Panorama of Years of Search and Research*. Springfield, Ill.: Thomas.

Gottfredson, M.R. and Hirschi, T. (1990) *A General Theory of Crime*. Stanford, California: Stanford University Press.

Gough, D. (2010) 'Multi-agency working in corrections: cooperation and competition' in Pycroft, A. and Gough, D. (eds) *Multi-Agency Working in Criminal Justice: Control and care in contemporary correctional practice*. Bristol: The Policy Press.

Graham, J. and Bowling, B. (1995) *Young People and Crime*. Home Office Research Study 145. Online. Available at: www.homeoffice.gov.uk/rds/pdfs2/hors145.pdf [Accessed: 14/12/2009].

Graham, J. and Utting, D. (1996) 'Families, Schools and Criminality Prevention' in Bennett, T. (ed.) *Preventing Crime and Disorder: Targeting Strategies and Responsibilities*, Cambridge Cropwood Series. Cambridge: Institute of Criminology.

Gray, P. (2005) 'The Politics of Risk and Young Offenders' Experiences of Social Exclusion and Restorative Justice' in *British Journal of Criminology*, 45: 938–57.

Greenberg, D.F. (1977) 'Delinquency and the Age Structure of Society' in *Contemporary Crises*, 1: 189–223.

Greener, I. (2002) 'Agency, social theory and social policy' in *Critical Social Policy*, 22 (4): 688–705.

Gregory, M. (2010) 'Reflection and Resistance: Probation Practice and the Ethic of Care' in *British Journal of Social Work*. Online. Available at: http://bjsw.oxfordjournals.org/cgi/reprint/bcq028v1 [Accessed: 26/04/2010].

Griffin, P. (2006) 'Getting Out of Trouble: The Pathways to Desistance Study' in *Pennsylvania Progress: Juvenile Justice Achievements in Pennsylvania*, 11 (4): 1–9.

Hagell, A., Newburn, T. and Rowlingson, K. (1995) *Financial Difficulties on Release from Prison*. London: PSI.

Haigh, Y. (2009) 'Desistance from crime: reflections on the transitional experiences of young people with a history of offending' in *Journal of Youth Studies*, 12 (3): 307–22.

Hale, C. and Fitzgerald, M. (2007) 'Social Exclusion and Crime' in Christian, J.N., Abrams, D. and Gordon, N. (eds) *Multidisciplinary Handbook of Social Exclusion Research*. Chichester: John Wiley and Sons.

Hales, J., Neville, C., Pudney, S. and Tipping, S. (2009) *Longitudinal analysis of the Offender, Crime and Justice Survey 2003–06*. Online. Available at: www.homeoffice.gov.uk/rds/pdfs09/horr19c.pdf [Accessed: 14/12/2009].

Halliday, J. (2001) *Making Punishments Work: Report of a Review of the Sentencing Framework for England and Wales*. London: Home Office.

Hannah-Moffat, K. (1999) 'Moral Agent or Actuarial Subject: Risk and Canadian Women's Imprisonment' in *Theoretical Criminology*, 3 (1): 71–94.

Hannah-Moffat, K. (2005) 'Criminogenic needs and the transformative risk subject: Hybridizations of risk/need in penality' in *Punishment and Society*, 7 (1): 29–51.

Harper, G. and Chitty, C. (2005) *The Impact of Corrections on Re-Offending: A review of 'what works', 3e*. Home Office Research Study 291. London: Home Office.

Harper, G., Man, L-H., Taylor, S. and Niven, S. (2004) 'Factors associated with offending' in Harper, G. and Chitty, C. (eds) *The Impact of Corrections on Re-Offending: A review of 'what works'. 3e*. Home Office Research Study 291. Online. Available at: www.homeoffice.gov.uk/rds/pdfs04/hors291.pdf [Accessed: 27/07/2008].

Harper, R. and Hardy, S. (2000) Research note. 'An evaluation of motivational interviewing as a method of intervention with clients in a probation setting' in *British Journal of Social Work*, 30 (3): 393–400.

Haslewood-Pocsik, I., Merone, L. and Roberts, C. (2004) *The Evaluation of the Employment Pathfinder: Lessons from Phase 1 and a survey for Phase 2*. London: Home Office.

Hayford, S. and Furstenberg, F. (2008) 'Delayed Adulthood, Delayed Desistance? Trends in the Age Distribution of Problem Behaviours' in *Journal of Research on Adolescence*, 18 (2): 285–304.

Hays, S. (1994) 'Structure and Agency and the Sticky Problem of Culture' in *Sociological Theory*, 12 (1): 57–72.

Healy, D. (2010) *The Dynamics of Desistance: Charting pathways through change*. Cullompton: Willan.

Healy, D. (2012) 'Advise, Assist and Befriend: Can Probation Supervision Support Desistance' in *Social Policy and Administration*, 46 (4): 377–94.

Healy, D. and O'Donnell, I. (2008) 'Calling time on crime: Motivation, generativity and agency in Irish probationers' in *Probation Journal*, 55 (1): 25–38.

Healy, K. (1998) 'Conceptualising Constraint: Mouzelis, Archer and the Concept of Structure' in *Sociology*, 32 (3): 509–22.

Hedderman, C. (1998) 'A critical assessment of probation research' in *Research Bulletin*, 39: 1–7.

Hedderman, C., Ellis, T. and Sugg, D. (1999) *Increasing Confidence in Community Sentences: The Results of Two Demonstration Projects*. Home Office Research Study 194. London: Home Office.

Hegney, D., Fallon, T. and O'Brien, M.L. (2007) 'Against all odds: a retrospective case-controlled study of women who experienced extraordinary breastfeeding problems' in *Journal of Clinical Nursing*, 17 (9): 1182–92.

Helyar-Cardwell, V. (2012) 'Fathers for good? Exploring the impact of becoming a father on young offenders' desistance from crime' in *Safer Communities*, 11 (4): 169–78.

Hirschi, T. and Gottfredson, M.R. (1983) 'Age and Explanation of Crime' in *American Journal of Sociology*, 89: 552–84.

Hirschi, T. and Gottfredson, M. (2001) 'Self-control theory' in Paternoster, R. and Bachman, R. (eds) *Explaining Criminals and Crime*. Los Angeles: Roxbury Press.

HM Government (2005) *Reducing Re-Offending Through Skills and Employment*. CM 6702. London: The Stationery Office.

HM Government (2006) *Reducing Re-Offending Through Skills and Employment: Next Steps*. Online. Available at: www.dfes.gov.uk/offenderlearning [Accessed: 27/03/2008].

HM Government (2009) *Cutting Crime Two Years On: An Update to the 2008–2011 Crime Strategy*. London: HM Government.

HM Prison Service (2009) *Prison Population and Accommodation Briefing For – 11th Dec 2009*. Online. Available at: www.hmprisonservice.gov.uk/resourcecentre/publicationsdocuments/index.asp?cat=85 [Accessed: 14/12/2009].

Hogg, E. and Baines, S. (2011) 'Changing Responsibilities and Roles of the Voluntary and Community Sector in the Welfare Mix: A Review' in *Social Policy and Society*, 10 (3): 341–52.

Holliday, A. (2007) *Doing and Writing Qualitative Research, 2e*. London: Sage.

Hollin, C.R. (1999) 'Treatment Programs for Offenders: Meta-Analysis, "What Works", and Beyond' in *International Journal of Law and Psychiatry*, 22 (3/4): 361–72.

Hollis, M. (1994) *The Philosophy of Social Science: An introduction*. Cambridge: Cambridge University Press.

Hollway, W. and Jefferson, T. (2000) *Doing Qualitative Research Differently: Free association, narrative and the interview method*. London: Sage.

Hollway, W. and Jefferson, T. (2001) 'Free Association, Narrative Analysis and the Defended Subject: The Case of Ivy' in *Narrative Inquiry*, 11 (1): 103–22.

Home Office (1998) *Prisons-Probation: Joining forces to protect the public*. London: The Stationery Office.

Home Office (2002a) *Narrowing the Justice Gap: Framework*. London: Home Office.

Home Office (2002b) *Justice for All*, CM 5563. London: Home Office.

Home Office (2004a) *Confident Communities in a Secure Britain: The Home Office Strategic Plan 2004–08*. London: The Stationery Office.

Home Office (2004b) *Prolific and Other Priority Offender strategy Initial Guidance Catch and Convict Framework*. London: Home Office.

Home Office (2004c) *Reducing Crime – Changing Lives: The Government's Plans for Transforming the Management of Offenders*. London: Home Office.

Home Office (2004d) *Reducing Re-offending National Action Plan*. London: Home Office.

Home Office (2006a) *A Five Year Strategy for Protecting the Public and Reducing Re-offending*. London: The Stationery Office.

Home Office (2006b) *Rebalancing the Criminal Justice System in Favour of the Law-abiding Majority: Cutting Crime, Reducing Reoffending and Protecting the Public*. London: Home Office.

Home Office Communications Directorate (2004) *Joint Inspectorate Report into Persistent and Prolific Offenders*. London: Home Office.

Home Office/Ministry of Justice (2010) *Integrated Offender Management: Key Principles*. Online. Available at: www.homeoffice.gov.uk/publications/crime/reducing-reoffending/IOM-Key-Principles-Guidance?view=Binary [Accessed: 27/02/2012].

Hope, T. and Sparks, R. (eds) (2000) *Crime, Risk and Insecurity*. Abingdon: Routledge.

Hopkins, M. and Wickson, J. (2012) 'Targeting prolific and other priority offenders and promoting pathways to desistance: Some reflections on the PPO programme using a theory of change framework' in *Criminology and Criminal Justice*. Online. Available at: http://crj.sagepub.com/content/early/2012/11/01/1748895812462595.abstract.

Horney, J., Osgood, D.W. and Haen Marshall, I. (1995) 'Criminal Careers in The Short Term: Intra-Individual Variability in Crime and Its Relation to Local Life Circumstances' in *American Sociological Review*, 60: 655–73.

House of Commons Justice Committee (2011) *The Role of the Probation Service. Eighth Report of Session 2012–12. Volume 1*. London: The Stationery Office.

Howard League for Penal Reform (no date) *Community Sentences Cut Crime – Factsheet*. Online. Available at: www.howardleague.org/fileadmin/howard_league/user/pdf/Community_sentences_factsheet.pdf [Accessed: 12/11/2009].

Hudson, B. (2003) *Justice in the Risk Society*. London: Sage.

Hudson, B. and Bramhall, G. (2005) 'Assessing the "other"' in *British Journal of Criminology*, 45: 721–40.

Hughes, M. (1998) 'Turning points in the lives of young inner-city men forgoing destructive criminal behaviours: A qualitative study' in *Social Work Research*, 22 (3): 143–51.

Hughes, M. (ed.) (2009) *Social Trends, No. 39*. Basingstoke: Palgrave Macmillan.

Hutchinson, S. (2006) 'Countering catastrophic criminology: Reform, punishment and the modern liberal compromise' in *Punishment and Society*, 8 (4): 443–67.

Hutto, T.D. (1990) 'The Privatization of Prisons' in Murphy, J.W. and Dison, J.E. (eds) *Are Prisons any Better? Twenty Years of Correctional Reform*. Newbury Park, California: Sage.

Jamieson, J., McIvor, G. and Murray, C. (1999) *Understanding Offending Among Young People*. Edinburgh: Scottish Executive.

Jordan, B. (1998) *The New Politics of Welfare: Social Justice in a Global Context.* London: Sage.

Kazemian, L. (2007) 'Desistance from Crime: Theoretical, Empirical, Methodological and Policy Considerations' in *Journal of Contemporary Criminal Justice*, 23 (1): 5–27.

Kempf, K. (1988) 'Crime severity and criminal career progression' in *Journal of Criminal Law and Criminology*, 79: 524–40.

Kempf, K.L. (1990) 'Career Criminals in the 1958 Philadelphia Birth Cohort: A Follow-Up of the Early Adult Years' in *Criminal Justice Review*, 15 (2): 151–72.

Kemshall, H. (2003) *Understanding Risk in Criminal Justice.* Maidenhead: Open University Press.

Kemshall, H. (2004) 'Risk, Dangerousness and Female Offenders' in McIvor, G. (ed.) *Women Who Offend.* London: Jessica Kingsley Publishers.

Kemshall, H. and Maguire, M. (2001) 'Public protection, "partnership" and risk penality' in *Punishment and Society*, 3: 237–54.

Kilcommins, S. (2011) 'Where Is Our Criminal Justice System Going?' in *Irish Probation Journal*, 8: 69–81.

Kim, K. (2009) 'Sanction Threats and Desistance from Criminality' in Savage, J. (ed.) *The Development of Persistent Criminality.* New York: Oxford University Press.

King, R.D., Massoglia, M., MacMillan, R. (2007) 'The context of marriage and crime: gender, the propensity to marry, and offending in early adulthood' in *Criminology*, 45: 33–65.

King, S. (2012) 'Transformative agency and desistance from crime' in *Criminology and Criminal Justice*, 13 (3): 317-335.

King, S. (2013a) 'Assisted desistance and experiences of probation supervision' in *Probation Journal*, 60 (2): 136-151.

King, S. (2013b) 'Early desistance narratives: a qualitative analysis of probationers' transitions towards desistance' in *Punishment and Society*, 15 (2): 147–165.

Kreager, D.A., Matsueda, R.L. and Erosheva, E.A. (2010) 'Motherhood and Criminal Desistance in Disadvantaged Neighbourhoods' in *Criminology*, 48 (1): 221–58.

Kruttschnitt, C., Uggen, C. and Shelton, C. (2000) 'Predictors of Desistance Among Sex Offenders: The Interaction of Formal and Informal Social Controls' in *Justice Quarterly*, 17 (1): 61–87.

Lash, S. and Urry, J. (1994) *Economies of Signs and Space.* Sage: London.

Laub, J.H. and Sampson, R.J. (1988) 'Unraveling Families and Delinquency: A Reanalysis of the Gluecks' Data' in *Criminology*, 26: 355–80.

Laub, J.H. and Sampson, R.J. (2001) 'Understanding Desistance from Crime' in *Crime and Justice: A Review of Research*, 28: 1–69.

Laub, J.H. and Sampson, R.J. (2003) *Shared Beginnings, Divergent Lives: Delinquent Boys to Age 70.* Cambridge, MA: Harvard University Press.

Laub, J.H., Nagin, D.S. and Sampson, R.J. (1998) 'Trajectories of Change in Criminal Offending: Good Marriages and the Desistance Process' in *American Sociological Review*, 63 (2): 225–38.

Lawrie, C. (2011) 'What happened to probation between 1997 and 2010? A probation professional's perspective' in Silvestri, A. (ed.) *Lessons for the Coalition: An end of term report on New Labour and criminal justice.* London: Centre for Crime and Justice Studies.

Leapman, B. (2006) 'Offenders on probation carry out 10,000 crimes a month' in *The Telegraph*, 14/05/2006. Online. Available at: www.telegraph.co.uk/news/uknews/1518301/Offenders-on-probation-carry-out-10000-crimes-a-month.html [Accessed: 12/02/2010].

LeBel, T., Burnett, R., Maruna, S. and Bushway, S. (2008) 'The "Chicken and Egg" of Subjective and Social Factors in Desistance from Crime' in *European Journal of Criminology*, 5 (2): 131–59.

Le Blanc, M., and Frechette, M. (1989) *Criminal Activity from Childhood through Youth: Multilevel and Developmental Perspectives*. New York: Springer-Verlag.

Le Blanc, M. and Loeber, R. (1998) 'Developmental Criminology Updated' in *Crime and Justice*, 23: 115–98.

Ledger, J. (2010) 'Rehabilitation revolution: Will probation pay the price?' in *Probation Journal*, 57 (4): 415–22.

Leibrich, J. (1993) *Straight to the Point: Angles on Giving Up Crime*. Otago: University of Otago Press.

Leibrich, J. (1996) 'The role of shame in going straight: A study of former offenders' in Galaway, B. and Hudson, J. (eds) *Restorative justice: International Perspectives*. Monsey, NY: Criminal Justice Press.

Lemert, E.M. (1951) *Social Pathology*. New York: McGraw Hill.

Lemert, E.M. (1967) *Human Deviance, Social Problems and Social Control*. Englewood Cliffs, NJ: Prentice-Hall.

Lewis, S. (2005) 'Rehabilitation: Headline or footnote in the new penal policy?' in *Probation*, 52 (2): 119–35.

Lewis, S. (2008) 'Adult Offenders: Policy Developments in England and Wales' in McIvor, G. and Raynor, P. (eds) *Developments in Social Work with Offenders*. London: Jessica Kingsley.

Lewis, S., Maguire, M., Raynor, P., Vanstone, M. and Vennard, J. (2007) 'What works in resettlement? Findings from seven Pathfinders for short-term prisoners in England and Wales' in *Criminology and Criminal Justice*, 7 (1): 33–53.

Liddle, M. (2001) 'Community penalties in the context of contemporary social change' in Bottoms, A., Gelsthorpe, L. and Rex, S. (eds) *Community Penalties: Change and Challenges*. Cullompton: Willan.

Lipsey, M.W. (1992) 'Juvenile delinquency treatment: A meta-analytic inquiry into the variability effects' in Cook, T.D., Cooper, H., Cordray, D.S., Hartmann, H., Hedges, L.V., Light, R.J., Louis, T.A. and Mosteller, F. (eds) *Meta-Analysis for Explanation: A casebook*. New York: Russell Sage Foundation.

Lipsey, M.W. (1995) 'What do we learn from 400 studies on the effectiveness of treatment with juvenile delinquents?' in McGuire, J. (ed.) *What Works: Reducing Reoffending*. Chichester: John Wiley and Sons.

Lipsey, M.W. (1999) 'Can rehabilitative programs reduce the recidivism of juvenile offenders? An inquiry into the effectiveness of practical programs' in *Virginia Journal of Social Policy and the Law*, 6 (3): 611–41.

Local Government Association (LGA) (2005) *Going Straight: Reducing Re-offending in Local Communities*. London: LGA.

Local Government Information Unit (LGiU) (2009) *Primary Justice: An Inquiry Into Justice in Communities*. Online. Available at: https://member.lgiu.org.uk/whatwedo/Publications/Documents/APPG%20report%20Primary%20Justice.pdf [Accessed: 12/11/2009].

Loeber, R. and Le Blanc, M. (1990) 'Toward a developmental criminology' in Tonry, M. and Morris, N. (eds) *Crime and Justice*. Chicago, IL: University of Chicago Press.

Loeber, R. and Stouthhamer-Loeber, M. (1986) 'Family Factors as Correlates and Predictors of Juvenile Conduct Problems and Delinquency' in Tonry, M. and Morris, N. (eds) *Crime and Justice: An Annual Review of Research 7*. Chicago: University of Chicago Press.

Loeber, R., Stouthamer-Loeber, M., Van Kammen, W. and Farrington, D. (1991) 'Initiation, escalation, and desistance in juvenile offending and their correlates' in *Journal of Criminal Law and Criminolology*, 82: 36–82.

Logan, C. (1990) *Private Prisons: Cons and Pros.* Oxford: Oxford University Press.

Logan, C. (1996) *Private Prisons: Cons and Pros, Second Edition.* Oxford: Oxford University Press.

Logan, C.H. and Rausch, S.P. (1985) 'Punish and Profit: The Emergence of Private Enterprise Prisons' in *Justice Quarterly*, 2 (3): 303–18.

Luhmann, N. (1988) 'Familiarity, confidence, trust: Problems and alternatives' in Gambetta, D.G. (ed.) *Trust.* New York: Basil Blackwell.

MacDonald, D. (1990) *Prisons for Profits: The privatization of corrections.* New Brunswick, NJ: Rutgers University Press.

MacDonald, D. (1992) 'Private penal institutions' in Tonry, M. (ed.) *Crime and justice: A review of research.* Chicago, IL: University of Chicago Press.

MacDonald, R. (2006) 'Social Exclusion, Youth Transitions and Criminal Careers: Five Critical Reflections on "Risk"' in *Australian and New Zealand Journal of Criminology*, 39 (3): 371–83.

Macdonald, Z. (2002) 'Official Crime Statistics: Their Use and Interpretation' in *The Economic Journal*, 112 (477): f.85-f.106.

Maguire, M. (2004) 'The Crime Reduction Programme in England and Wales: Reflections on the vision and the reality' in *Criminal Justice*, 4 (3): 213–37.

Maguire, M. (2012) 'Response 1: Big Society, the voluntary sector and the marketization of criminal justice' in *Criminology and Criminal Justice*, 12 (5): 483–94.

Maguire, M. and Raynor, P. (2006a) 'Will new resettlement programmes succeed?' in Paper presented at the ESRC/Scottish Executive Public Policy Seminar, *Reducing reoffending in Scotland: targets and solutions.* Online. Available at: www.esrc.ac.uk/ESRCInfoCentre/Images/Reducing%20re-offending%20in%20Scotland%20-%20%20targets%20and%20solutions_tcm6–17729.pdf [Accessed: 27/08/2008].

Maguire, M. and Raynor, P. (2006b) 'How the resettlement of prisoners promotes desistance from crime: Or does it?' in *Criminology and Criminal Justice*, 6 (1): 19–38.

Mair, G. (ed.) (2004) *What Matters in Probation.* Cullompton: Willan.

Mair, G. and May, C. (1997) *Offenders on Probation.* London: Home Office.

Mair, G. and Mills, H. (2009) *The Community Order and the Suspended Sentence Order three years on: The views and experiences of probation officers and offenders.* London: Centre for Crime and Justice Studies.

Mair, G., Cross, N. and Taylor, S. (2007) *The Use and Impact of the Community Order and the Suspended Sentence Order.* London: Centre for Crime and Justice Studies.

Maley, S., Narey, J., O'Sullivan, J. and Williams, E. (2007) *Getting Out to Work: A guide to good practice.* Barrow Cadbury Trust/Business in the Community. Online. Available at: www.barrowcadbury.org.uk/pdf/Getting%20out%20to%20work%20-%20employers'%20guide.pdf [Accessed: 06/06/2008].

Marshall, V.W. (2005) 'Agency, Events and Structure at the End of the Life Course' in *Advances in Life Course Research*, 10: 57–91.

Martinson, R. (1974) 'What works? Questions and answers about prison reform' in *The Public Interest*, 35: 22–54.

Martinson, R. (1979) 'New findings, new views: a note of caution regarding sentencing reform' in *Hofstra Law Review*, 7: 243–58.

Maruna, S. (1997) 'Going Straight: Desistance from crime and life narratives of reform' in *The Narrative Study of Lives*, 5: 59–93.

Maruna, S. (1999) 'Desistance and Development: The Psychosocial Process of "Going Straight"' in *The British Criminology Conferences: Selected Proceedings. Volume 2. Papers from the British Criminology Conference, Queen's University Belfast, 15–19 July 1997*. Online. Available at: www.britsoccrim.org/volume2/003.pdf [Accessed: 30/11/2005].

Maruna, S. (2000) 'Desistance from crime and offender rehabilitation: a tale of two research literatures' in *Offender Programs Report*, 4 (1): 1–13.

Maruna, S. (2001) *Making Good: How Ex-Convicts Reform and Rebuild Their Lives*. Washington, DC: American Psychological Association Books.

Maruna, S. (2006) 'Who owns resettlement? Towards restorative re-integration' in *British Journal of Community Justice*, 4 (2): 23–33.

Maruna, S. and Immarigeon, R. (eds) (2004) *After Crime and Punishment: Pathways to Ex-Offender Reintegration*. Cullompton: Willan.

Maruna, S. and King, A. (2008) 'Selling the Public on Probation: Beyond the Bib' in *Probation*, 5 (4): 337–52.

Maruna, S. and Roy, K. (2007) 'Amputation or Reconstruction? Notes on the Concept of "Knifing-Off" and Desistance From Crime' in *Journal of Contemporary Criminal Justice*, 23 (1): 104–24.

Maruna, S. and Toch, H. (2005) 'The Impact of Imprisonment on the Desistance Process' in Travis, J. and Visher, C. (eds) *Prisoner Reentry and Crime in America*. Cambridge: Cambridge University Press.

Maruna, S., Immarigeon, R. and LeBel, T.P. (2004) 'Ex-offender reintegration: theory and practice' in Maruna, S. and Immarigeon, R. (eds) *After Crime and Punishment: Pathways to offender reintegration*. Cullompton: Willan.

Maruna, S., LeBel, T., Mitchell, N. and Naples, M. (2004) 'Pygmalion in the Reintegration Process: Desistance from Crime Through the Looking Glass' in *Psychology, Crime and Law*, 10 (3): 271–81.

Maruna, S., Porter, L. and Carvalho, I. (2004) 'The Liverpool Desistance Study and Probation Practice: Opening the Dialogue' in *Probation*, 51 (3): 221–32.

Mason, P. and Prior, D. (2008) *Engaging Young People who Offend*. YJB Source Document. London: Youth Justice Board.

Massoglia, M. (2006) 'Desistance or Displacement? The Changing Patterns of Offending from Adolescence to Young Adulthood' in *Journal of Quantitative Criminology*, 22 (3): 215–39.

Massoglia, M. and Uggen, C. (2007) 'Subjective Desistance and the Transition to Adulthood' in *Journal of Contemporary Criminal Justice*, 23 (1): 90–103.

Massoglia, M. and Uggen C. (2010) 'Settling Down and Aging Out: Toward an Interactionist Theory of Desistance and the Transition to Adulthood' in *American Journal of Sociology*, 116 (2): 543–82.

Matthews, R. (2005) 'The myth of punitiveness' in *Theoretical Criminology*, 9 (2): 175–201.

Matza, D. (1964) *Delinquency and Drift*. New York: Wiley.

Maume, M., Ousey G., and Beaver, K. (2005) 'Cutting the grass: A reexamination of the link between marital attachment, delinquent peers, and desistance from marijuana use' in *Journal of Quantitative Criminology*, 21: 27–53.

Mawby, R.C. and Worrall, A. (2011a) '"They were very threatening about do-gooding bastards": Probation's changing relationships with the police and prison services in England and Wales' in *European Journal of Probation*, 3 (3): 78–94.

Mawby, R.C. and Worrall, A. (2011b) *Probation Workers and their Occupational Cultures*. Summary report of ESRC project findings. Leicester: University of Leicester. Online. Available at: http://www2.le.ac.uk/departments/criminology/documents/Final_report_Nov_2011%20-17%20Nov%202011.pdf [Accessed: 27/05/2012].

May, C. and Cooper, A. (1995) 'Personal Identity and Social Change: Some Theoretical Considerations'. Review Essay in *Acta Sociologica*, 38: 75–85.

McAdams, D.P. (1992) *Coding Autobiographical Episodes for Themes of Agency and Communion, 3e*. Evanston, IL: Foley Center for the Study of Lives, Northwestern University.

McAdams, D.P. (2001) 'Coding Autobiographical Episodes for Themes of Agency and Communion'. Online. Available at: www.sesp.northwestern.edu/docs/Agency_Communion01.pdf [Accessed: 28/07/2009].

McAra, L. and McVie, S. (2007) 'Youth Justice? The Impact of System Contact on Patterns of Desistance from Offending' in *European Journal of Criminology*, 4 (3): 315–45.

McCord, J., Widom, C.S., and Crowell, N.A. (eds) (2001) *Juvenile Crime, Juvenile Justice. Panel on Juvenile Crime: Prevention, Treatment, and Control*. Washington, DC: National Academy Press.

McCulloch, T. (2005) 'Probation, social context and desistance: Retracing the relationship' in *Probation Journal*, 52 (1): 8–22.

McCulloch, T. (2010) 'Realising Potential: Community service, pro-social modeling and desistance' in *European Journal of Probation*, 2 (2): 3–22.

McDowell, L. (2003) *Redundant Masculinities? Employment Change and White Working Class Youth*. Oxford: Blackwell.

McGuire, J. (ed.) (1995) *What Works: Reducing Reoffending*. Chichester: John Wiley and Sons.

McGuire, J. (ed.) (2002) *Offender Rehabilitation and Treatment*. Chichester: John Wiley and Sons.

McGuire, J. and Priestley, P. (1985) *Offending Behaviour: Skills and Stratagems for Going Straight*. London: Batsford.

McGuire, J. and Priestley, P. (1995) 'Reviewing "What Works". Past, present and future' in McGuire, J. (ed.) *What Works: Reducing Reoffending*. Chichester: John Wiley and Sons.

McLaughlin, E. and Muncie, J. (2005) *The Sage Dictionary of Criminology, 2e*. London: Sage.

McNeill, F. (2003) 'Desistance-Focused Probation Practice' in Chui, W.H. and Nellis, M. (eds) *Moving Probation Forward: Evidence, Arguments and Practice*. Harlow: Pearson Education Limited.

McNeill, F. (2004) 'Supporting desistance in probation practice: A response to Maruna, Porter and Cavalho' in *Probation Journal*, 51 (3): 241–47.

McNeill, F. (2006a) 'A desistance paradigm for offender management' in *Criminology and Criminal Justice*, 6 (1): 39–62.

McNeill, F. (2006b) 'Community Supervision: Contexts and Relationships Matter' in Goldson, B. and Muncie, J. (eds) *Youth Crime and Justice*. London: Sage.

McNeill, F. (2009) 'What Works and What's Just?' in *European Journal of Probation*, 1 (1): 21–40.

McNeill, F. and Maruna, S. (2007) 'Giving Up and Giving Back: Desistance, Generativity and Social Work with Offenders' in McIvor, G. and Raynor, P. (eds) *Developments in Social Work With Offenders*. London: Jessica Kingsley Publishers.

McNeill, F. and Whyte, B. (2007) *Reducing Reoffending: Social work and community justice in Scotland*. Cullompton: Willan.

McNeill, F., Anderson, K., Colvin, S., Overy, K., Sparks, R. and Tett, L. (2011) 'Inspiring desistance? Arts projects and "what works?"' in *Justitieleverkenningen*, 37 (5): 80–101.

McNeill, F., Batchelor, S., Burnett, R. and Knox, J. (2005) *21st Century Social Work: Reducing Re-offending: Key Practice Skills*. Edinburgh: Scottish Executive.

McNeill, F., Farrall, S., Lightowler, C. and Maruna, S. (2012) 'Re-Examining "Evidence-Based Practice" in Community Corrections: Beyond "a confined view" of what works' in *Justice, Research and Policy*, 14 (1): 35–60.

McWilliams, W.W. (1983) 'The mission to the English police courts 1876–1936' in *The Howard Journal of Criminal Justice*, 22 (3): 129–47.

McWilliams, W.W. (1985) 'The Mission Transformed: Professionalisation of Probation Between the Wars' in *The Howard Journal of Criminal Justice*, 24 (4): 257–74.

McWilliams, W.W. (1986) 'The English Probation System and the Diagnostic Ideal' in *The Howard Journal of Criminal Justice*, 25 (4): 241–320.

McWilliams, W.W. (1987) 'Probation, Pragmatism and Policy' in *The Howard Journal of Criminal Justice*, 26 (2): 97–121.

Mears, A.R. (2008) 'Rehabilitation of offenders – does the 1974 Act help them?' in *Probation Journal*, 55 (2): 161–70.

Meisenhelder, T. (1989) 'Reading 38: Becoming Normal: Certification as a Stage in Exiting from Crime' in Bryant, C.D. (ed.) *Deviant Behaviour: Readings in the Sociology of Norm Violations*. London: Taylor and Francis.

Metcalf, H., Rolfe, H. and Anderson, T. (2001) *Barriers to Employment for Offenders and Ex-offenders*. London: Department for Work and Pensions.

Michalsen, V. (2011) 'Mothering as a Life Course Transition: Do Women Go Straight For Their Children?' in *Journal of Offender Rehabilitation*, 50 (6): 349–66.

Miethe, T.D. and Meier, R.F. (1994) *Crime and its Social Context: Toward an Integrated Theory of Offenders, Victims, and Situations*. Albany, NY: State University of New York Press.

Ministry of Justice (2007a) *Penal Policy – A Background Paper*. London: MoJ.

Ministry of Justice (2007b) *Performance Report on Offender Management Targets (PROMT) April 2006 – September 2006*. London: Home Office.

Ministry of Justice (2008a) *Community Sentencing – Reducing reoffending, changing lives: Cutting crime in our communities*. Online. Available at: www.justice.gov.uk/publications/docs/community-sentencing.pdf [Accessed: 27/08/2008].

Ministry of Justice (2008b) *Re-offending of adults: new measures of re-offending 2000–2005: England and Wales: Ministry of Justice Statistics Bulletin*. Online. Available at: www.justice.gov.uk/publications/docs/re-offending-adults-2000–05.pdf [Accessed: 12/11/2009].

Ministry of Justice (2008c) *Prison Population Projections 2008–2015: Ministry of Justice Statistics Bulletin*. Online. Available at: www.justice.gov.uk/about/docs/stats-prison-pop-sep08.pdf [Accessed: 14/12/2009].

Ministry of Justice (2008d) *Punishment and Reform: Our Approach to Managing Offenders*. London: Ministry of Justice.

Ministry of Justice (2009a) *Sentencing Statistics 2007, England and Wales: Ministry of Justice Statistics Bulletin*. Online. Available at: www.justice.gov.uk/publications/docs/sentencing-statistics-2007-revised.pdf [Accessed: 14/12/2009].

Ministry of Justice (2009b) *Reoffending of Adults: Results from the 2007 cohort England and Wales – Ministry of Justice Statistics Bulletin*. Online. Available at: www.justice. gov.uk/publications/docs/reoffending-adults-2007.pdf [Accessed:14/12/2009].

Ministry of Justice (2009c) *Story of the prison population 1995–2009: Ministry of Justice Statistics Bulletin*. Online. Available at: www.justice.gov.uk/about/docs/story-prison-population.pdf [Accessed: 14/12/2009].

Ministry of Justice (2009d) *About us: Protecting the public and reducing reoffending*. Online. Available at: www.justice.gov.uk/about/protecting-public.htm [Accessed: 12/11/2009].

Ministry of Justice (2009e) *Offender Management Caseload Statistics 2008: Ministry of Justice Statistics bulletin*. Online. Available at: www.justice.gov.uk/publications/docs/offender-management-caseload-statistics-2008-2.pdf [Accessed: 14/08/2009].

Ministry of Justice (2012a) *Criminal Justice Statistics Quarterly Update to December 2011. Ministry of Justice Statistics bulletin*. London: Ministry of Justice.

Ministry of Justice (2012b) *Punishment and Reform: Effective Probation Services*. Consultation Paper CP7/2012. London: Ministry of Justice.

Ministry of Justice (2013) *Proven Re-offending Statistics Quarterly Bulletin April 2010 to March 2011, England and Wales*. Online. Available at: www.justice.gov.uk/downloads/statistics/reoffending/proven-reoffending-apr10-mar11.pdf [Accessed: 25/03/2013].

Ministry of Justice and Department for Work and Pensions (2011) *Offending, employment and benefits – emerging findings from the data linkage project*. Online. Available at: www.justice.gov.uk/downloads/statistics/mojstats/offending-employment-benefits-emerging-findings-1111.pdf [Accessed: 24/01/2012].

Mischkowitz, R. (1994) 'Desistance From A Delinquent Way of Life?' in Weitekamp, E.G.M. and Kerner, H.J. (eds) *Cross-National Longitudinal Research on Human Development and Criminal Behaviour*. London: Kluwer Academic Publishers.

Mishra, A.K. (1996) 'Organizational Responses to Crisis: The Centrality of Trust' in Kramer, R. and Tyler, T. (eds) *Trust in Organizations: Frontiers of Theory and Research*. Thousand Oaks, California: Sage.

Misztal, B.A. (2001) 'Trust and cooperation in the democratic public sphere' in *Journal of Sociology*, 37 (4): 371–87.

Mobley, A. and Geis, G. (2001) 'The Corrections Corporation of America aka The Prison Realty Trust, Inc.' in Shichor, D. and Gilbert, M.J. (eds) *Privatization in criminal justice*. Cincinnati, OH: Anderson.

Moffitt, T.E. (1993) 'Adolescence-Limited and Life-Course-Persistent Antisocial Behavior: A Developmental Taxonomy' in *Psychological Review*, 100 (4): 674–701.

Moffitt, T.E. (1994) 'Natural Histories of Delinquency' in Weitekamp, E.G.M. and Kerner, H-J. (eds) *Cross-National Longitudinal Research on Human Development and Criminal Behaviour*. Dordrecht: Kluwer Academic Publishers.

Moffitt, T.E. (2003) 'Life-course persistent and adolescence-limited antisocial behaviour: A 10-year research review and a research agenda' in Lahey, B., Moffitt, T.E. and Caspi, A. (eds) *The Causes of Conduct Disorder and Serious Juvenile Delinquency*. New York: Guilford.

Moffitt, T.E. (2008) 'A Review of Research on the Taxonomy of Life-Course Persistent Versus Adolescence-Limited Behavior' in Cullen, F.T., Wright, J.P. and Blevins, K.R. (eds) *Taking Stock: The Status of Criminological Theory*. New Brunswick, NJ: Transaction Publishers.

Moffitt, T.E. and Caspi, A. (2001) 'Childhood predictors differentiate life-course persistent and adolescence-limited antisocial pathways among males and females' in *Developmental Psychopathology*, 13 (2): 355–75.

Moffitt, T.E. and Walsh, A. (2003) 'The adolescence-limited/life course persistent theory of antisocial behavior: What have we learned?' in Walsh, A. and Ellis, L. (eds) *Biosocial Criminology: Challenging Environmentalism's Supremacy*. New York: Anderson Publishing.

Moore, R. (2012) 'Beyond the prison walls: Some thoughts on prisoner "resettlement" in England and Wales' in *Criminology and Criminal Justice*, 12 (2): 129–47.

Mulvey, E.P., Steinberg, L., Fagan, J., Cauffman, E., Piquero, A.R., Chassin, L., Knight, G.P., Brame, R., Schubert, C.A., Hecker, T. and Losova, S.H. (2004) 'Theory and Research on Desistance from Antisocial Activity Among Serious Adolescent Offenders' in *Youth Violence and Juvenile Justice*, 2 (3): 213–36.

Murray, C. (2008) 'Conceptualising Young People's Strategies of Resistance to Offending as "Active Resilience"' in *British Journal of Social Work*, 40 (1): 115–32.

Murray, C. (2009) 'Typologies of Young Resisters and Desisters' in *Youth Justice*, 9 (2): 115–29.

Nagin, D.S. (2004) *Group-Based Modeling of Development over the Life Course*. Cambridge, Mass: Harvard University Press.

Nagin, D.S., and Farrington, D.P. (1992) 'The Stability of Criminal Potential from Childhood to Adulthood' in *Criminology*, 30: 235–60.

Nagin, D.S., and Paternoster, R. (1991) 'On the Relationship of Past to Future Delinquency' in *Criminology*, 29: 163–89.

Nagin, D.S., Farrington, D.P. and Moffitt, T.E. (1995) 'Life-Course Trajectories and Different Types of Offenders' in *Criminology*, 33: 111–39.

NAPO (2011) *Criminal Justice in Meltdown*. London: NAPO.

Nash, M. (2004) 'Probation and Community Penalties' in Muncie, J. and Wilson, D. (eds) *Student Handbook of Criminal Justice and Criminology*. London: Cavendish Publishing Limited.

National Association for the Care and Resettlement of Offenders (NACRO) (2003) *Recruiting Ex-Offenders: The Employers' Perspective*. London: NACRO.

National Audit Office (2002) *Reducing Prisoner Reoffending*. London: The Stationery Office.

National Audit Office (2008a) *The Supervision of Community Orders in England and Wales*. London: The Stationery Office.

National Audit Office (2008b) *Meeting needs? The Offenders' Learning and Skills Service*. London: The Stationery Office.

National Offender Management Service (NOMS) (2005) *The National Reducing Reoffending Delivery Plan*. London: Home Office.

National Offender Management Service (NOMS) (2006a) *The NOMS Offender Management Model*. London: Home Office.

National Offender Management Service (NOMS) (2006b) *The NOMS Offender Management Model*. London: Home Office.

National Probation Directorate (2005a) *National Standards 2005: Probation Circular 15/2005*. London: National Probation Directorate.

National Probation Directorate (2007) *A Century of Cutting Crime 1907–2007*. Online. Available at: http://probationassociation.co.uk/media/3766/a_20century_20of_20cutting_20crime_201907_20__202007.pdf [Accessed: 12/05/2007].

National Probation Service (2006) *NPS Offender Employment Target 2006/07, PC16/06*. Online. Available at: www.probation.homeoffice.gov.uk/files/pdf/PC16_2006.pdf [Accessed: 27/03/2008].

National Probation Service (2008) *National Probation Service for England and Wales Annual Report 2007–2008*. Online. Available at: www.parliament.co.uk [Accessed: 08/09/09].

Nayak, A. (2006) 'Displaced Masculinities: Chavs, Youth and Class in the Post-Industrial City' in *Sociology*, 40 (5): 813–31.

Neilson, A. (2010) 'Counterblast: Ships Ahoy? What the New Coalition Government Might Do With Penal Policy' in *The Howard Journal of Criminal Justice*, 49 (3): 282–85.

Nellis, M. (2002) 'Community penalties in historical perspective' in Bottoms, A., Gelsthorpe, L. and Rex, S. (eds) *Community Penalties: Change and Challenges*. Cullompton: Willan.

Nellis, M. (2005) 'Dim prospects: Humanistic values and the fate of community justice' in Winstone, J. and Pakes, F. (eds) *Community Justice: Issues for Probation and Criminal Justice*. Cullompton: Willan.

Nellis, M. (2006) 'NOMS, contestability and the process of technocorrectional innovation' in Hough, M., Allen, R. and Padel, U. (eds) *Reshaping Probation and Prisons: The New Offender Management Framework*. Bristol: The Policy Press.

Newburn, T. and Jones, T. (2007) 'Symbolizing crime control: Reflections on Zero Tolerance' in *Theoretical Criminology*, 11 (2): 221–43.

Newman, J. and Nutley, S. (2003) 'Transforming the probation service: "what works", organisational change and professional identity' in *Policy and Politics*, 31 (4): 547–63.

Nicholls, M. and Katz, L. (2004) 'Michael Howard: a life in quotes' in *The Guardian*, 26/08/2004. Online. Available at: www.guardian.co.uk/politics/2004/aug/26/conservatives.uk [Accessed: 22/03/2007].

Nicholson, D. (2011) *Cooperating out of Crime*. London: CentreForum.

Niven, S. and Olagundoye, J. (2002) *Jobs and Homes – A Survey of Prisoners Nearing Release. Home Office Findings No. 173*. London: Home Office.

Niven, S. and Stewart, D. (2005) *Resettlement Outcomes on Release from Prison 2003, Home Office Findings 248*. London: Home Office.

Nixon, D. (2009) '"I Can't Put A Smiley Face On": Working-Class Masculinity, Emotional Labour and Service Work in the "New Economy"' in *Gender, Work and Organization*, 16 (3): 300–22.

Noaks, L. and Wincup, E. (2004) *Criminological Research: Understanding Qualitative Methods*. London: Sage.

Nugent, B. and Loucks, N. (2011) 'The Arts and Prisoners: Experiences of Creative Rehabilitation' in *The Howard Journal of Criminal Justice*, 50 (4): 356–70.

O'Donnell, I. and O'Sullivan, E. (2003) 'The Politics of Intolerance – Irish Style' in *British Journal of Criminology*, 43 (1): 41–62.

Office for National Statistics (2009) *Labour Force Survey: Unemployment by Age and Duration (16+ and working age) (SA)*. Online. Available at: www.statistics.gov.uk/STATBASE/xsdataset.asp?vlnk=1385 [Accessed: 11/11/2009].

Oldfield, M. (2002) *From Welfare to Risk: Discourse, Power and Politics in the Probation Service*. London: NAPO.

Oldfield, M. and Grimshaw, R. (2007) *Probation Resources, Staffing and Workloads, 2001–2008*. London: Centre for Crime and Justice Studies.

O'Malley, P. (1998) *Crime and Risk Society*. Dartmouth: Dartmouth Publishing.

O'Malley, P. (2004) *Risk, Uncertainty and Government*. London: Glasshouse Press.

Osborn, S.G. (1980) 'Moving home, leaving London and delinquent trends' in *British Journal of Criminology*, 20 (1): 54–61.

Osgood, D.W. and Lee, H. (1993) 'Leisure activities, age, and adult roles across the life-span' in *Society and Leisure, 16:* 181–208.

Palmer, E.J. (2003) *Offending Behaviour: Moral Reasoning, Criminal Conduct and the Rehabilitation of Offenders.* Cullompton: Willan.

Partridge, S. (2004) *Examining Case Management Models for Community Sentences.* London: Home Office.

Paternoster, R. (1989) 'Decisions to participate in and desist from four types of common delinquency: Deterrence and the rational choice perspective' in *Law and Society Review,* 23: 7–40.

Paternoster, R. and Brame, R. (1997) 'Multiple routes to delinquency? A test of developmental and general theories of crime' in *Criminology,* 35(1): 49–84.

Patterson, G. and Yoerger, K. (1993) 'A model for early onset of delinquent behavior' in Hodgins, S. (ed.) *Mental Disorder and Crime.* Newbury Park, CA: Sage.

Perry, A.E., Newman, M., Hallam, G., Johnson, M., Sinclair, J. and Bowles, R. (2009) *A Rapid Evidence Assessment on the evidence of the effectiveness of interventions with persistent/prolific offenders in reducing re-offending.* Online. Available at: www.justice.gov.uk/publications/docs/persistent-prolific-offenders-research-report.pdf [Accessed: 09/11/2009].

Petersilia, J. (1980) 'Criminal Career Research: A Review of Recent Evidence' in Morris, N. and Tonry, M. (eds) *Crime and Justice: An Annual Review of Research. Vol. 2.* Chicago: University of Chicago Press.

Petersilia, J. (2003) *When Prisoners Come Home: Parole and Prisoner Reentry.* Oxford University Press: New York.

Petras, H., Nieuwbeerta, P., and Piquero, A. (2010) 'Participation and frequency during criminal careers across the life span' in *Criminology,* 48 (2): 607–37.

Phillips, J. (2011) 'Target, audit and risk assessment cultures in the probation service' in *European Journal of Probation,* 3 (3): 108–22.

Piliavin, I., Thornton, C., Gartner, R. and Matsueda, R.L. (1989) 'Crime, deterrence and rational choice' in *American Sociological Review,* 51: 101–19.

Piper, E. (1985) 'Violent recidivism and chronicity in the 1958 Philadelphia cohort' in *Journal of Quantitative Criminology,* 1: 319–44.

Piquero, A.R., Farrington, D.P. and Blumstein, A. (2003) 'The criminal career paradigm' in *Crime and Justice: a Review of Research,* 30: 359–506.

Piquero, A.R., Farrington, D.P. and Blumstein, A. (2007) *Key Issues in Criminal Career Research: New Analyses of the Cambridge Study in Delinquent Development.* Cambridge: Cambridge University Press.

Piquero, A.R., Hawkins, J.D. and Kazemian, L. (2012) 'Criminal Career Patterns' in Loeber, R. and Farrington, D.P. (eds) *From Juvenile Delinquency to Adult Crime.* Oxford: Oxford University Press.

Potter, J. and Hepburn, A. (2005) 'Qualitative interviews in psychology: problems and possibilities' in *Qualitative Research in Psychology,* 2: 1–27.

Pratt, J. (2002) *Punishment and Civilization.* London: Sage.

Prime, J., White, S., Liriano, S., and Patel, K. (2001) *Criminal Careers of those Born between 1953 and 1978.* Home Office Statistical Bulletin 4/01. London: Home Office.

Prior, D., Farrow, K., Hughes, N., Kelly, G., Manders, G., White, S. and Wilkinson, B. (2011) *Maturity, Young Adults and Criminal Justice: A Literature Review.* Birmingham: University of Birmingham.

Prison Reform Trust (2005a) *Prison Factfile.* London: Prison Reform Trust.

Prochaska, J.O. and DiClemente, C.C. (1992) 'Stages of change in the modification of problem behaviors' in Hersen, M., Eisler, R.M. and Miller, P.M. (eds) *Progress in Behavior Modification*. Sycamore, IL: Sycamore Press.

Prochaska, J.O. and Levesque, D.A. (2003) 'Enhancing Motivation of Offenders at Each Stage of Change and Phase of Therapy' in McMurran, M. (ed.) *Motivating Offenders to Change: A Guide to Enhancing Engagement in Therapy*. Chichester: Wiley & Sons.

Prochaska, J.O., DiClemente, C.C. and Norcross, J.C. (1992) 'In Search of How People Change: Applications to Addictive Behaviors' in *American Psychologist*, 47 (9): 1102–14.

Pycroft, A. (2010) 'Consensus, complexity and emergence: the mixed economy of service provision' in Pycroft, A. and Gough, D. (eds) *Multi-Agency Working in Criminal Justice: Control and care in contemporary correctional practice*. Bristol: The Policy Press.

Quinn, J. (2009) 'Rethinking "failed transitions" to higher education' in Ecclestone, K., Biesta, G. and Hughes, M. (eds) *Transitions and Learning Through the Lifecourse*. Abingdon: Routledge.

Raine, A., Brennan, P., and Mednick, S. (1994) 'Birth complications combined with early maternal rejections at age 1 year predispose to violent crime at age 18 years' in *Archives of General Psychiatry*, 51: 984–88.

Ramsay, M. (ed.) (2003) *Prisoners' Drug Use and Treatment: Seven Studies*. Findings 186. London: Home Office.

Rand, A. (1987) 'Transitional Life Events and Desistance From Delinquency and Crime' in Wolfgang, M.E., Thornberry, T.P. and Figlio, R.M. (eds) *From Boy to Man, From Delinquency to Crime*. Chicago, IL: University of Chicago Press.

Raynor, P. (1996) 'Effectiveness now' in McIvor, G. (ed.) *Working with Offenders*. London: Jessica Kingsley Publishers.

Raynor, P. (2002a) 'Community penalties and social integration: "community" as solution and as problem' in Bottoms, A., Gelsthorpe, L. and Rex, S. (eds) *Community Penalties: Change and Challenges*. Cullompton: Willan.

Raynor, P. (2002b) 'Community Penalties: Probation, Punishment and "What Works"' in Maguire, M., Morgan, R. and Reiner, R. (eds) *The Oxford Handbook of Criminology, 3e*. Oxford: Oxford University Press.

Raynor, P. (2007a) 'Theoretical perspectives on resettlement: what it is and how it might work' in Hucklesby, A. and Hagley-Dickinson, L. (eds) *Prisoner Resettlement: Policy and practice*. Cullompton: Willan.

Raynor, P. (2007b) 'Risk and need assessment in British probation: the contribution of LSI-R' in *Psychology, Crime and Law*, 13 (2): 125–38.

Raynor, P. (2008) 'Community penalties and Home Office research: On the way back to "nothing works"?' in *Criminology and Criminal Justice*, 8 (1): 73–87.

Raynor, P. and Vanstone, M. (1996) 'Reasoning and Rehabilitation in Britain: The Results of the Straight Thinking on Probation (STOP) Programme in *International Journal of Offender Therapy and Comparative Criminology*, 40 (4): 272–84.

Raynor, P. and Vanstone, M. (2002) *Understanding community penalties: Probation, policy and social change*. Buckingham: Open University Press.

Reyna, V.F. and Farley, F. (2006) 'Risk and rationality in adolescent decision-making: Implications for theory, practice, and public policy' in *Psychological Science in the Public Interest*, 7 (1): 1–44.

Rex, S. (1999) 'Desistance from Offending: Experiences of Probation' in *The Howard Journal of Criminal Justice*, 38 (4): 366–83.

Rhodes, J. (2008) 'Ex-Offenders, Social Ties and the Routes into Employment' in *Internet Journal of Criminology*, 1–20. Online. Available at: www.internetjournalofcriminology.com/Rhodes%20-%20Ex-offenders%20and%20Employment.pdf   [Accessed: 27/11/2008].

Riley, D. and Shaw, M. (1985) *Parental Supervision and Juvenile Delinquency*. Home Office Research Study 83. Online. Available at: www.homeoffice.gov.uk/rds/pdfs05/hors83.pdf [Accessed: 14/12/2009].

Robbins, I. (1988) *Legal Dimensions of Private Incarceration*. Washington, DC: American Bar Association.

Roberts, J.V. (2008) *Punishing Persistent Offenders: Exploring Community and Offender Perspectives*. Oxford: Oxford University Press.

Roberts, S. (2012) 'Boys Will Be Boys … Won't They? Change and Continuities in Contemporary Working-class Masculinities' in *Sociology*, Online First: DOI: 10.1177/0038038512453791.

Robinson, G. (1999) 'Risk Management and Rehabilitation in the Probation Service: Collision and Collusion' *The Howard Journal of Criminal Justice*, 38 (4): 421–33.

Robinson, G. (2003) 'Risk and Risk Assessment' in Chui, W.H. and Nellis, M. (eds) *Moving Probation Forward: Evidence, Arguments and Practice*. Harlow: Pearson Education.

Robinson, G. (2005) 'What Works in Offender Management' in *The Howard Journal of Criminal Justice*, 44 (3): 307–18.

Robinson, G. (2008) 'Late-modern rehabilitation: The evolution of a penal strategy' in *Punishment and Society*, 10 (4): 429–45.

Robinson, G. and Crow, I. (2009) *Offender Rehabilitation: Theory, Research and Practice*. London: Sage.

Robinson, G. and Dignan, J. (2004) 'Sentence management' in Bottoms, A., Rex, S. and Robinson, G. (eds) *Alternatives to Prison: Options for an insecure society*. Cullompton: Willan.

Robinson, G. and McNeill, F. (2008) 'Exploring the dynamics of compliance with community penalties' in *Theoretical Criminology*, 12 (4): 431–49.

Robinson, G. and McNeill, F. (2012) 'The dynamics of compliance with offender supervision' in McNeill, F., Raynor, P. and Trotter, C. (eds) *Offender Supervision: New directions in theory, research and practice*. Abingdon: Routledge.

Robinson, G. and Raynor, P. (2006) 'The future of rehabilitation: What role for the probation service?' in *Probation Journal*, 53 (4): 334–46.

Robinson, S.L. and O'Leary-Kelly, A.M. (1998) 'Monkey See, Monkey Do: The Influence of Work Groups on the Antisocial Behavior of Employees' in *Academy of Management Journal*, 41 (6): 658–72.

Roe, S. and Ashe, J. (2008) *Young people and crime: findings from the 2006 Offending, Crime and Justice Survey*. Home Office Statistical Bulletin 09/08. Online. Available at: www.homeoffice.gov.uk/rds/pdfs08/hosb0908.pdf [Accessed: 14/12/2009].

Ross, J.I. and Richards, S.C. (2009) *Beyond Bars: Rejoining Society After Prison*. London: Alpha.

Ross, R.R., Fabiano, E.A. and Ross, R.D. (1986) *Reasoning and Rehabilitation: A Handbook for Teaching Cognitive Skills*. Ottawa: University of Ottawa.

Rumgay, J. (2004) 'Scripts for Safer Survival: Pathways Out of Female Crime' in *The Howard Journal of Criminal Justice*, 43 (4): 405–19.

Ryan, M. (2011) 'Counterblast: Understanding Penal Change: Towards the Big Society?' in *The Howard Journal of Criminal Justice*, 50 (5): 516–20.

Ryan, M. and Ward, T. (1989) *Privatisation and the Penal System*. Milton Keynes: Open University Press.

Sainsbury Centre for Mental Health (2006) *The Future of Mental Health: a Vision for 2015*. London: The Sainsbury Centre for Mental Health.

Sampson, R.J. and Laub, J.H. (1990) 'Crime and Deviance Over the Life Course: The Salience of Adult Social Bonds' in *American Sociological Review*, 55: 609–27.

Sampson, R.J. and Laub, J.H. (1992) 'Crime and Deviance in the Life Course' in *Annual Review of Sociology*, 18: 63–84.

Sampson, R.J. and Laub, J.H. (1993) *Crime in the Making: Pathways and Turning Points through Life*. London: Harvard University Press.

Sampson, R. J. and Laub, J. H. (1995) 'Understanding variability in lives through time: Contributions of life-course criminology' in *Studies on Crime and Crime Prevention*, 4: 143–58.

Sampson, R.J. and Laub, J.H. (2005a) 'A Life-Course View of the Development of Crime' in *The ANNALS of the American Academy of Political and Social Science*, 602 (1): 12–45.

Sampson, R. J., and Laub, J. H. (2005b) 'A general age-graded theory of crime: Lessons learned and the future of the life-course criminology' in Farrington, D.P. (ed.) *Integrated Developmental and Lifecourse Theories of Offending*. New Brunswick, NJ: Transaction.

Sampson, R.J., Laub, J., and Wimer, C. (2006) 'Does marriage reduce crime? A counterfactual approach to within-individual causal effects' in *Criminology*, 44 (3): 465–506.

Samuels, P. and Mukamal, D. (2004) *After Prison: Roadblocks to Reentry*. New York: Legal Action Center.

Sanders, T. (2007) 'Becoming an Ex-Sex Worker: Making Transitions Out of a Deviant Career' in *Feminist Criminology*, 2 (1): 74–95.

Sapouna, M., Bisset, C. and Conlong, A. (2011) *What Works to Reduce Reoffending: A Summary of the Evidence*. Justice Analytical Series. Online. Available at: http://scotland.gov.uk/Resource/0038/00385880.pdf [Accessed: 03/08/2012].

Sarno, C., Hearnden, I., Hedderman, C., Hough, M., Nee, C. and Herrington, V. (2000) *Working Their Way Out of Offending: An Evaluation of Two Probation Employment Schemes*. Home Office Research Study 218. London: Home Office.

Sarno, C., Hough, M., Nee, C. and Hetherington, V. (1999) *Probation Employment Schemes in Inner London and Surrey, an evaluation*. London: Home Office.

Schroeder, R.D., Giordano, P.C. and Cernkovich, S.A. (2007) 'Drug Use and Desistance Processes' in *Criminology*, 45 (1): 191–222.

Sen, A. (1999) *Development as Freedom*. New York: Knopf.

Serin, R.C. and Lloyd, C.D. (2009) 'Examining the process of offender change: the transition to crime desistance' in *Psychology, Crime and Law*, 15 (4): 347–64.

Serin, R.C., Lloyd, C.D. and Hanby, L.J. (2010) 'Enhancing Offender Re-Entry: An integrated model for enhancing offender re-entry' in *European Journal of Probation*, 2 (2): 53–75.

Shannon, L. (1991) *Changing Patterns of Delinquency and Crime: A Longitudinal Study in Racine*. Boulder, Co: Westview Press.

Shannon, S.K.S. and Abrams, L.S. (2007) 'Juvenile offenders as fathers: perceptions of fatherhood, crime and becoming an adult' in *Families in Society: The Journal of Contemporary Social Services*, 88 (2): 183–91.

Shapland, J. and Bottoms, A.E. (2011) 'Reflections on social values, offending and desistance among young adult recidivists' in *Punishment and Society*, 13 (3): 256–91.

Shapland, J., Atkinson, A., Atkinson, H., Dignan, J., Edwards, L., Hibbert, J., Howes, M., Johnstone, J., Robinson, G. and Sorsby, A. (2008) *Does Restorative Justice Affect Reconviction? The fourth report from the evaluation of three schemes*. Ministry of Justice Research Series 10/08. London: Ministry of Justice.

Shapland, J., Bottoms, A., Farrall, S., McNeill, F., Priede, C. and Robinson, G. (2012) *The Quality of Probation Supervision – A Literature Review*. Sheffield: University of Sheffield, Centre for Criminological Research.

Sharpe, G. (2011) 'Beyond youth justice: Working with girls and young women who offend' in Sheehan, R., McIvor, G. and Trotter, C. (eds) *Working with Women Offenders in the Community*. Abingdon: Willan.

Shaw, M. and Hannah-Moffat, K. (2000) 'Gender, diversity and risk assessment in Canadian corrections' in *Probation Journal*, 47: 163–72.

Shichor, D. (1995) *Punishment for Profit*. London: Sage.

Shover, N. (1983) 'The Later Stages of Ordinary Property Offender Careers' in *Social Problems*, 31 (2): 208–18.

Shover, N. (1996) *Great pretenders: Pursuits and Careers of Persistent Thieves*. Boulder, CO: Westview.

Shover, N. and Thompson, C.Y. (1992) 'Age, Differential Expectations, and Crime Desistance' in *Criminology*, 30: 89–104.

Silvestri, A. (2012) 'Austerity, spending cuts and the "frontline"' in Silvestri, A. (ed.) *Critical Reflections: Social and criminal justice in the first year of Coalition government*. London: Centre for Crime and Justice Studies.

Simmonds, A.P. (1989) 'Ideological Domination and the Political Information Market' in *Theory and Society*, 18 (2): 181–211.

Simons, R.L. and Barr, A.B. (2012) 'Shifting Perspectives: Cognitive Changes Mediate the Impact of Romantic Relationships on Desistance from Crime' in *Justice Quarterly*, Available Online First, DOI: 10.1080/07418825.2012.704388.

Skarohamar, T. and Hovde Lyngstad, T. (2009) *Family Formation, Fatherhood and Crime: An invitation to a broader perspective on crime and family transitions*. Discussion paper No. 579, Statistics Norway, Research Department. Online. Available at: www.ssb.no/publikasjoner/DP/pdf/dp579.pdf [Accessed: 27/08/2012].

Smith, C. (2001) 'Trust and Confidence: Possibilities for Social Work in "High Modernity"' in *British Journal of Social Work*, 31 (2): 287–305.

Smith, D.J. (2005) 'The effectiveness of the juvenile justice system' in *Criminology and Criminal Justice*, 5 (2): 181–95.

Smith, D.J. (2006a) *Social Inclusion and Early Desistance from Crime*. Edinburgh Study of Youth Transitions and Crime, Research Digest No. 12. Edinburgh: Centre for Law and Society, University of Edinburgh.

Smith, D.J. (2006b) *School Experience and Delinquency at Ages 13–16*. Edinburgh Study of Youth Transitions and Crime, Research Digest No. 13. Edinburgh: Centre for Law and Society, University of Edinburgh.

Smith, D.J. and McVie, S. (2003) 'Theory and Method in the Edinburgh Study of Youth Transitions and Crime' in *The British Journal of Criminology*, 43 (1): 169–95.

Social Exclusion Unit (2002) *Reducing Re-offending by Ex-prisoners*. London: Office of the Deputy Prime Minister.

Soothill, K., Ackerley, E. and Francis, B. (2003) 'The persistent offenders debate: A focus on temporal changes' in *Criminal Justice*, 3 (4): 389–412.

Soothill, K., Fitzpatrick, C. and Francis, B. (2009) *Understanding Criminal Careers*. Cullompton: Willan.

Squires, P. (2006) 'New Labour and the politics of antisocial behaviour' in *Critical Social Policy*, 26 (1): 144–68.

Stenson, K. and Sullivan, R.R. (eds) *Crime, Risk and Justice: The Politics of Crime Control in Liberal Democracies*. Cullompton: Willan.

Stevens, A. (2012) ' "I am the person now I was always meant to be": Identity reconstruction and narrative reframing in therapeutic community prisons' in *Criminology and Criminal Justice*. Online. Available at: http://crj.sagepub.com/content/early/2012/01/0 3/1748895811432958.full.pdf+html [Accessed: 16/01/2012].

Stewart, D. (2008) *The Problems and Needs of Newly Sentenced Prisoners: Results from a National Survey*. London: Ministry of Justice.

Sugarman, J. (2005) 'Persons and Moral Agency' in *Theory and Psychology*, 15 (6): 793–811.

Tarry, N. (2006) 'Introduction and Executive Summary' in Tarry, N. (ed.) *Returning to its roots? A new role for the Third Sector in Probation*. London: The Social Market Foundation.

Taylor, I., Walton, P. and Young, J. (1973) *The New Criminology: For a Sociology of Deviance*. London: Routledge.

Taylor, I., Walton, P. and Young, J. (1975) *Critical Criminology*. London: Routledge.

Teague, M. (2012) 'Neoliberalism, Prisons and Probation in the United States and England and Wales' in Whitehead, P. and Crawshaw, P. (eds) *Organising Neo-liberalism: Markets, Privatisation and Justice*. London: Anthem Press.

Tett, L., Anderson, K., McNeill, F., Overy, K. and Sparks, R. (2012) 'Learning, rehabilitation and the arts in prisons: a Scottish case study' in *Studies in the Education of Adults*, 44 (2): 171–85.

Thakker, J., Ward, T. and Navathe, S. (2007) 'The Cognitive Distortions and Implicit Theories of Child Sexual Abusers' in Gannon, T.A., Ward, T., Beech, A.R. and Fisher, D. (eds) *Aggressive offenders' cognition: Theory, Research and Practice*. Chichester: John Wiley and Sons.

Thomson, M. (2009) *Reducing Re-offending: Calculating reconviction rates*. Online. Available at: www.clinks.org/(S(i5mvmfjhk5wgnr3xq52fcimr))/downloads/publications/ReportsConsColls/090312ReducingReoffendingStatistics.pdf [Accessed: 14/12/2009].

Tittle, C.R., Antonaccio, O., Botchkovar, E. and Kranidioti, M. (2010) 'Expected utility, self-control, morality and criminal probability' in *Social Science Research*, 39 (6): 1029–46.

Tracy, P.E., and Kempf-Leonard, K. (1996) *Continuity and Discontinuity in Criminal Careers*. New York: Plenum.

Trades Union Congress (2001) *Employment and Ex-Offenders*. London: TUC.

Travis, J. (2005) *But They All Come Back: Facing the Challenges of Prisoner Reentry*. New York: Urban Institute.

Tripodi, S., Kim J., and Bender, J. (2010) 'Is employment associated with reduced recidivism? The complex relationship between employment and crime' in *International Journal of Offender Therapy and Comparative Criminology*, 54 (5): 706–20.

Trotter, C. (1993) *The Supervision of Offenders: What Works*. Sydney: Victorian Office of Corrections.

Trotter, C. (1996) 'The impact of different supervision practices in community corrections: cause for optimism' in *Australian and New Zealand Journal of Criminology*, Vol. 29: 29–46.

Trotter, C. (1999) *Working with Involuntary Clients: A Guide to Practice*. London: Sage.

Uggen, C. (1999) 'Ex-Offenders and the Conformist Alternative: A Job Quality Model of Work and Crime' in *Social Problems*, 46 (1): 127–51.

Uggen, C. (2000) 'Work as a Turning Point in the Life Course of Criminals: A Duration Model of Age, Employment, and Recidivism' in *American Sociological Review* 65(4): 529–46.

Uggen, C. and Kruttschnitt, C. (1998) 'Crime in the Breaking: Gender Differences in Desistance' in *Law and Society Review*, 32 (2): 339–66.

Uggen, C. and Massoglia, M. (2003) 'Desistance from Crime and Deviance as a Turning Point in the Life Course' in Mortimer, J.T. and Shanahan, M.J. (eds) *Handbook of the Life Course*. Kluwer Academic/Plenum: New York.

Uggen, C., Manza, J. and Angela, B. (2004) 'Less than the Average Citizen: Stigma, Role Transition, and the Civic Reintegration of Convicted Felons' in Maruna, S. and Immarigeon, R. (eds) *After Crime and Punishment: Pathways to Offender Reintegration*. Cullompton: Willan.

Ugwudike, P. (2010) 'Compliance with community penalties: the importance of interactional dynamics' in McNeill, F., Raynor, P. and Trotter, C. (eds) *Offender Supervision: New directions in theory, research and practice*. Abingdon: Routledge.

Vanstone, M. (2004) *Supervising Offenders in the Community: A History of Probation Theory and Practice*. Aldershot: Ashgate.

Vanstone, M. (2010) 'New Labour and criminal justice: Reflections on a wasteland of missed opportunity' in *Probation*, 57 (3): 281–85.

Vaughan, B. (2000) 'Punishment and conditional citizenship' in *Punishment & Society*, 2 (1): 23–39.

Vaughan, B. (2007) 'The Internal Narrative of Desistance' in *British Journal of Criminology*, 47 (3): 390–404.

Veit-Wilson, J. (1998) *Setting Adequacy Standards*. Bristol: Policy Press.

Vennard, J. and Hedderman, C. (2009) 'Helping offenders into employment: How far is voluntary expertise valued in a contracting-out environment?' in *Criminology and Criminal Justice*, 9 (2): 225–45.

Visher, C.A. and Travis, J. (2003) 'Transitions from Prison to Community: Understanding Individual Pathways' in *Annual Review of Sociology*, 29: 89–113.

Walker, L. (2010) '"My Son Gave Birth to Me": Offending Fathers – Generative, Reflective and Risky?' in *British Journal of Social Work*, 40 (5): 1402–18.

Warburton, F. (2010) 'Crime and justice after the election: what are the parties proposing?' in *Safer Communities*, 9 (2): 20–7.

Warr, M. (1998) 'Life-course transitions and desistance from crime' in *Criminology*, 36: 183–215.

Weaver, B. (2009) 'Communicative punishment as a penal approach to supporting desistance' in *Theoretical Criminology*, 13 (1): 9–29.

Weaver, B. (2012) 'The Relational Context of Desistance: Some Implications and Opportunities for Social Policy' in *Social Policy and Administration*, 46 (4): 395–412.

Weaver, B. and McNeill, F. (2007a) 'Desistance' in Canton, R. and Hancock, D. (eds) *Dictionary of Probation and Offender Management*. Cullompton: Willan.

Weaver, B. and McNeill, F. (2007b) *Giving Up Crime: Directions For Policy*. The Scottish Consortium on Crime and Criminal Justice, Briefing Paper. Online. Available at: www.scccj.org.uk [Accessed: 03/06/09].

Weaver, B. and McNeill, F. (2010) 'Travelling hopefully: desistance theory and probation practice' in Brayford, J., Crowe, F. and Deering, J. (eds) *What Else Works? Creative Work with Offenders*. Cullompton: Willan.

Webster, C., Macdonald, R. and Simpson, M. (2006) 'Predicting Criminality? Risk Factors, Neighbourhood Influence and Desistance' in *Youth Justice*, 6 (1): 7–22.

Webster, C., Simpson, D., MacDonald, R., Abbas, A., Cieslik, M., Shildrich, T. and Simpson, M. (2004) *Poor Transitions: Social Exclusion and Young Adults*. Bristol: The Policy Press.

Webster, R., Hedderman, C., Turnbull, P.J. and May, T. (2001) *Building Bridges to Employment*. Research Study 226. London: Home Office.

West, D.J. and Farrington, D.P. (1973) *Who Becomes Delinquent?* London: Heinemann.

White, M. (1994) 'Blair defines the new Labour' in *The Guardian*, 05/10/1994. Online. Available at: www.guardian.co.uk/politics/1994/oct/05/speeches.michaelwhite [Accessed: 14/02/2013].

Whitehead, P. (2007) *Modernising Probation and Criminal Justice: Getting the Measure of Cultural Change*. Kent: Shaw and Sons.

Wikstrom, P-O. (1987) *Patterns of Crime in a Birth Cohort: Age, Sex and Class Differences. Project Metropolitan: A Longitudinal Study of a Stockholm Cohort no. 24*. Stockholm: University of Stockholm, Department of Sociology.

Wikstrom, P-O. and Treiber, K. (2007) 'The Role of Self-Control in Crime Causation: Beyond Gottfredson and Hirschi's General Theory of Crime' in *European Journal of Criminology*, 4 (2): 237–64.

Wikstrom, P-O. and Treiber, K. (2009) 'What drives persistent offending? The neglected and unexplored role of the social environment' in Savage, J. (ed.) *The Development of Persistent Criminality*. Oxford: Oxford University Press.

Williams, A.E. and Ariel, B. (2012) 'The Bristol Integrated Offender Management Scheme: a Pseudo-Experimental Test of Desistance Theory' in *Policing*. Available Online First. DOI: 10.1093/police/pas053.

Williams, F., Popay, J. and Oakley, A. (1999) 'Changing Paradigms of Welfare' in Williams, F., Popay, J. and Oakley, A. (eds) *Welfare Research: A Critical Review*. London: UCL Press.

Winnick, T.A. and Bodkin, M. (2008) 'Anticipated stigma and stigma management among those to be labeled "ex-con"' in *Deviant Behavior*, 29: 295–333.

Wolfgang, M., Thornberry, T. and Figlio, R. (1987) 'From boy to man, from delinquency to crime: A follow-up of delinquents in a birth cohort'. Report. Chicago, IL: University of Chicago Press.

Worrall, A. and Hoy, C. (2005) *Punishment in the Community: Managing Offenders, Making Choices*. Cullompton: Willan.

Wright, J.P. and Cullen, F.T. (2004) 'Employment, Peers and Life Course Transitions' in *Justice Quarterly*, 21 (1): 183–205.

Young, J. (2002) 'Crime and Social Exclusion' in Maguire, M., Morgan, R. and Reiner, R. (eds) *The Oxford Handbook of Criminology, 3e*. Oxford: Oxford University Press.

Young, J. (2003) 'Winning the fight against crime? New Labour, populism and lost opportunities' in Matthews, R. and Young, J. (eds) *The New Politics of Crime and Punishment*. Cullompton: Willan.

Young, J. and Matthews, R. (2003) 'New Labour, crime control and social exclusion' in Matthews, R. and Young, J. (eds) *The New Politics of Crime and Punishment*. Cullompton: Willan.

Young, P. (1987) *The Prison Cell*. London: Adam Smith Institute.

Zamble, E. and Quinsey, V. (1997) *The Criminal Recidivism Process*. Cambridge: Cambridge University Press.

Zedner, L. (2002) 'Dangers of dystopia in penal theory' in *Oxford Journal of Legal Studies*, 22 (2): 341–66.

Index

Page numbers in *italics* denote tables, those in **bold** denote figures.

personal responsibility, issue of 117–20;
job prospects as barrier to 123–5;
marriage and 105–9; neighbourhoods,
estates or areas, ties with 112–16; from
projective to practical-evaluative agency
158–65; secure accommodation, issue of
117–20
street-level bureaucracy, Lipsky's notion
of 180
supervision, one-to-one 16, 21, 72, 128,
131–4, 137, 143–5, 158, 166, 170–1,
173
'surveillant managerial' discourse 17, 177
suspended maturity 26
Suspended Sentence Order (SSO) 16, 79,
81, 98

target culture, notion of 19, 170
thoughtfully reflective decision making
(TRDM) 52–3
transition towards desistance 1–2, 153–4;
human agency and 63–8, 70–2, 73,
85–95; instigating 85–101; phases of
102; practical-evaluative dimension of

agency and 162; probation constraining
138–50; probation helping 70–2, 150;
regret, shame and remorse 89; self-
confidence during 133; social cues and
96–101
Turner, Victor 60, 64

Uggen, C. 28–9, 31, 35, 37, 75
unpaid work 15–16, 18, 128
uptariffing, issue of 16

Warr, M. 31
'What Works' movement 15
willingness to desist 34
would-be desisters 2, 37, 39–40, 58–61,
115, 117, 125–6, 151, 153, 168–9,
171–2, 177, 181, 183; impact of
probation on 165–6; personal and social
problems 61; personal identity of 57,
156, 178–80; relationship between
supervising officer and 165–6; strategies
for staying away from crime 72;
transformative agency 174

For Product Safety Concerns and Information please contact our EU
representative GPSR@taylorandfrancis.com
Taylor & Francis Verlag GmbH, Kaufingerstraße 24, 80331 München, Germany

www.ingramcontent.com/pod-product-compliance
Lightning Source LLC
Chambersburg PA
CBHW070406270326
41926CB00014B/2719

9 781138 922372